Variations on a Blue Guitar

Variations on a Blue Guitar

The Lincoln Center Institute Lectures on Aesthetic Education

Maxine Greene

TEACHERS
COLLEGE
PRESS

Teachers College, Columbia University
New York and London

Library of Congress Cataloging-in-Publication Data

Greene, Maxine.
  Variations on a blue guitar : the Lincoln Center Institute lectures on aesthetic education / Maxine Greene.
      p.   cm.
  Includes bibliographical references.
      ISBN 0-8077-4136-1 (cloth : alk. paper) — ISBN 0-8077-4135-3 (paper : alk. paper)
      1. Art teachers—Training of—New York (State)—New York.   2. Aesthetics—Study and teaching—New York (State)—New York.   3. Arts—Study and teaching—New York (State)—New York.   4. Artists as teachers—New York (State)—New York.   I. Lincoln Center Institute.   II. Title.
  NX284.4.N7 G74 2001
  791'.071'17471—dc21   2001027325

Copyright page is continued on p. xiii.

ISBN 0-8077-4135-3 (paper)
ISBN 0-8077-4136-1 (cloth)

Printed on acid-free paper
Manufactured in the United States of America
08   07   06   05   04   03   02   01   8   7   6   5   4   3   2   1

Contents

Reflection on
Variations on a Blue Guitar

These lectures were given over a period of twenty-five years of self-discovery and continuing efforts to move a diversity of teachers to discover new dimensions of themselves. One paper was prepared for large public audiences concerned with education and the arts; another was intended to introduce school administrators to aesthetic education and the arts in their plurality. Most, however, were presented to the teachers attending Summer Session at Lincoln Center Institute for the Arts in Education.

Beginning in the early 1970s, I was privileged to work with Mark Schubart, Director of the Institute, June Dunbar, Associate Director, and a number of particularly talented representatives of the arts and art institutions in the city; among others, Paula Kahn, Joanne Robinson (Hill), Jonathan Levy, David Shookhoff, Madeleine Cohen, and Barbara Ellmann, each working from her or his own point of view. As will be evident throughout this text, I have been exploring philosophy in the context of teacher education (at Teachers College, Columbia University) and teaching courses in educational philosophy, the arts and American education, and aesthetics and education. It must be understood that the essays to follow are not of the sort I would have prepared for journals in philosophy or classes in advanced philosophic thought. I have tried to connect with the thinking, the questions, the views of practice of elementary and secondary public school teachers, relatively few of whom have had backgrounds in philosophy or aesthetics. They have been, I must point out, largely self-selected for the Institute, and I have been able to assume a high degree of enthusiasm, curiosity, and wonder on the part of my audiences or readers. It may be of some interest that, where the talks at the Institute were concerned, I have always provided the texts of those talks the day after they were given. At a time when there is considerable probing about the relationship between talking and writing, writing and reading, this probably should be taken into account.

Themes have developed throughout the book, sometimes overlapping, expanding, repeating themselves. I suspect that this happens in most people's intellectual and emotional lives as time passes, experiences multiply, perspectives change. What does not change, however, is my core commitment to the activity (or the process, or the undertaking) we call aesthetic education and the growth of mind and spirit and what John Keats called "the soul." What does not change, as well, is the regard for diversity, for the distinctiveness of different cultures and for our ongoing obligation to do justice to multiplicity and difference, even as we keep alive our engagement with the art forms in the context of which we create our identities.

Aware of the changes in approaches in the arts—most particularly the rejection of pure formalism—I have tried to be attentive to the context, while insisting on personal transactions with actual works of art. Acknowledging our links to constructivism, to the idea that meanings must be achieved and not simply found, that they can only be achieved against the backgrounds of lived lives, I celebrate the ways in which what is called "active learning" is nourished and stimulated by the involvement (and integration) of body, mind, and emotion in the work with the teaching artists in the Institute workshops. I celebrate, as well, the growing concern for the centrality of imagination, for the work being done to clarify the relationship between imagination and embodiment, between imagination and the pursuit of what John Dewey called "intellectual possibility." Throughout (and this is repeated over and over again) I have recalled Dewey's view that the opposite of "aesthetic" is "anaesthetic." Anaesthesia, for me, implies numbness, an emotional incapacity, and this can immobilize, prevent people from questioning, from meeting the challenges of being in and naming and (perhaps) transforming the world.

Acknowledgments

The journey would have been unthinkable if I had embarked on it alone. At the start, there were Mark Schubart, June Dunbar, Trevor Cushman, Paula Kahn, and I coming together to invent aesthetic education and a new role for the arts in the schools. Later came the wondrous Cathryn Williams, Christine Goodheart, Alison Lehner-Quam, and Beverly Emmons. There were others, good friends and companions all: those we came to call "teaching artists"—Joanne Robinson (Hill), Madeleine Cohen, Tom Bullard, David Shookhoff, Jonathan Levy, Eric Booth, Susan Thomassen, Barbara Ellmann, Holly Fairbank, and others who know I would name them if there were room. Also, those wonder workers in book production: MaryAlice Rocks, Catherine Rogers, Josie Shafer, Jack Cadwallader, Kevin Dhaniram, and many volunteers, all of whom put in countless hours researching, copyediting, and retyping. Of course, the foundation of all this work was set by Carole Saltz, dear friend and publisher at Teachers College Press, and Catherine Bernard, her brilliant young associate.

Then the two who made this book possible—Scott Noppe-Brandon and Madeleine Holzer.

Scott Noppe-Brandon and I have been together at the Institute for fifteen years, and there is no one I can think of better qualified to carry on Mark Schubart's work and extend it in new directions. Nor is there anyone I can think of who could have encouraged me more as a writer, workshop leader, and "Philosopher-in-Residence."

Madeleine Holzer joined us most recently—poet, friend, intellectual, all I could have hoped for in a collaborator. She shaped, edited, and honed this manuscript, and nurtured my hopes and confidence in the months that have passed. I want to write her name in shimmering blue and gold—suggesting the way she weds thought and imagination, the way she is in the world.

My gratitude to all the above is bottomless.

M.G.

Permissions

Maxine Greene and Lincoln Center Institute: Setting the Context

Scott Noppe-Brandon and Madeleine F. Holzer

L incoln Center Institute for the Arts in Education grew out of a fourteen-year history of an evolving educational program, an intensive study of arts institutions and young people, and the deliberations of many artists and educators working with the organization. In 1960, even before the first building at Lincoln Center was completed, the pilot phase of its educational initiative had been launched. Under the title Lincoln Center Student Program, performing artists began bringing their works to secondary schools throughout the city, and the organization worked to bring more students directly to Lincoln Center performances.

As the organization evolved, Lincoln Center became increasingly aware that the program lacked educational depth and continuity, in part because the presentations were not sufficiently oriented to the needs of young people and teachers, and in part because most schools had neither teaching staff nor educational materials for teaching the performing arts as part of the general curriculum. Moreover, despite a genuine interest in the program, many educators regarded activities in the performing arts as additives to what is generally considered "essential" education. To help overcome this difficulty, the Center became increasingly involved in the educational process, recruiting and training young professional composers, choreographers, playwrights, and directors to work with students and teachers before and after performances in an effort to help young people get at the fundamentals of the artistic experience.

Nationally during this period, the general position of the arts in education began to change. Largely through the impetus of federally funded programs—notably those under Title III of the Elementary and Secondary Education Act of 1965—performing arts activity in the schools increased. Throughout the country, school districts experimented with ways to integrate the performing arts into the experiences of young people—through humanities programs, interdisciplinary and team-teaching approaches, and a more flexible approach to the curriculum. Furthermore, the political and educational leadership of the nation began to consider a larger role for the arts and the humanities in the educational process.

Though Lincoln Center continued to work closely with school systems, the administration believed that the programs, however successful and deserving, were still not likely to effect significant change in the basic status of the arts and education. On the other hand, it was unclear how the work of the Student Program needed to change.

In 1970, with the assistance of a grant from the Carnegie Corporation, Education Director Mark Schubart undertook a one-year study to address issues of how most effectively to reach young people. In addition, issues concerning repertory, the artist-student relationship, the teaching process, and the relationship between Lincoln Center and schools were examined. Two major recommendations emerged from the study. The goals of Lincoln Center's educational programs, the study concluded, had been too narrowly defined in terms of exposure to the arts. Opening students to the aesthetic dimension in human experience, rather than simple exposure, should be the objective. Moreover, in order to attain this objective, it was recommended that the Center establish a new kind of arts institution to be called Lincoln Center Institute, one dedicated solely and specifically to meeting the needs of young people and their teachers. As a result, Lincoln Center began to reorient its existing student program activities, particularly artist-led workshops with students and teachers, toward goals of increased aesthetic awareness.

At the same time, it was decided that, rather than reach out to a limited number of young people who would not be in a position to effect institutional change, the Institute's primary task would be to partner with adults—teachers, school leaders, community leaders, and artists—who would develop programs in aesthetic education for students in their own organizations. In this way, larger numbers of students could be reached. To this day, the design of Lincoln Center Institute reflects that basic policy decision.

To better fulfill the new expectations, in 1975 the Institute established a partnership with Teachers College, Columbia University. A faculty committee worked out the details of the collaboration, and the college president, Lawrence Cremin, appointed one key faculty member, Dr. Maxine Greene, distinguished philosopher and authority in the field of aesthetic education, to serve as liaison with the Institute. When the Institute's Summer Session for teachers and school administrators was established a year later, a series of workshops and lectures by Dr. Greene dealing with the philosophy of aesthetic education and its role within the broader educational experience became an integral part. And so, the role of philosophy within the Institute, led by the esteemed Maxine Greene, was born.

* * *

Imagine, if you will, studios at the Juilliard School in New York City filled with teachers from the metropolitan area. They are dressed informally, many wearing warm-up clothing and running shoes. They are spending three weeks immersing themselves in music, theater, visual art, and dance accompanied by aesthetic education workshops with Lincoln Center Institute teaching artists. Imagine even further: the teachers are dancing a pas de deux in their workshops; they are doing improvisational theater; they are composing a song; they are making silhouettes. They see the Alvin Ailey Repertory Ensemble, a performance of Beckett's *Krapp's Last Tape,* hear the Emerson String Quartet, and visit The Museum of Modern Art. They go back to studios, reflect with teaching artists about their experiences, and discuss how the experiences relate to their teaching. In the middle of all this, they all assemble to hear Maxine Greene, who, with her poetic cadence, personal asides, and powerful connections to their lives as teachers, holds them in rapt attention.

For the twenty-five years of the existence of Lincoln Center Institute's Summer Session, Maxine Greene has inspired teachers to think in new ways about the aesthetic experiences they have at the Institute, urging them to transform their learning into innovative classroom teaching that recognizes perception, cognition, affect, and the imagination as ways of knowing. In the early years, Dr. Greene prepared a series of six or seven lectures. These lectures outlined and developed the basic themes of aesthetic education as she defined it, and as it continues to be practiced by teaching artists at Lincoln Center Institute. In later years, Dr. Greene gave three lectures, one during each week of Summer Session. These all built on the concepts developed in the late 1970s and early 1980s, refining them, and applying them to current educational concerns and issues.

The lectures are not only essential to understanding aesthetic education, but they also serve as rich sources of Dr. Greene's unique style of imaginative thinking that combines references to philosophy, art criticism, literature, and education, and builds on the works of art in the Institute's repertory and the New York City cultural scene. These references are never linear, and for teachers who return to the Institute summer after summer, they become familiar touchstones—John Dewey, Dennis Donoghue, Hannah Arendt, and Wallace Stevens's blue guitar and sombrero hats, among others. Yet, in the context of the different works of art performed, the touchstones are illuminated somewhat differently than they had been when mentioned before. With the added context of pressing educational issues, such as standards, education reform, and cultural diversity, Dr. Greene makes aesthetic experience and the life of the imagination essential to all that goes on in schools.

After listening to these lectures in the context of Lincoln Center Institute's Summer Session, countless teachers have asked new questions, viewed ideas in a different way, and even transformed some part of their life or work. As you enter this world, asking only one question beginning with "What if?" will set you off on the journey Maxine Greene intends.

PART I

DEFINING AESTHETIC EDUCATION

How are we to understand "aesthetic education"? How does it differ from what is called "art education"? From "art appreciation"? It is important to understand that "aesthetics" is the term used to single out a particular field in philosophy, one concerned about perception, sensation, imagination, and how they relate to knowing, understanding, and feeling about the world. For some, "aesthetics" has primarily to do with the kinds of experiences associated with reflective and conscious encounters with the arts. Or it may focus on the way in which a work of art can become an object of experience and the effect it then has in altering perspectives on nature, human beings, and moment-to-moment existence. "Aesthetic," of course, is an adjective used to describe or single out the mode of experience brought into being by encounters with works of art.

"Education," as I view it, is a process of enabling persons to become different, to enter the multiple provinces of meaning that create perspectives on the works. To enter these provinces (be they those identified with the arts, the social sciences, the natural sciences), the learner must break with the taken-for-granted, what some call the "natural attitude," and look through the lenses of various ways of knowing, seeing, and feeling in a conscious endeavor to impose different orders upon experience. It is important to understand that the concepts and precepts available to the learner stem from the funded meanings or ways of knowing designed over the years by artists, teachers, and philosophers. We enter traditions as we engage with such perspectives, becoming members of a culture changing on many levels throughout history. Or, to say it differently, we learn to make sense, all kinds of sense, but we make the culture's symbol systems our own, including those associated with the arts.

"Aesthetic education," then, is an intentional undertaking designed to nurture appreciative, reflective, cultural, participatory engagements with the arts by enabling learners to notice what is there to be noticed, and to lend works of art their lives in such a way that they can achieve them as variously meaningful. When this happens, new connections are made in experience: new patterns are formed, new vistas are opened. Persons *see* differently, resonate differently; as Rilke wrote in one of his poems, they are enabled to pay heed when a work of art tells them, "You must change your life" (1940/1974, p. 93).

Art education, it should be clear, focuses upon exploration of the different media. Young people experience what it signifies to give their feelings and perceptions embodiment in paint, clay, movement, sound. It allows for many modes of expression, many modes of learning a craft, many ways of leaving an imprint on the world. Certainly, people who know the joy and strain of working with a medium are in a position to respond to the work of a professional artist in that medium—and in consequence, to pose the questions about their own aesthetic experiences with which aesthetic education begins. Always, we try to encourage more and more connections, so that art educators reach out for the presence of works of art, and aesthetic educators open spaces for explorations of the materials of art.

At the heart of our Institute, of course, are the workshops taught by professionals in the various fields—choreographers, actors, musicians, painters, others more than well-equipped to make accessible the languages, the mysteries, of the various art forms. Teachers begin to internalize new modalities for expression. They explore patterns, rhythms, effort-shape, tonalities, to such an extent that when they attend performances at the Institute or see art exhibitions, they can attend not only cognitively and according to rule, but with their emotions, their nervous system, their body-minds brought new and in startling relation to the world.

Notes on Aesthetic Education

(1980)

An Initiation into New Ways of Seeing, Hearing, Feeling, and Moving . . .

We are interested in education here, not in schooling. We are interested in openings, in unexplored possibilities, not in the predictable or the quantifiable, not in what is thought of as social control. For us, education signifies an initiation into new ways of seeing, hearing, feeling, moving. It signifies the nurture of a special kind of reflectiveness and expressiveness, a reaching out for meanings, a learning to learn.

Our core concern, of course, is with aesthetic education; but we do not regard aesthetic education as in any sense a fringe undertaking, a species of "frill." We see it as integral to the development of persons—to their cognitive, perceptual, emotional, and imaginative development. We see it as part of the human effort (so often forgotten today) to seek a greater coherence in the world. We see it as an effort to move individuals (working together, searching together) to seek a grounding for themselves, so that they may break through the "cotton wool" of dailyness and passivity and boredom and come awake to the colored, sounding, problematic world.

Sometimes I think that what we want to make possible is the living of lyrical moments, moments at which human beings (freed to feel, to know, and to imagine) suddenly understand their own lives in relation to all that surrounds. Young people, older people are constantly prevented from doing this. Their lives, even the things they are taught, are broken into fragments, categorized, compartmentalized. I remember Elizabeth Bishop's translation of Octavio Paz's poem on Joseph Cornell's boxes, particularly the following verse:

Minimal, incoherent fragments:
the opposite of History, creator of ruins,
out of your ruins you have made creations.

("Objects and Apparitions: For Joseph
Cornell," 1997, pp. 275–276)

In some strange way, that describes for me some of what we shall be doing
here.

But what is aesthetic education? How *can* it lead to the discovery of new
vistas, to the bringing of severed parts together and making things (for a
moment) whole? Most simply, most directly, it is education for more discriminating appreciation and understanding of the several arts. The first
concern of those of us engaged in aesthetic education is to find ways of
developing a more active sensibility and awareness in our students. To bring
this about, we believe, we have somehow to initiate them "into what it feels
like to live in music, move over and about in a painting, travel round and
in between the masses of a sculpture, dwell in a poem." (Reid, 1969, p. 302).
This is the starting point: the ability to feel from the inside what the arts are
like and how they mean. Experiences of this sort cannot but become the
ground of an illumination of much that lies beyond, and we are preoccupied with allowing such illumination to occur.

We are hardly, however, in a position to develop a heightened sensitivity
in others if we ourselves do not know what it is like to live inside, to move
around within the range of art forms. And few of us are in a position to
communicate what this is like to others if we who are teachers have not
reflected upon our own experiences with music, dance, theater, and the rest.
I am reminded of the play *Children of a Lesser God*, and of the impassioned,
eloquent effort made by the teacher to communicate to his non-hearing wife
what it has meant to him to listen to Bach. It is not only that he knew how
to listen, how to notice what there was to be noticed. He had lived inside
it; he had allowed it to permeate his experience, and what he was trying to
express was the manner in which a particular mode of listening, of paying
heed, had illuminated his very existence. He did not (as so many do) offer
a variation of "Man!" or "Wow!" or "Cool!" He did not say the performance was gorgeous, that he was thrilled, that all presumably sophisticated
and right-minded people felt—or ought to have felt—exactly as he did. He
made it very clear that the wonder he experienced—and the illumination—
were in part due to the way in which he had attended to the music, what he
had brought to his listening. The frustration he expressed was due to his

recognition that the non-hearing woman could only feel the beat, and that Bach in his fullness would never be a possibility for her.

Our classroom encounters are not so desperate, but most of us can find an analogy in that scene. We have often found ourselves confronted by young people who have felt something equivalent to the beat, to whatever level of acoustic pitch the non-hearing woman could feel. Like that woman, many students are quite satisfied with what they have heard. They may, in fact, assert that there is something "real" and "cool" about their experience that teachers (caught up in the conventional "hearing" culture) are too remote to understand. Yet most of us know, at least theoretically, that— although we have to be moved in some fashion in order to appreciate what works of music or plays or dance pieces are about—the aesthetic experience is not simply an affair of feeling or sensation or responsiveness to a beat. Even as we welcome declarations that a specific work has been prized and enjoyed, whatever the reason, we nevertheless hope to communicate the notion that heightened understanding might well heighten enjoyment and extend the range of what is prized.

Many of us have had the kinds of experiences that have helped us realize the connection between cognitive understanding and our capacity to hear and to see and to attend. We may be reminded of this every time we are fortunate enough to have a second or third encounter with a complex work, especially if we have made some intervening effort to comprehend it a bit more. Some of us have gone several times to see the Picasso exhibition with precisely this in mind. We have viewed, say, the acrobats, or the portrait of Gertrude Stein, or the *Guernica* on different days, at different moments in our lives. And, if we have pondered at all, read at all, we are likely to have discerned more in each painting, *felt* more in response to it, each time we have been in its presence. It may be that we suddenly began seeing the acrobats as something other than frail, blue figures arranged in a kind of frieze. Perhaps we became more sensitive to the interplay of color and line and form; perhaps (having attended, and continuing to attend to shapes and nuances) we found a new subject matter emerging for us—acrobats as outcasts, on the outskirts of ordinary society, strangely dignified in their isolation, touched by the grace of their craft. Perhaps we saw something else emerging. Who knows? Surely, we were more likely to respond to the symbols in the *Guernica,* the images of suffering and the destructiveness of pain. We were more intent on noticing the electric bulb, the sun, the torch, things we may not have seen before because we did not know quite how to engage in the special sort of noticing that permits a painting to show itself as something other than a commentary or a topical account or a representation of something "out there," "in the world."

Similar things may be said about the Mozart Clarinet Quintet, *Madame Bovary,* Martha Clarke's *Haiku,* a movie like *Citizen Kane.* Not only is an active and informed perceiving required; an attentiveness to the qualities of the medium is required, and this, in turn, depends upon the kind of understanding many of us are about to gain through our work with teaching artists. I mean an understanding of the elements of perception, of the kinds of qualities that distinguish each of the languages of art: tone, color, sonority, texture, contour, volume, light and shade, rhythm, beat. I mean an understanding brought about, not simply by means of information and explanation, but by means of actual and personal engagements with the several arts.

Our view is that understanding can only be enriched when we actually work with the raw materials of music, dance, and drama: the medium of sound; the medium that is the body in motion; the medium of language or gesture or movement in space. You are going to discover, sometimes with a veritable shock of awareness, the degree to which such understanding enables you to move out toward, to be present at performances and created works, the degree to which knowing can open perceptual possibilities and, indeed, enable us to feel more, to sense more, to be more consciously in the world.

But that is not all. It is not only a matter of discovering something about the qualities of the diverse art forms with which we intend to deal, nor even of realizing that something new is likely to be disclosed every time we encounter a given work of art—something that always lies beyond. There is also the importance of knowing that works of art exist in their own space, what some call an "art world," apart from the mundane and the routinized and the everyday. This being so, they can be achieved and made meaningful only when those who attend are willing to leap out of the ordinary and be present, as authentic and incomplete beings, to the works at hand.

Surely we have to know enough not to apprehend a dance called *Haiku* mainly as a philosophical statement, for all the fact that it deals ostensibly with the life cycle. We have to bracket out, put in parentheses at least for a time, what we *know* about the life cycle, even what we have learned about the haiku in Japanese culture. Otherwise, we may find ourselves unable to attend to the work as a privileged object, made for our delectation and delight. Too involved with summoning up what we have read about the haiku (and about Japan, anthropology, and even Pilobolus and modern dance), we may be unable to attend to the gestures, movements, surfaces, patterns in space, the weaving in of musical sound, the play of light. The recognitions, associations, meanings will come later; and the richness of them, the depth of them, may well be a function of the intensity of our attending.

So we need to know something about aesthetic space and the significance of distancing or uncoupling, to the end of grasping a work in its integrity and its autonomy. But we need to know something else too, and this brings me back to my beginning. We need to understand what is involved as we move (as we should) from attending to the work in its integrity to moments of presence, of felt relation to the work, when we allow our imagination to play on what we have perceived, when we incarnate it and make it ours. It is at this point that the work may infuse our consciousness, bring new and unexpected patternings into our reflected-on experience, offer us new vantage points on the world.

I was talking, at the start, about a closing of gaps, a making of patterns and effecting of connections. Only we—live, situated human beings—can make such patterns and connections, and the making of them may be thought of as identical with the creation of meanings or, if you like, the making of creations. Not only do new orderings lie ahead for all of us, but an intensified pursuit of meanings. The subjective dimension of our knowing, our awareness, will be brought into play, that part of us which is so discouraged by those intent on making us conform to official descriptions of a so-called objective "reality." We ourselves, unique persons living in a shared world, will be enlisted in the sense-making process, as we must be every time we attend to a play, listen to a quartet, watch a dance. And this is one of the things we will want to learn how to communicate to those we teach. Through the awareness, through the wide-awakeness brought about by aesthetic education (or by authentic teaching conducted to that end), our students will in some sense be free to find their own voices, as they find their eyes and ears. They may even find themselves free for a time to possess their own lived worlds.

Multiple Visions:
Aesthetic Moments and Experiences

Think of the whiteness, the tension of a dancer's legs on point under a shining red skirt; think of a lithe black figure leaping and of the sound of wind instruments, flutes, and strings, the sound of Bach. Think of the pale, crouching, sliding, protrusive shapes of *Haiku* and those diverse images in half-lit space. Recall the melodic line, the transparent textures of the Ravel quartet, the rhythms and charged energies in *Games.*

Experiencing works like these in a particular way, we are very likely to encounter bright examples of what might be called the aesthetic moment—perhaps living through lyrical moments of our own as we do so. Yes, it is possible to have aesthetic experiences with the sight of trees, animals, sunsets, thunderstorms, babies' hands, the rush of children on a street. But certain kinds of objects and events are particularly suited for aesthetic regard. They are made by living persons for living persons; they offer each of us visions *for us*—if we are willing to open ourselves to them, to attend.

Each work—the *Brandenburg Concerto,* a scene from *A Midsummer Night's Dream,* a Picasso painting—is a selection from the appearing world. By that I mean the shaped, colored, sounding world through which we move, day to day, as we live, and to which we so seldom pay heed. I do not mean the world of numbers or electrons or molecules, the Xs and the Ys. Wallace Stevens, in his poem called "The Motive for Metaphor," wrote about the motive for metaphor shrinking from "the A B C of being" (1982, p. 288). He meant that it is in the world as it *appears* to us that we look for resemblances, seek out connections, identify possibilities, go in quest of meanings. The poet is moved to make metaphors when, after exploring and paying imaginative attention to aspects of the phenomenal field (the world as it impinges on his/her consciousness, as it presents itself, as it appears), he/she selects out that which seems to call out to him/her, to hold potential meaning, to give off a kind of light.

Many works of art may be understood to begin with such selecting from the world of sounds and colors and shapes. Then the ordering takes place, the composing of sensuous and formal elements, the embodying of what has been perceived and felt and imagined in musical notes, particular kinds of movements, deliberate actions, words. The work to which this gives rise—the object or the event—must be grasped, perceived, attended to in a certain way if it is to arise in another's experience as a work of art.

Perceiving, it is often said, is the beginning, the ground. It is important to think about what this means, because it is so fundamental to aesthetic grasping and apprehension. We need to recognize that perception involves a direct apprehension of some complex totality as it is given and presented to our viewing or listening consciousness. It enables us to look at *Games,* for instance, not as a shifting arrangement of distinct sensory images (faces at a window, singing voices, yellow and green and pink dresses, blue jeans, angular movements, thrusts, leaps) that we are asked to interpret mentally and link together into a whole called "dance," but as light, sound, moving shapes, gestures in their particularity and, at once, aspects of a structure, a design. Opening ourselves as perceivers to the work, entering into it kinaesthetically, we free ourselves to grasp it in its vital fullness and complexity. It is not a matter of linking disparate pieces together piece by piece, like beads on a string. Rather, it is a matter of discovering a vision of wholeness in the making, of "incoherent fragments" becoming coherent in dynamic form.

Encountering *Games* again, pondering the problem of awareness, I thought of the approach taken by the choreographer of that piece, Donald McKayle. He wrote:

> In my own work, I always demand a certain vibrancy, an inner vitality that communicates through the viscera, not the mind. While the mind is never dormant, it does not hold sway in all areas, and definitely should not in dance. The senses must be reached before the mind. The reflection afterward, which is then basically a process of the mind, should—if the experience has been meaningful—once more awaken this sensory network. (1969, pp. 55–57)

We would be unable to come in touch with such "vibrancy" and "vitality" if we were unable to address ourselves, with our own energy, to what is being enacted on the stage. *Games,* according to McKayle, opens with "songs and dances of play." Beer cans are imaginatively converted into toys, but then the dance becomes a dance of hunger and finally "a sordid dance of terror." If we could not attend to the dance as a whole, we could not have seen or sensed such transmutations. We would not have known the intrinsic gratification that accompanies the recognition of a totality, a completed design. Nor would we have experienced the strange coming together of some of our own memories and feelings—the perception of new meanings in our own lived worlds.

Perceiving a dance, a painting, a quartet means taking it in and going out to it. The action required is at the furthest remove from the passive gaze that is the hallmark of our time: the blank receptivity induced by the television set, the "laid-back" posture of which the young are so proud. Perceiving is an active probing of wholes as they become visible. It involves, as it goes on, a sense of something still to be seen, of thus far undisclosed possibility. It requires a mental and imaginative participation (even when the mind does not "hold sway"), a consciousness of a work as something there to be achieved, depending for its full emergence on the way it is attended to and grasped.

Ernst Gombrich, the art historian, has often written about the ways in which a beholder must collaborate with a visual artist to transform a colored canvas into a semblance of the visible world (Gombrich, 1965). So it is with other arts, including literature. Georges Poulet, writing about the act of reading, has said:

> At the beginning of Mallarmé's unfinished story, *Igitur,* there is the description of an empty room, in the middle of which, on a table there is an open book. This seems to me the situation of every book, until someone comes and begins to read it. Books are objects. On a table, on bookshelves, in store windows, they wait for someone to come and deliver them from their materiality, from their immobility. When I see them on display, I look at them as I would at animals for sale, kept in little cages, and so obviously hoping for a buyer. For— there is no doubting it—animals do know that their fate depends on a human intervention. . . .Isn't the same true of books? Made of paper and ink, they lie where they are put, until the moment some one shows an interest in them. They wait. Are they aware that an act of man might suddenly transform their existence? They appear to be lit up with that hope. Read me, they seem to say. I find it hard to resist their appeal. (1969, pp. 53–68)

This suggests something that applies to many works of art—objects or events that take on aesthetic existence only in transaction with some human consciousness.

It is not just a matter of showing an interest, however. It is, as I have said, a matter of perceiving, noticing in a certain way. The noticing I have in mind also involves an awareness of the medium, the material out of which the particular work of art is made: the textures of Bartók's musical sounds; the forcefulness and pensiveness of the instruments in their virtuosity; the lights and colors and kinetic patterns of the movement that is dance. The qualities of each medium depend for their disclosure upon someone singling them out, identifying them for a particular kind of attention.

We might look at the auditorium we are inhabiting at this moment. Under ordinary observation, there are material things all around, set out in some kind of metrical order in physical space. Also, there are things we understand in terms of their use value and practicality: the seats, the doors, the light. Now it is possible to shift our perspective as we look around, to uncouple the shapes and textures and lights and the rest from the ordinary and the practical. It is possible to focus attention on the redness, the texture of the seats; on the linear forms in the panelling; on the glimmer of faces in the shadows; on the glint of silk on a sleeve or the spurt of green on a shirt; on echoing, whispering sounds; on the dark oblongs at the back of the stage. Doing so, we become sensitive, as we ordinarily are not, to the appearances of things and the sounds and the feel of things against our skin. Attending to, "prehending" qualities in this fashion, as Aldrich (1963) says, we may discover the shades of red, say, the slope of the seats, or even the feel of carpet on the steps to be interesting for their own sakes, worthy of some kind of contemplation. Once this occurs, we will have located the theater itself in a kind of aesthetic space, a space determined by the intensities or the values of the colors and sounds and shapes of which we may have become suddenly aware.

It is not that the physical room becomes unreal or non-existent. It exists in its configurations and can be restored, once we regain our ordinary perspective on what lies around. I simply want to suggest the dependence of the qualitative aspect of things on a certain sort of noticing. And I want to underline the notion that aesthetic qualities are perceptible attributes of actual objects and events (of chairs, teacups, street-corner meetings), attributes that are made to appear intrinsically interesting and significant when they are allowed to exist in an aesthetic space. Think of the significance of Cézanne's monumental forms, his grays and blues, in one of his renderings of Mount St. Victoire, for instance, when the painting is permitted to exist in aesthetic space. Think of how intrinsically interesting the colors of the costumes were and the movements of the dancers in *Games,* at least for those of us who attended, who paid heed. Recall some of the street scenes in a production of *Romeo and Juliet:* the swirling young bodies; the color contraries; the shine of buckles; the sweep of swords.

The crucial and fascinating point is that works of art are deliberately created for the kind of perceiving we are called on to engage in with respect to the theater. They are, for that reason, conceived of as privileged objects. They are created not solely for the sake of making visible and audible and palpable the stuff out of which they were fashioned, the colors and sounds and shapes, but to communicate something by means of that display—something that can only be grasped by those who attend, something that opens vistas on what lies beyond.

I have been emphasizing the fact that the work or the performance can only emerge as an aesthetic object or event in encounters with some human consciousness. Works of art do not reveal themselves automatically, you see. I have been suggesting that they have to be achieved. And they are most likely to be achieved by those who know how to notice, how to actively perceive. Ordinarily, it takes time, if consciousness is to be informed by what is seen and heard. It occurs in a "vivid present," in which inner and outer time are somehow unified:

> Living in the vivid present . . . the working self experiences itself as the origi-
> nator of the ongoing actions and, thus, as an undivided total self. It experiences

its bodily movements from within; it lives in ... experiences which are inaccessible to recollection and reflection; its world is a world of open anticipations. (Schutz, 1967, p. 216)

These experiences may be associated with the sense of our personal histories, against the background of which we move into the presence of works of art. They are, for the moment, inaccessible, because we suppress our awareness of them when we move out toward a painting, a sonata, a play. In that moment, similarly, we suspend what we know about art history and the contexts in which the works were made. We do not, of course, erase what we have learned about the arts or about ourselves. It is obvious that such learning, when assimilated, enriches our perception and our pleasure; indeed, whatever relevant knowledge we have amassed provides more points of contact with any given work. It may open channels of aesthetic awareness, blocked, say, by our ignorance of the twelve-tone scale or the meaning of collage or the uses of imagery in poems. The point is that what we have come to know need not be in the forefront of our minds at the moment of our encounter with a work of art. If it is, we are likely to be distracted, preoccupied; our attention is likely to be diffused.

But our lives remain the ground against which we experience works of art. There is a sense in which coming in contact with a work is like meeting another human being. Meetings of this sort can never take place in a vacuum, in isolation from lived biography. But when persons open themselves to one another, there is always a sense of new profiles to be experienced, new aspects to be understood. So it often is in encounters with the arts, if we are open, if we take the time. If we attend from our own centers, if we are present as living, perceiving beings, there is always, always more.

Imagination Transmutes "Antic Fables" ...

We have been resonating to performances, one after the other. We have explored the materials out of which the pieces performed were made: the medium of sound; the stuff of language; the body in motion. We have explored the uses of tension and release in creating the qualitative surfaces of what is seen upon a stage; we have discovered how they contribute to what we feel. We have attended to visible metaphors of various kinds: the stricken gesture at the end of *Games;* the dancer's foot on point in the *Four Temperaments* pas de deux; the two-dimensional cut-outs of human shapes on the walls of one of the art classrooms. We have begun listening differently to the conversation among the instruments in a string quartet. Several of us have heard a vibrato for the first time; some have, for the first time, found themselves able to single out developing and recurring themes; still others have heard, as never before, the beauty of a clarinet's melodic line.

And many of us, somewhat to our surprise, have begun to find our way in the complex work of musical art called *Ancient Voices of Children.* We have done so by relating to the voice at first, or to the Lorca poetry, or to the bolero rhythm pounding below; and gradually, gradually, we have come to see the point of the circular notation with its markings for mandolin, oboe, piano, singer, and with its evocations of Mahler and Bach. Gradually, gradually, we have come to realize that the dialogue between the woman and the boy is an integral part of the developing meaning and of the musical structure as well.

All this signifies that we are experiencing the transformation of increasing numbers of works of art into what may become aesthetic objects for us, objects of *our* aesthetic experiencing. We are breaking through to new horizons of sound and feeling. We are beginning, just beginning, to suspect what still lies beyond.

Consider what William Shakespeare's *A Midsummer Night's Dream* is becoming—familiar though it may be. We can see it as a play of coruscating fictions, having to do with maskings, pretendings, what Titania calls "forgeries" and Oberon "shaping"—if not "hateful"—fantasies. All of these, we now realize, are direct and indirect ways of talking about the arts. Remember Theseus with his "antic fables," his reminder that:

> . . . *as imagination bodies forth*
> *The forms of things unknown, the poet's pen*
> *Turns them to shapes, and gives to airy nothing*
> *A local habitation and a name.*

We may have been reminded now and then of the strange images, the fearful images, the "things unknown" so often released by unbridled fantasy. Shakespeare spoke of the fantasies of the madman and the frenzied lover. Some of us might think of the addict or the seeker after sensory shocks and the thrill of violence. If we do, we might recognize again the special powers of the poet, the artist, who orders and embodies such images, who forms deliberately and transmutes and names. These activities, these achievements (the giving to "airy nothing a local habitation and a name") have been, in some core fashion, our primary concern.

Our focus has been on what the poet can do, and the choreographer, the playwright, the composer. It has been on what, in turn, the performer or the interpreter can do to make their texts and scores and scripts into something visible, audible, palpable, accessible to persons willing to pay heed. So much depends on the ways we go out to what is offered to us, on our participation, our openness to the qualities of what we hear and see—to what has been, for many of us, heretofore unsuspected, unheard, unseen.

But what accounts for all of this? And how, as the moments go on, does this phenomenon affect us, work in our experience, open new vistas to what may often strike us as astonishing? And why should we wonder? Why should we even ask?

Reflective encounters with performances that mark our days are enabling us to find out more and more about particular art forms and about the ways in which they are made. Because we know more, we are seeing and hearing more. On the surface, that would seem to be enough. Nevertheless, we feel bound to concern ourselves with the complexities of aesthetics, with the range of troubling questions that have to do with the languages of art and the nature of the artistic-aesthetic itself. And, somehow, the questioning appeals to many of us: the wonder, the astonishment that there can be *Prometheus Bound* and *Mourning Becomes Electra* and Rembrandt's self-portraits and William Blake's poetry and Martha Graham's *Appalachian Spring,* and that they all exist in some extended present and retain the capacity to make visions possible. How can this come to be? How do such works take on aesthetic existence for us? How do they bring illumination into our lives? How do they bring us in touch with ourselves?

Were it not for our questioning and our efforts to respond, what we are doing here might seem like a mode of art education linked to what is thought of as art appreciation. Granted, it may be carried on at a particularly high level of excellence, because of the quality of the teaching artists involved. Granted, too, the ambience of a space like Lincoln Center makes many of us feel like initiates, credentialed members of the contemporary "art world." But our focal concerns go beyond art education in any traditional sense. This is why we are so interested in the shifting meanings of art in human life and in the multiple ways there are of focusing on and grasping diverse works of art. We are interested, also, in what happens after we have pondered our experiences with them. We are eager to understand what it is that allows us to perceive new aspects of our condition, after we have reflected on them "in tranquillity," what it is that permits us to find fresh significance in our being in the world.

We do not want our encounters to take place in the sealed-off, hermetic atmosphere sometimes associated with the "high" arts. Nor do we want to accede to the widespread view that involvements with the arts are somehow magical, intuitive, subjective—beyond understanding, beyond words. Only as we conceptualize what is happening to us as we teachers participate can we be clear about the experiences we want to make possible for our students. Only as we become somewhat clear about the relationship between what we are learning here and the buzzing, booming confusion of ordinary things can we talk about the place of the arts in education, as education is carried on today.

We are all aware that, for generations, the arts have been treated either as didactic forms or as decorative devices in education, intended either to improve or to motivate. They have been relegated to figurative back alleys in places where cognitive activity, practical concerns, and moral behaviors have been considered central, and even in places where there has been a presumably idealistic social concern. What is thought of as art-making—or creativity—has been used therapeutically, sometimes for the sake of pure self-expression or sensory play, both of which are surely valuable but may have little to do with the arts. They have been located, more often than not, in an affective realm, with the implication that the affective is alternative to the cognitive, that educators are fated to think in terms of either/or.

Very commonly, the arts are linked to a type of self-indulgence, to fun and games that are not serious; they are treated as a kind of midsummer night's dream. In a few places, usually in elite schools, the handling of the artistic-aesthetic encourages a bland consumerism. A kind of haughty connoisseurship develops, and there remains little relevance for what transpires when persons are freed to engage in a discriminating way with works of art. Or, because of an odd confusion between the aesthetic and the moral, people may distance themselves and treat politics, say, as theater, a revolution as spectacle, the plight of refugees as a pitiable media event. And the terms become confused. It is not long since people were prone to say, "He/she is a beautiful human being," not even pondering the difference between saying that someone is physically beautiful and judging that person to be compassionate or humane. Even today, we put stress on the image of the public figure rather than on his/her capabilities or worth.

If we learn anything at Lincoln Center Institute, we learn the appropriateness of specific vocabularies when talking about art and non-art—and the inappropriateness of others. Even more important, we learn the degree of

craftsmanship and care and discipline required for the making and interpretation of art forms. We need only recall the members of the Emerson
Quartet discussing their work with us, or what we now know went into the
making of *Citizen Kane* and Kenneth Rinker's *Four*. It cannot but seem
strange to us, at this juncture, to hear people speak of the arts as fundamentally playful, accidental, *easy*—the chance results of intuitive responses
or spiritual insights or moments of inspiration or even semi-automatic marks
on a canvas or a page. This is why it is so necessary for us to pose our own
questions with regard to what we ourselves have done and experienced,
with the end of granting the arts at long last their proper place in the schools.
Surely we can learn to articulate more clearly what it is about making and
attending that so often opens up new perspectives, that allows people to perceive new experiential possibilities, that offers them new symbolic languages
through which to express themselves. Surely, when we are aesthetically educated, we can break through the either/or.

Yes, we all want to encourage and must encourage more exploration of
media under the guidance of artists and art teachers. We all want to stimulate the making of images, the putting of words together, the notating of
songs, the editing of film, the shaping of gestures in available space. And
many of us realize by now how such explorations can be related, far more
than they presently are, to aware encounters with the several arts, allowing
for students' levels of development, but not excluding the younger child.

But there is more. Many of us, reflecting upon our experiences here, realize once again that a pas de deux or pieces of music like the Mozart quintet (*Clarinet Quintet in A-Major, K. 581*) do not reveal all they have to
reveal naturally or automatically. There is pleasure to be found in letting the
sound flow through and around one, moving into reverie, sitting passively
and allowing the sweetness of it (or the sprightliness or percussiveness) make
one feel good. We know that there is delight simply in watching dancers
reaching, stretching, curving their bodies, becoming images of kinetic beauty
on a lighted stage. Once we begin *thinking*, however, about what it signifies
to engage with musical works and dance works, we soon realize how much
remains to be discovered by those who can notice what there is to be noticed.
We realize how far we can go beyond "feeling good" once we become aware
of qualities, once we learn what it actually means to be attentive, to go out
to the works at hand, to take the risk of going deeper and deeper to gain a
sense of what lies beyond.

I am talking, of course, about the relevance of aesthetic education when
it comes to full apprehension of works of art. It is clear to many of us by
now that involvement with aesthetic questioning heightens awareness of

what is demanded of us as listeners, as beholders. Such involvement heightens our consciousness of the mystery as well, as it discloses possibilities we could not have anticipated before. We cannot but realize that teachers who have thought about their own experiencing, their own moments of joy, are the ones in a position to make significant choices where the arts are concerned. This is because they *know* in some profound sense; they have "been there"; they are committed to opening doors.

Teachers of this sort are likely to exert themselves in the creation of something resembling an art space in their schools: a space accessible to all kinds of children, to their fellow teachers, to the parents who come by. All depends upon a willingness to recognize how much engagement with the arts has to do with wide-awakeness, perceptual aliveness, the sense of discovery, the desire to learn and thereby go beyond. Those truly concerned, authentically concerned, understand that it is not merely a matter of providing performances now and then, not simply a matter of hanging a Monet here, a Jackson Pollock there, or turning the light on over the reproduction of the Raphael *Madonna and Child*.

They know about the circles of quietness that have to be drawn to enable persons to take their own time in grasping the appearance, the shape and sound of things. They know about the need to create the kinds of situations that release spontaneity and the desire to articulate what has been made visible in the everyday world. I mentioned earlier what a few moments from *Children of a Lesser God* made me think about teaching, about communication, about the gulfs between the hearing and the non-hearing, about the gaps some of us may never cross. What I found in that play did not resolve the complexity of teaching those who cannot connect or the problem of communicating what one values to those who prefer other things. But it made me more perceptive of what is entailed by such an effort. It made me more intent on making my own interpretations of situations like that when they arise in classrooms, becoming more present to them when they occur.

Again, it must be evident that participation in this dimension of aesthetic questioning and reflection adds to the wonder as it increases the complexity. Crucial, for example, in most aesthetic inquiry is the problem of the relation between subject and object where works of art and their realization are concerned. Think for a moment of how much there is to ponder, once we acknowledge that subject and object are the two poles of the aesthetic encounter. We must ask ourselves what there is about human consciousness that allows for such encounters, not to speak of the pleasures and the visions they make possible, at least for some. We must ask ourselves about the differences among human subjects and the degree to which they are the same. We must confront the mystery of one subjectivity's grasping another, especially when the other has found expression through shaped content, embodied form. We must try to comprehend how each of us, unique persons with unique life histories, can move inside works created by quite different human beings and actually discover ourselves there. We have asked ourselves and must continue asking ourselves what it *is* about the work of art that allows this to happen, what it *is* about a painting or a dance or a piece of music that seems to command attention, that may sometimes change a life. We must ponder further the matter of the aesthetic point of view, the special mode of attending that permits certain kinds of objects, certain events to emerge as works of art.

It may seem dissonant for people who have sailed so high in classes or workshops to have to take pause and think about it all. There are always those who believe that analysis or reflective thought interferes with the experience of art. My point, however, is that self-reflection and critical consideration can be as liberating as they are educative. They, too, have the potentiality of opening multiple worlds.

The languages and images and sounds found in art, it has been said, make perceptible, visible, and audible that which is no longer or not yet "perceived, said, and heard in everyday life." Herbert Marcuse wrote that art makes "the petrified world speak, sing, perhaps dance" (1977/1978, p. 73). To be petrified is to be incapable of learning, impervious to change. If the artistic-aesthetic can indeed open up a petrified world, provide new standpoints on what is taken for granted, those who are empowered to engage with the arts cannot but pose a range of questions that never occurred to them before. They cannot but do so in the light of what they themselves are living, what they themselves are discovering, what they themselves want to know. And it is surely those who can pose their own questions, pose them in person, who are the ones ready to learn how to learn.

At a moment when so many forces are working to thrust young people into passivity, the open-mindedness and the sense of exploration fostered by aware aesthetic involvements may well move them to break with "the cotton wool" of dailyness—to use Virginia Woolf's language in *Moments of Being* (1985)—the plain ordinariness of things. To give up stock and stereotyped responses is, at any age, to achieve a new readiness. Not only may there be a consciousness of things in their multiplicity and particularity; there may also be a consciousness of them as they actually present themselves to the individual thinker and perceiver, the person grounded in his/her own lived world. And this may well lead to a fresh orientation to the search for meanings, for new modes of sense-making. If all this is coupled with an awareness that each human being can become different as he/she moves on his/her way—and that things can be otherwise than they are—new sorts of possibilities may be disclosed. They cannot be predicted, of course. Nothing can be predetermined *or* predicted in the artistic-aesthetic domain. But anything is possible. We have only to free ourselves, to choose.

Learning and Development, Tacit Awareness, and the Enlargement of Possibility

The questions have been coming, I am glad to say. They have to do with criticism and its relation to aesthetics and to the "art world" we are inhabiting at this time. Also, they have to do with the matter of curriculum and what an aesthetic education curriculum might signify. Finally, they have to do with the connection between what we actually *know* about learning and development and what we ought to try to do if we want to engage young persons with the arts.

We might begin by reopening the question of what must be taken into account by those eager to create art spaces in their schools, how we all might *think* about developing whatever awarenesses are possible among those we try to teach. We do not only want to make possible enhanced enjoyment of the arts; we want, in addition, to cultivate the disposition to choose to engage with diverse art forms, to attend and explore and take risks. Wonderful things can happen when the artists conduct workshops around artworks like *Little Improvisations* and *Haiku* and the Mozart quintet; wonderful things can also happen when the artists leave. We cannot, however, help but be interested in what might happen when our students leave their classrooms, when they go beyond what they have been taught. We know so well that much of the learning comes later—when a young person tries out a gesture (or a fling, or a slashing movement) at the end of the corridor, when someone tries to pick out the theme of the Mozart on a piano or a guitar, when someone tries to recapture a fragment of dialogue before a mirror at home. How do we invent the kinds of situations that release people for moments like these?

If we, as teachers, are not clear about what discriminating awareness signifies, we will have no way of clarifying our aims or identifying our ends
when we teach in the art fields. We will have no way of recognizing aesthetic
sensitivity when we see it expressed; we may ourselves be naive. To be naive
is to be prone to reject immediately what displeases: an atonal work of
music, for example; an abstract modern dance; a play without an ordinary
beginning, middle, and end. To be naive is to be likely to lapse into merely
sentimental reverie when the music sounds sweet, when the ballerina is beautiful, when the play confirms hopes and expectations, when the film ends
"happily." To be naive is to be unable to distinguish between a sculpture
and a glacier-eroded rock, between Monet's painted poplars and the poplars
as viewed on a misty morning along the Seine. It is, in other words, to be
incapable of distinguishing between those "privileged objects" we have called
aesthetic objects and natural things perceived aesthetically.

One of our dominant concerns is to counter such naiveté—in the interests of the children, in the interests of ourselves. Teachers need to become
increasingly aware of the distinctive possibilities and limitations of the arts
if they are to make them in any manner accessible to children and young
persons, if the arts are to make a signal difference in anyone's life. Our experiences have already helped us discover what it means to attend in such a
way that the works we see and hear speak out more and more fully to us as
living beings. We are beginning to realize, too, that each of us has at some
point to make critical decisions. We hope, as one writer on aesthetics says,
that such decisions are made "as precipitates of a voluminous experience of
apprehension rather than as consequences of an instantaneous interaction
between the object and fixed preconceptions that often have little to do with
art or art criticism" (Gotshalk, 1962, p. 161). He goes on to make the point
that "disciplined art experience is ordinarily much more pure, sustained, and
active than naive experience. At its best, it treats the work of art with the
single-mindedness, vigor, and respect that the creative artist presumably
bestowed on it" (1962, p. 161). Working with practicing artists, many of us
have learned what such people "bestow" on the works they make (or interpret, or perform). And we have come to recognize how much depends upon
the quality of our attending—and what pervades that attending in the course
of an encounter with a work of art.

How are we to understand criticism? More important than a study of our
relation to professional art critics is the realization that the undertaking that
is criticism is a mode of thinking or inquiry in which teachers, most particularly, must learn to engage. Of course there are academic critics of all sorts,
professional journal critics, so-called "experts" of all kinds, people whose

talk about art provides some of the context in which we do our work. And there are identifiable critical approaches (impressionist, expressionist, formalist, experiential) which govern some of our own readings of various works of art.

I am mainly concerned about the communicating that we, as teachers, are bound to do. I am concerned with the experiences about which we try to speak—and which we sometimes try to share. This speaking ought to become more precise, more imaginative, more articulate, the more we become absorbed in and understanding about the arts. Criticism may be conceived as talk about—and elucidation of—particular works of art (*Ancient Voices of Children,* an Emily Dickinson sonnet, the Ravel *Bolero,* Woody Allen's *Manhattan,* William Styron's *Sophie's Choice*). Sometimes it is linked to and enriched by talk about styles and movements in art: Romanticism, say, or Cubism, or Theatre of the Absurd. Sometimes, obviously, it is not. The point is that we *do* perform some mode of criticism whenever we talk about specific works and attempt to make them available on various levels, in various modes.

Aesthetics draws on such reflection and such talk. It has often been called a "second order" mode of study, since it involves inquiry into or clarification of critical talk and writing, as it involves reflection upon personal experiences with the several arts. As you realize, we "do" aesthetics when we probe such matters as the meaning of the aesthetic experience, distancing or uncoupling, qualitative perceiving, imaginative awareness, the aesthetic point of view. But we can "do" all this only on the ground of actual experiences and in the context of some sort of critical talk. And as we become increasingly familiar with aesthetic thinking, we become increasingly adept at looking at the assumptions underlying our own and various critics' judgments: assumptions about the nature of art and the place of the arts; assumptions about beauty and significance and subject matter and form. Criticism, like the talking we do in our classrooms, is always grounded in certain assumptions of this kind. It can be illuminating (and even liberating) to be clear about them, to be able to articulate where we stand.

This is another reason for our interest in provoking you to clarify your own notions of what the arts can do and be. You realize, by this time, that careful attending must precede any authentic effort to act as teacher-critic. If we are to point to (for the sake of disclosing) aspects of a painting or a piece of music, if we are to share our perceptions of what we have seen or heard, we must first have noticed what there was to be noticed. We must have *begun,* at least, to impart aesthetic existence to the work, to be present to it, to make it live *for us.* Of course we may consult scholars on occasion (art historians, musicologists, critics, iconographers). We may even take the time to study some theories of art. But whatever studying we do ought to feed into and focus our perceiving, enhance the attentiveness with which we address ourselves to particular works. It is out of that sort of attentiveness, not out of a mediated expertise, that we ought to come to our students. Our aim, after all, is to help them become more wide-awake, more aware.

In my own case, no matter how many times I have encountered a given work of art, I try to approach my teaching of it on the ground of some immediate satisfaction, the kind of satisfaction John Dewey said is simply had. This summer, for instance, I have been working with a number of Hawthorne short stories, all of which I have read over and over through the years. Nevertheless, before I go to class, I read each one again. I try to respond to its command somehow, as if it were wholly new. I consciously move into an imaginary mode of awareness so that I can enter into the illusioned world, say, of "Ethan Brand" or "Young Goodman Brown." Not only do I uncouple myself from my ordinary twentieth-century world; I set aside the multiple criticisms I have read (even as I hope they have enhanced my attentiveness, allowed me to "see" more). I try, all over again, to perceive the story as a shape, a content given a particular form. I seek the internal connections in it, in the story-as-I-experience-it. I often go into class with a feeling of wonder at what I have found. And I go in with a conviction that there is value in the work, value I want my students, too, to feel.

But that initial response (even after so many years) remains corrigible, as judgments of immediate value ought always to be corrigible. I realize, on some level, that my excitement about the piece, my resonating to it may have made the original judgment unreliable. I may have felt myself in some sense compelled to value it, because of prescribed canons in American Studies, because of habit, because all teachers of American literature are expected to cherish Hawthorne's work. So I have to ponder my response again. I have to pay heed again to the design as it completes itself in my experience. I have to seek out the expressive significance once more. Only then, I suppose, do I find myself in a position to move my students to take their own journeys through the work. Only then can I decide, with some degree of authenticity, what to do to help them notice certain qualities, discriminate certain details, engage imaginatively with the text.

There is no guarantee that they will value it, anymore than there is any guarantee that they will have an aesthetic experience with it. But all I can do, as a teacher-critic, is to find a language that may help them attend. I have to have some notion of the mode of understanding necessary for the attainment of awareness. I have to be able to speak about the medium and the distinctiveness of the medium. And I have to know when to be still. The critical process, the process of making available, is what is important. It is far more important than the conclusions we might come to, certainly more important than some measurable "success."

Whether we teach the very young or the adult, we obviously have to have some clear idea of what a developed capacity in a particular symbolic medium is like. To say this is to suggest that we have to have in mind some conception of human development where the arts are concerned. There are, for all of us, sequences to have in mind, steps to take. Even in a college class, the teacher has to be cognizant of the examples, problems, themes appropriate at particular stages of development—in my case, of literary comprehension. At our Institute, the teaching artists have certainly taken into account the various stages of our development when it comes to the understanding of musical notation, say, dance movements, the building up of dramatic scenes. It has not been a matter of skill mastery; certainly, no one has relied upon formulas or recipes. But we have all come to realize the importance of some foundational understanding, some knowledge that cannot always be totally specified. The kinds of knowledge that can be made available and that feed into what we have called "tacit awareness" (Polanyi, 1967) clearly have a good deal to do with the stage at which the learners involved have arrived.

To recognize this is to recognize the need for another kind of exploration. Each of us, in our own classrooms, has to discover the kind of knowledge, the kind of formulation that effectively responds to what students at different levels want to know. At once, each of us has to discover something about the kinds of insights such knowledge may make possible. Thinking back over our own learning experience in order to learn at this Summer Session, we may find many clues. Were we not, in effect, childlike the first time we heard *Ancient Voices of Children*? Were we developed viewers when we first encountered *Four*?

The question of curriculum relates to all of this. We want to create situations in classrooms that will release our students for live and informed encounters. We want to make the richest sorts of experiences possible; we want choices to be made. The ordinary planning we have been taught to do probably has to be reconceived. The orientation to predetermined objectives has to be set aside. As we have seen, there is a kind of logic within each art form: certain kinds of awarenesses and certain modes of technical mastery are required if works like *Ancient Voices* or *Four* are to be achieved. And, yes, patterns of development have to be held in mind. For all that, what happens must be conceived of as an emergent, as a realized possibility. It cannot be preplanned or predicted, no matter how carefully wrought are the occasions created, no matter how much we take into account.

A curriculum in aesthetic education, then, is always in process, as we who are teachers try to make possible a continuing enlargement of experience. There must be open-mindedness and a sense of exploration; there must be breaks with ordinariness and stock response. If this is how we approach curriculum, there may be a new readiness, a new ripeness in our students and even in ourselves. There may be an increasing awareness of things in their particularity, of beauty and variety, and form. People may be brought to watch and to listen with heightened attentiveness and care. The questions may keep coming. We can ask no more of ourselves.

The Phases of Imaginative Action, the Feeling of Beauty

I have been suggesting that our own intensifying awareness of particular works—the Shakespeare, the George Crumb, the Balanchine, the Bach, the Martha Clarke—especially when reflected upon over time, ought to suggest an end to have in view when we return to our classrooms. I was trying to suggest as well that, whatever the age of those we teach, we will be making an effort to disclose, to direct attention to certain aspects of works like these. We will be making an effort to enhance the perceptiveness of those around us, to intensify interest, to widen understanding, always with some sensitivity to levels of development, the accumulated experience of the young persons with whom we are concerned. We will be, in other words, doing something resembling criticism—developing languages that help individuals recognize things, leading their eyes to look and find. We will have made ourselves into teacher-critics once we are able to free others to perceive and hear patterns, to discern relationships when they are exposed to such phenomena as *A Midsummer Night's Dream* or *Four* or the Mozart quintet.

It would seem to be evident that we are in a better position to empower students to notice what there is to be noticed if we have pondered the significance of such noticing. We may even be better teachers once we have thought, not solely about the particular works we have witnessed and explored, but about the domain of the artistic-aesthetic in general—the distinctive province of meaning into which this Institute has ushered us, making it possible for some of us to take new perspectives upon our own lived worlds.

We "do" aesthetics, once again, when we think about what it means to release ourselves into an art space, an alternative reality. We "do" aesthetics when we consider the challenge of transmuting a given work—*Games,* let us say, or the *French Suite in G*—into an aesthetic object, an object of our own aesthetic experiencing: something that offers a particular kind of pleasure, that illuminates in a distinctive way, that can be cherished in a distinctive way. The insights, the modes of attending that allow that kind of transmutation to take place are not the sort that can be translated into statements of competencies or quantifiable skills. Well, I suppose they *can* be by certain kinds of people; but I think you will agree that, no matter how exhaustive the list, there is no guarantee that the exercise of the competencies mentioned will lead to the enjoyment, the discriminating awareness, the sense of disclosure most of us have in mind. Nor is there any guarantee that the work of art at hand *will* be transmuted into an aesthetic object, no matter what the level of skill nor how extravagant the claims.

Of course we believe that the more we know, the more we are likely to see and hear. Your experiences in the workshops have already taught you that. You are aware, as most of you never were, of the significance of space in relation to movement, of sonorous images and tonal qualities, of the connection between meaning and rhythm in spoken lines, of visual metaphors in film. What we hope is that what you are learning continues to feed into the tacit awareness I have spoken of, that subsidiary kind of knowledge that feeds into your focal experience with a work. It is not a matter of recapitulating or summoning up what you have learned in your workshops about, say, Bartók's atonality or the ethnic themes that appear in his work, not a matter of having the beat of iambic pentameter in mind when listening to Shakespeare. You are not asked to be ready to reproduce what you have learned from your experiments with masks or your studies of *Haiku* or even your growing comprehension of the use of poetry in musical works. The idea is to use what you have learned to see and to hear differently: to allow, for example, your awareness of the details of a dance to feed into your awareness of the dance in its totality; to *dwell* in details such as the contours and protruding forms in the Cézanne painting for the sake of moving from such awareness to the still life in its resplendent fullness. So it is with what you are learning about aesthetic space and the importance of the qualitative and the idea of the imaginary.

We want all this to enrich your actual encounters, to make the transmutation I keep speaking of more likely. The end in view, I need not repeat, is intensified consciousness, heightened appreciation. It is *not* the ability to replicate, to recite, to demonstrate the mastery of skills. What we are trying to bring about is neither measurable nor predictable. How could it be if our desire is to enable persons to be personally present to works of art? How could it be if we want so deeply to enable persons to reach out, each one in his/her freedom, to release his/her imagination, to transmute, to transform?

We have talked little about imagination; yet, in some sense, it may be the most focal of our concerns. Imagination is not only the power to form mental images, although it is partly that. It is also the power to mold experience into something new, to create fictive situations. It is, as well, the power—by means of sympathetic feeling—to put oneself in another's place. How else to identify with a non-hearing woman, a Theseus, an unmarried sister, a man hitting his head against a wall? It has often been said that ours is a culture that discourages the use of imagination, especially if imagination is understood to involve a capacity to see new possibilities in things, to perceive alternative realities, to open windows in the actual and discover what might be. It is not only that a technical culture tends to focus on abstract explanations; stress is laid upon objectivity and neutrality, on impersonal ways of looking upon the world. The enterprise of schooling too often emphasizes the need to *accede* to the world as "given," as officially and expertly described. The media give the impression that they provide windows on what is unquestionable—really real, really *there*. Young people, for all their restless searches for new sensations, are constantly pulled back (once they go to school, once they come home) to what might be called "the plain sense of things." I cannot but think of Wallace Stevens and his poem of the same name. The metaphor for human being in this poem is, strangely, an inquisitive rat.

> After the leaves have fallen, we return
> To a plain sense of things. It is as if
> We had come to an end of the imagination,
> Inanimate in an inert savoir. . . .
>
> Yet the absence of the imagination had
> Itself to be imagined. The great pond,
> The plain sense of it, without reflections, leaves,
> Mud, water like dirty glass, expressing silence

> *Of a sort, silence of a rat come out to see,*
> *The great pond and its waste of the lilies, all this*
> *Had to be imagined as an inevitable knowledge,*
> *Required, as a necessity requires.*
>
> (1982, pp. 502–503)

And somewhere else, Stevens wrote about "The Man with the Blue Guitar," and here the blue guitar became a metaphor for the imagination:

> *They said, "You have a blue guitar,*
> *You do not play things as they are.*
>
> *The man replied, "Things as they are*
> *Are changed upon the blue guitar."*
>
> (1982, p. 165)

Imagination, Stevens help us see, is the mode of grasping, of reaching out that allows what is perceived to be transformed. It is what allows four older actresses, each a personality, each a star, to be transformed into a gathering of elderly sisters, interwoven with one another, creating a pattern, a structure, a phalanx with one another. It is what permits a number of plain crossed beams and a platform to be transformed into the porch of a southern homestead (in *Home*). It makes it possible for an actress who is herself non-hearing to be transformed into a young woman who rebels in the name of signing, an outraged inhabitant of an unreal world. And it is imagination that involves the ability to pull together the diverse strands of a Copland piece, to constitute *Four* as event, as design. Without this ability, there could scarcely be aesthetic experience.

We presume that there are phases of imaginative awareness (Rader, 1974, p. 136), and we also presume that each phase can be encouraged as we teach. The first phase involves the paying attention we have stressed: the focusing, the careful noticing; the phase that permits the dance or the musical piece to emerge in its uniqueness and integrity. It is the phase in which utilitarian and moral and historical considerations are suppressed or set aside, so that the pas de deux can disclose its qualities, the changing sound of the soprano come clear. We can talk, point, disclose in such a way that this phase of awareness is provoked, extended; we can move people to pay heed.

But there is more. There is the savoring in inner time, the elaboration of what has been seen or heard, the seeping down. What has been encountered becomes an event within personal consciousness; it may begin shining toward the lived world. Clearly, we cannot *make* that happen; nor can we intrude when people are becoming aware in this way. We cannot grade them on whether or not such a phenomenon does occur. All we can do is to try to invent situations that make it more likely—allowing for time, for privacy, for silences. We have to try to move persons to think about alternative ways of being alive, possible ways of inhabiting the world. And then we may be able to help them realize the sense in which an active imagination involves transactions between inner and outer vision. And, indeed, all sorts of relationships may be created between the world of the work at hand and the worldhood of the one who attends. I spoke at the beginning of the quest for meaning as a quest for patternings, new orders in experience; and, in some way, each emergent pattern, each new order comes as a surprise. Stevens's poem on the blue guitar ends:

> *You as you are? You are yourself.*
> *The blue guitar surprises you.*
>
> (1982, p. 183)

If I could create more situations in my classroom in which this sort of surprise became palpable—in which persons could truly see alternatives, perceive connections, create new orders—I would not only feel that I was learning how to do aesthetic education. I would feel that I was on the road to becoming a teacher—at last.

Aesthetic pleasure involves many of the values I have been attempting to describe. There has been much probing of aesthetic pleasure in the literature since the days of Immanuel Kant. Kant himself wrote of pure delight in appearances, and about what could happen when people learned to hold particular objects or events in attention, when they allowed themselves to become more and more fully aware of such phenomena without thinking deliberately about them. There were other thinkers who talked of classes of pleasure and wondered whether the arts appealed to the "superior senses" or simply to the sense of play. Still others said that aesthetic pleasure was not really different from ordinary pleasure, except for the fact that it was less utilitarian and more intense. And there were those who insisted that aesthetic pleasures, being intrinsic, were not like bodily pleasures; because the organs in use—the eye, the ear, the hand—had to be transparent, so that attention could be carried directly to the object or the event or the performance. Most agree that no object can be beautiful if it gives no pleasure, even as they assert that we have to be moved in some fashion by a work if we are fully to appreciate what it is about and means to set before us, if we are to have any sort of aesthetic pleasure with what we see and hear (Hofstadter & Kuhns, 1964).

But what does it mean to be moved in this way, to respond emotionally to a work? What does it mean to encounter a work as a marvelous artifact, a presence that may fill us with wonder, with a kind of awe? What does it mean to encounter it as an expressive form, speaking to us, as it were, making us feel in unexpected ways, addressing itself to our subjectivities? There are many occasions on which we come at a work from the outside, perceiving its qualities, knowing it as an expression, but not as if it were our own, feeling a predominantly aesthetic emotion—a cool delight. I think of some of Balanchine's dances (as compared, perhaps, with Martha Graham's). I think of Barnett Newman's minimal art (as compared, perhaps, with Rembrandt's or Cézanne's work). I think of a poem by William Butler Yeats about the terrors of the world and the futility, the uselessness of art. It is called "Lapis Lazuli," and it tells of a kind of gaiety that transfigures dread. It present two Chinamen carved in lapis lazuli and a servant with a musical instrument climbing toward a little house.

> *... and I*
> *Delight to imagine them seated there;*
> *There, on the mountain and the sky,*
> *On all the tragic scene they stare.*
> *One asks for mournful melodies;*
> *Accomplished fingers begin to play.*
> *Their eyes mid many wrinkles, their eyes,*
> *Their ancient, glittering eyes, are gay.*
> (1997, p. 300)

There are other works, quite different, that call upon us to experience them from within: not as Wordsworth's personal cry of ecstasy, not as Mahler's private utterance of grief, not as Camus' own existential anguish when his character Meursault recognizes the indifference of the sky, but a human experience we ourselves can constitute for ourselves as we attend.

For an example of this, I would summon up an Elizabeth Bishop poem, "Sleeping Standing Up":

> *As we lie down to sleep the world turns half away*
> *through ninety dark degrees;*
> *the bureau lies on the wall*

> *and thoughts that were recumbent in the day*
> *rise as the others fall,*
> *stand up and make a forest of thick-set trees.*
> *The armored cars of dreams, contrived to let us do*
> *so many a dangerous thing,*
> *are chugging at its edge*
> *all camouflaged and ready to go through.*
> (1997, p. 30)

She says "we," inviting us to place ourselves in imagination at the point from which the poet is related to the world, the bureau, her own thoughts, her dreams. We can take up a "we" like that and involve ourselves in the poet's situation. We can experience what she is expressing, and the emotion informing it from the vantage point of a woman fending off sleep; and this would be quite different from admiring it (as we might admire "Lapis Lazuli") from without. The strange sensation the poet has is not our own strange feeling about getting to sleep, but the ambivalence, the dislocation are in some way present in ourselves when we realize the poem in our experience. I do feel as if I were somehow inhabiting the poet's tired, uneasy body when I read it, thinking with her voice, experiencing what she was experiencing on her own behalf, and I believe that this comes as close for me to understanding the connections between expression and emotion as anything can. And I would stress again, as I hope you would as well, how necessary it is to be open-minded about a work like this—and exploratory and involved. And there remains the need to be attentive, to release ourselves into another space when we read, an amazing space, when you think of it. Can we not but be surprised?

There is a connection between the feelings we have in the presence of certain works and what can be called beauty. "Beauty," since the days of Plato, has meant a multitude of things, very often clustering around perfection of form, harmony, synchrony, perfection of expression; and notions of beauty tend to change as notions of art change. Some have connected it with a domain of pure aesthetic exaltation, apart from all human interests, linked to "austere and thrilling raptures." Others have linked it to the general spiritual life of mankind finding expression in art. And still others have refused to see either beauty *or* art as existing in some separate realm.

Louis Arnaud Reid, who pays great attention to embodied content in the work of art, talks about the ways in which the affective value of every element in a work may bear upon, harmonize with, and help to constitute the affective value of the whole. He writes about the ways in which images cluster around interesting themes and about the ways in which their values fuse with and enhance the meaning of the total work (Reid, 1958). There is significance to be found, very often, in the enjoyment of the values arising out of an elaborate working out in form, as in a Bach fugue. But still another kind of significance is to be found when the viewer or the listener becomes deeply interested in the feeling side of what he/she apprehends. We can find an example in listening to slow music, when we dwell on the sounds of single notes and chords and, as it were, taste their affective meanings. We can find another example in looking at a painting with a particular focus on the color, or in paying particular attention to the word-sounds in a poem.

The crucial point is that significance in art, however found, must be seen as emergent. It is not something buried in a work; it is not something inherent in the subject, distinct from its form. We know that whatever affective meanings we enjoy must be apprehended through and by means of form, as we know that the form must express some effective meanings. We need only recall *Ancient Voices of Children* once again to recall how expressiveness and significance are interwoven, how meaning grows and swells in the course of the experience. There is no meaning-product; there can be no summary of or statement of the significance to be found. There is only the work to be realized by the one willing to pay heed; and there is the possibility that what emerges from the formed sounds and words and movements and vibrations might be called beautiful.

Perceiving, imagining, searching for meaning: these are the leitmotifs in what we are doing here. We realize now that the worlds presented to us, made available to us by works of art, are not the worlds of ordinary reality, of the commonplace. But they are not worlds of total gossamer or fantasy either, because they contain nothing that does not also exist in our lived worlds— once we are enabled to see what they are and what they might be. What we have discovered in *Ancient Voices* and *Haiku* and Cézanne's *The Cardplayers* is qualitatively other than the everyday. Being other, offering us new vantage points, it has made us hear as never before; it has enabled us to see.

The Maker and the Perceiver: Embodied Meanings

There can be no adequate summing up of experience in aesthetic education. There can be no packaging of what has been experienced, what has been learned. Indeed, the very notion of packaging—like the notion of a finished product—is antithetical to all that aesthetic education has come to mean. We have discovered that the more informed our encounters with the arts become, the more perspectives open for us—on the works themselves and on our lives. We not only see more and hear more as the days go by; we have (almost without realizing it) discerned new shapes, new rhythms, new significances in the ordinary world. And, if we are attentive, if we are lucky, all of this will continue on.

So many things have happened to us. Attending as we have to so many created works, we have found all sorts of occasions for new and rich experiencing. Our interest has intensified, very often, when we have been enabled to view such works as testimony to their own making. Their making—George Crumb's composing, Kenneth Rinker's choreographing, Emily Dickinson's writing of poetry, Paul Cézanne's painting—may be seen as a distinctive mode of human action and human choice. Whatever the differences among them, all these artists lived or are living lives of intellectual and moral wide-awakeness. They have created or are creating themselves *as* artists by means of the projects they have chosen or are choosing to pursue, the projects that constitute their ways of being in and acting on the world.

We who make an effort to go out to their works can only do so in terms of freely chosen projects of our own. We can only do so by means of our own will and in the contexts of our own particular lives. It might be said that, through this summer's learning, we, too, have embarked upon a new kind of life work, a new kind of choosing. There is no way of saying that it is finished, that our exploring has come to an end, not if we have chosen ourselves authentically as lovers of the arts. To think even of our experiences with *A Midsummer Night's Dream* as over and done with would be to falsify. It does not matter how often we have seen performances of the play, read and analyzed the several texts, studied the critical interpretations. We still cannot assert that we have "done" it in the manner people say they have "done" Paris or the Picasso exhibition or Louise Nevelson's chapel in the Whitney Museum. In every case, in spite of what is said, there is always, always more.

Each time we witness a performance of a play or see a painting exhibition or hear a concert (or visit Paris), we do so at a distinctive stage in our own life histories. Because we are different at different moments of our lives, the works that we encounter can never be precisely the same. Viewed as open possibilities each time we come to them, they will begin to appear as events in the ongoing human career, not objects or sediments or *things*. We who are teachers, working with newcomers, cannot but be aware of the diverse realizations that lie ahead for the works of art we make accessible. At once, we recognize that the quality and the fullness of those realizations will depend on the kind of attending we can make possible. So we ponder, as we must, the ways there are of providing the sorts of experiences we ourselves have had: experiences that lead to transformations, that open new vistas, that allow for new ways of structuring the lived world.

How can we speak of endings or summations when so much lies ahead? That is why I want to speak of beginnings on this last day of Summer Session, beginnings that *"must be thought possible. . .must be taken to be possible"* (Said, 1978, p. 35). And surely you remember T. S. Eliot:

> *What we call the beginning is often the end*
> *And to make an end is to make a beginning.*
> *The end is where we start from.*
>   (1952, p. 144)

We hope you will think about beginnings as you complete this Summer Session, not only for your students but for yourselves. We hope that you will go on encountering each piece of music, each dance, each theatrical performance with which you choose to engage as if it were a new occasion, calling upon you personally to attend, to be present, to wonder, to explore. If you can do this in the classroom, your sense of openness may well be contagious. Your students may be drawn more readily into the open-ended process of noticing, paying heed, trying to see and to hear. They too, before very long, may feel the breath of possibility.

It seems so evident that we, as teachers, must keep our questions open—the thronging questions about particular art forms and about art itself and about the place of art in human life. Only if we do so are we likely to clarify what we hope to bring about in our classrooms, whether we call it enhanced awareness, heightened understanding, enlightenment, or a new mode of literacy.

Yes, there is the realization of the relationship between increasingly informed exploration of a medium—sound and its potentialities, spoken verse, bodies in movement—and wide-awake attending. Yes, there is the importance of moments of collusion, like the moments of collusion with the musicians, when we listened in such a way as to create (we were told) a new kind of space. We are entirely cognizant by now of the manner in which the disparate and once unfamiliar sounds of *Ancient Voices of Children* became patterned for us, and more audible and distinct the more the patterning emerged. But we need to ponder what happened in our learning to listen. We need to think about the way in which the audible world expanded, as it did in our encounters with the Crumb piece, as it did for many when we heard the sounds made by the tap-dancer, Sandman Sims.

Indeed, just as Cézanne's paintings or Cubist paintings may alter our visions of the visible world, just as we learn to read nature in new ways by contemplating such paintings, so may encounters with music lead to a new informing of perception "not only of other sounds but also of the rhythms and patterns of what we see" (Goodman, 1988, p. 260). Think, for a moment, of what this implies for learning. All of us know something about the connection between felt curiosity and learning. But think of the curiosity that moved so many to find out what it was about *Ancient Voices*—how the voice made sounds like that, what the role of the poetry was, how the bolero beat connected with the harp, the bells, the saw. And recall the relation between our need to find out these things and the kind of illumination and enlightenment we hoped to achieve. Is not learning, authentic learning, a matter of going beyond? Is it not an exploration generated by wonder, curiosity, open questions? Is there not always a drive to reach beyond what is deliberately taught? Is it not the case that learning really begins when people begin teaching themselves? And is there not a special pleasure, a delight found in the discovery, in the sometimes startling realization, that what is being learned affects the manner in which we make sense of our world?

I cannot but reach back into my own personal history (as I hope you will) when I try to rediscover what all this means. There were not only the "aha" experiences that accompanied mathematical learning at certain times for me; there were not only the moments when I began grasping what it meant to "do" philosophy. I think of how learning to look through a Cubist perspective changed my view of objects and spaces and the relations between forms. I think of how T. S. Eliot (1952) made me see London Bridge anew (with the crowd flowing over it to the "Unreal City") and even the Brooklyn Bridge, and how he helped me reconceive Conrad's *Heart of Darkness* and that phrase, still nagging at me, "Mistah Kurtz—he dead" (1999, p. 87). And I remember how I learned to look at men scraping fish from reading Elizabeth Bishop on the old man with the sequins on his vest and his thumb, scraping the scales ("the principal beauty") from unnumbered fish with that "black old knife" (1997, pp. 64–66). (Clearly, I did not learn how to scrape fish; nor did I learn anything about the sociology or psychology of Nova Scotia fishermen. I was, though, helped to apprehend a dimension of life and nature I never had suspected before. And because this particular poem ends with talk of the feel, the taste of knowledge, knowledge as clear and flowing and dark, like cold moving water, I was enabled to reach far beyond what I saw and to enter places I had never been.) So it has been for me with the forms of the human body disclosed through watching Martha Graham and, later, Twyla Tharp. So it has been with the aspects, the forms of human striving, human action made visible through engagements with such plays as *Moon for the Misbegotten,* or *No Exit,* or *Death of a Salesman,* or *Six Characters in Search of an Author,* or *Antigone.* (How much less, I always think, I would know about the world—and authority and free choice and human pride—if I had never encountered *Antigone.* How much more sure of myself I would have been: I might even have been able to give you tight little answers to all the questions today, to imagine I could give you Truth.)

Now it is clear, I hope, that none of these works would have become so potent in my life if I did not know something about engaging with them. They would not have attained so much significance for me if I had not learned the differences, say, between the symbols used to construct the universe of *Antigone* and those used to render Plato's *Republic* or Sartre's *Being and Nothingness,* not to speak of the language Martha Graham had at hand, the language of gestures and movement she shaped to give us *Lamentation* and *Appalachian Spring.*

It remains altogether important to work for a sensitivity of discrimination where the various symbol systems are concerned, to discern the relationships within the distinctive forms. It remains important to enable persons to move out, to read paintings as well as poems, to locate both in an aesthetic space. I had to learn, as we all had to learn, to uncouple from the mundane and the routine in order to perceive the qualities in a play or painting or poem or sonata, in order properly to pay heed. Nelson Goodman tells us that the "aesthetic 'attitude' is restless, searching, testing—is less attitude than action: creation and re-creation" (1988, p. 242). I have been suggesting that we, as teachers, must be restless in this fashion, searching in this fashion. There is no other way of inciting the young to take this "attitude." We want to help them utter sounds, shape the sounds, learn how to listen, as we want to free them to learn how to move and attend to movement. We want to enable them to recognize some of the ways in which the formal elements in *Games,* say, or *Haiku* present very specific emotional qualities. We want to urge them to try themselves to translate wonder or the sense of mourning into gestures, to order those gestures into a design. We want to move them to seek out sounds that express surprise or anger or loss, and to come to the point at which they can link those sounds and pattern them into phrases. We have ourselves discovered here that it is not simply the words— "Every afternoon in Granada / a child dies, every afternoon" (Lorca,

1940/1995, p. 243). It is the expressiveness of the sounds, the definiteness of their expressiveness, and the forming of those words and the assimilation of them into the complex musical scheme of the whole.

We have been talking, of course, about the importance of the aesthetic point of view and the aesthetic situation, and about what is involved in introducing young people to their distinctiveness and their demands. I have also tried to suggest that it is not only a matter of attending to and interpreting works of art, but of "reorganizing the world in terms of works and works in terms of the world" (Goodman, 1988, p. 241). I do not believe that aesthetic contemplation or attending can take place apart from lived life. I do not believe that the significance of a work lies wholly in or is intrinsic to its form, that *Ancient Voices of Children* or *A Midsummer Night's Dream* can or should be encountered outside the contexts of our experience or the contexts in which they were made.

Of course it is important to avoid the tendency to read in meanings and expressions that are irrelevant. It is important not to psychologize or over-intellectualize. Not one of us, I am sure, would be inclined to explore George Crumb's childhood for the sake of elucidating *Ancient Voices*. It would be a waste of energy to seek out Freudian symbols in *A Midsummer Night's Dream*, as it would be a distortion to reject Picasso's minotaur prints because of Picasso's treatment of women. The same is true with regard to Elizabeth Bishop: surely, it would be foolish to criticize her because seals do not appear before Nova Scotia fishhouses—or, worse, because no seal, in our experience, has been "interested in music." (We might, of course, accept the claim that a seal is a "believer in total immersion," as we might be.) "I used to sing him Baptist hymns," Bishop wrote in her poem "At the Fishhouses" (1997, p. 65):

> I also sang "A Mighty Fortress is our God."
> He stood up in the water and regarded me
> steadily, moving his head a little.

To teach persons to attend, however, to remain within the form, to uncouple psychically from the everyday, is not to tell them that the emotions they experience, the visions they see, must be purely aesthetic. We do not want to communicate the formalist creed that aesthetic experiences have nothing to do with other kinds of feelings, with life histories, with the world. I, for one, would not care so much about the art forms I care about (or find them particularly significant) if they offered me only the pleasures I associate with the perception of decorative values or intricate shapes and forms. Yes, I want to know enough about qualitative perceiving to be aware of those values and those forms, and it takes a good deal of hard work to come to know these things. In my case, it is somehow necessary to explore styles and traditions and impinging technologies. I need to be conscious of my own mental sets, my expectations; and I need to find clues and cues in a range of criticisms and engage, to a degree, in some acts of criticism. Sometimes there seems to be no end to the inquiries I feel I have to undertake—in order to impart an aesthetic existence to a picture, an utterance, a dance, an arrangement of sounds—truly to listen, truly to hear.

The point is that if I could not listen, could not see, was not informed, the significance I seek would scarcely exist for me; and it is the significance of art forms, not simply their decorative value or complexity, that gives them staying power in experience. I look for embodied meanings; I look for significance in the work and not apart from it. I find it in the transformations effected by each artist, the transformations that make a Cézanne still life something other than decoration, that make the Mozart quintet something other than pleasurable sound. The fascinating thing, of course, is that the significance I am speaking of, the meanings that may be released in the course of an encounter, cannot be spelled out in words or even in music— apart from the encounter. This is the source of the difficulty some of us have with our school boards, our superintendents—with anyone who has never truly engaged with the arts.

So many do not realize that aesthetic objects arise in the course of voluntary transaction with works of art, that they cannot be packaged or neatly summarized, that meanings do not exist apart from their embodiments in color, language, movement, or sound. Arguments, as you well know, come to conclusions. Works of art do not. You might be able to tell someone in a few words what I have tried to say at Summer Session; you might even make a summary statement of what I have set forth. You cannot conceivably tell someone the meaning of *Ancient Voices* or the *Brandenburg Concerto;* you cannot make a summary statement about *Four* or *Games* or the play called *Home* and in any sense do justice to the piece. To grasp it, to achieve its meaning, each individual has to be personally present to the work at hand.

Nevertheless, the arts must be understood to be modes of sense-making. Perceiving as we have learned to do, using the symbol systems (or the languages) of the various arts, we extend our knowledge of the world. But, even to satisfy the requirements of those in charge, we must not try to assimilate the arts into other forms of knowledge. They are not "true" in the sense of conforming to some reality we know very well in common sense or in other ways. Shakespeare does not give us a picture of the night before a marriage that any of us can see any day or any night. He gives us the kind of picture that will shake people up if they ever risk attending to it. It will make them see and feel some dimension of life (and marriage and sexuality and art) they may never have suspected before: but this does not mean that dimension is untrue. Herman Melville and Elizabeth Bishop and Paul Cézanne are not giving us correct statements, statements that can be verified. They are urging us, disturbing us, moving us to experience the world differently, and that is something else.

To engage with works of art is to go in search of fresh connections, unsuspected meanings, to engage in acts of continuing discovery. The more informed these are, the more sensitive we are likely to be to the complexity of the world and the suggestiveness of it, to color and texture and qualities of sound and the relations of shapes in space, to untapped possibilities. As I have said, there is always more—more awakening to the world on the part of those willing to act, to come alive, to choose.

"The insights of art are not testable by 'public' sense experience," wrote Louis Arnaud Reid. "Since appreciative understanding of art involves the whole person, relatively impersonal tests of anything of a kind remotely resembling experiment and observation are 'out'. Again, judgments of art are value-judgments. . . . But when judgments of value are crucially involved, as they are in art, there is no such impersonal way of testing. Even if there are many 'observers' . . . each has to enter into the experience of the work with a proper involvement, as a person, with all his capacities working as a whole" (1968, p. 75). It is not merely the judgment of an art form itself. Most of us know enough to realize the importance of going to certain critics, even as we try to test works of art from within their own integrity, even as we explore the sense in which particular works feed our own understanding of life.

How do we demonstrate that young persons come to apprehend reality differently when they learn how to engage with art? What measures can we find for the additions to, the extensions of what is ordinarily conceived to be real? How can we test for explorations, for continuing creations? There must be new sensitivities among those eager to evaluate. There must be new ways of listening to what children say, to how children express what they feel. There must be new modes of discovering what young persons choose to choose.

There must be a new regard for the pursuit of meanings, for education as a pursuit of meanings. There must be new beginnings for each of us, in each of our lives. I shall end with words from Eliot's poem "Little Gidding" (1952, p. 145):

> *We shall not cease from exploration*
> *And the end of all our exploring*
> *Will be to arrive where we started*
> *And know the place for the first time.*

Eliot talked of what is not known because it is not looked for. We have all begun looking. The exploring must go on.

Opening to Alternative Realities . . .

(1981)

There are some lines from Emily Dickinson (1960, p. 327) that help me set my theme:

> *I dwell in Possibility—*
> *A fairer House than Prose—*
> *More numerous of Windows—*
> *Superior—for Doors—*

We are concerned with possibility, with opening windows on alternative realities, with moving through doorways into spaces some of us have never seen before. We are interested in releasing diverse persons from confinement to the actual, particularly confinement to the world of techniques and skill training, to fixed categories and measurable competencies. We are interested in breakthroughs and new beginnings, in the kind of wide-awakeness that allows for wonder and unease and questioning and the pursuit of what is not yet. The seminars with which you are involved, the performances that await you, the lectures, the dialogues: all these are intended to create new insights and perspectives, the kinds of insights and perspectives that often change people's lives.

The poet Rilke, having looked upon the "Torso of an Archaic Apollo" through the sculptor Rodin's eyes, ends his poem about the glowing stone and the lucent body with the words, "You must change your life" (1940/1974, p. 93). He means that a work, when fully perceived and carefully attended to, makes a demand upon beholders—a demand that they change, look with new eyes, hear with new ears, become something they have not been before. It is this sort of work (be it a sculptured torso, a dance, a musical piece, a theatrical event) that is our text, our focus, our starting

44

point; and there are, as you have seen, varieties of works that will make their own demands upon us: the Beethoven *Hammerklavier Sonata,* David Mamet's *Duck Variations,* Strindberg's *Miss Julie,* Paul Taylor's *Aureole,* Schoenberg's *Verklärte Nacht,* Kenneth Rinker's *Four.* Now our point is that, if such works are to become aesthetic objects, if they are to emerge in our experience as art, they have to be deliberately achieved. By that I mean that they have to be noticed, heeded in a particular way; they have to get the perception they solicit and deserve.

"To perceive aesthetically is to perceive faithfully," writes Mikel Dufrenne. "Perception is a task, for there are inept perceptions which fall short of the aesthetic object and only an adequate perception realizes its aesthetic qual ity" (1973, p. lii). Aesthetic education is a process of initiating persons into faithful perceiving, a means of empowering them to accomplish the task— from their own standpoints, against the background of their own awarenesses. Taylor's *Aureole* may be danced before your eyes, listed in your programs, talked about in your seminars; but it cannot exist as a full work of art for *you* if you are unable, say, to notice Taylor's use of space, the pressing movements, the flinging movements, the distinctive language of gesture, the qualities of the body in motion all this makes visible and palpable as well. We believe that the perceiving, the noticing are enhanced if you yourself are provided opportunities for moving in space, exploring gestures and kinetic patterns, discovering dynamic images, finding out what tension and contraction mean—and gliding, thrusting, flicking, the many ways of moving that are accessible to us, once the possibilities are made clear. And so it is with the other art forms we are exploring here: music, drama, and painting as well. To work with the structures and textures of musical sound is to sharpen discrimination in listening; to devise your own variations in language or in dramatic action is to enhance your ability to perceive what is happening in *Duck Variations,* perhaps even to enable you to create metaphors of your own, to find your own shapes or symbols, to make connections in your experience never made before.

There is a peculiar liveliness and energy with which the mind is activated when works of art are attended to so that the qualitative details emerge and come together, until there is a perception of a whole. That liveliness and energy are in part due to the fact that, in an authentic aesthetic encounter, we are able to recognize how much depends upon our presentness, our attentiveness, our willingness to go out to the work at hand. In some sense, the enjoyment we experience is a function of the work we are willing to do, as it is a function of our capacity to use our imaginations—to break with the routine and the useful and the conventional and enter into another, often magical, space. It is in that space, that aesthetic space, where *Miss Julie* or *Aureole* or the Emily Dickinson poem or Debussy's *Poissons d'or* must be allowed to exist in wholeness and fullness, disclosing their qualities as we attend to them and focus on them in their integrity. Imagination cannot function in this way if we look upon the work or listen to it as something to be used or marketed or even (later) taught. Our view is that you who are teachers will only be in a position to make such experiences available to your students if you take the time to cultivate your own informed awareness, if you allow *your* own minds to be activated, *your* feelings to be aroused, *your* imaginations to be released for the sake of bringing these works into being for yourselves. Only if you do take the time for faithful perceiving, for careful attending, will the work become significant enough for you to elaborate on what you see and hear within your own experience, make new associations, find new allusions and new openings, come more and more in touch with your own realities. Later, having had such experiences, having reflected back upon them—and on your own perceiving and imagining and thinking in the presence of these works—you will be able to choose yourselves as the kind of teachers ready to release others from confinement to the actual, able to invent your own ways of working with artists and making the languages of art significant in your schools.

I think sometimes of Tennyson's "Ulysses":

> ... *experience is an arch wherethrough*
> *Gleams that untraveled world whose margin fades*
> *Forever and forever when I move.*
> *How dull it is to pause, to make an end.*
>   (1962, p. 1464)

For me, that is a metaphor for the aesthetic experience, at least for those who recognize their own part in bringing works of art into being, in giving them full existence in their own lives. It is a metaphor, because we soon come to know that every experience, with the Beethoven, say, or the Taylor, holds within it a sense of the not-yet, of the untraveled—the suggestion that there is something undiscovered, not yet heard or seen. So it is with novels like *Moby-Dick* or *The Sound and the Fury, Anna Karenina* or *Madame Bovary,* or new ones like the two I have recently read, *July's People* and *The White Hotel.* And we are bound to say, as we would like our students to say: "How dull it is to pause, to make an end" (Tennyson, 1962, p. 1464).

This is why I believe that the learning provoked by what we call aesthetic education is paradigmatic for the learning many of us would like to see:

learning stimulated by the desire to explore, to find out, to go in search. This is the learning that goes beyond teaching—the only significant learning, I believe. It is self-initiated at some point, permeated by wonder, studded by moments of questioning, always with the sense that there is something out there, something worthwhile beyond. Those of you who have attended Summer Session before will recognize this as the kind of learning often made possible here. Some of you will remember the effort you chose to exert, the feeling that you were being asked to stretch, to extend yourself, to live up to certain standards, to do (as it were) a good job of work—whether in the effort to apprehend the designs of Rinker's *Four* or to understand the intricacies of George Crumb's *Ancient Voices of Children*. Surely you recognize that this kind of thing seldom happens naturally. Situations have to be created that release the energies required, that provoke interest, that move persons to reach beyond themselves. Individuals of all ages have to be empowered to learn how to learn with a sense of presentness and a consciousness of craft. They have to be helped to master appropriate ways of proceeding, of attending, of inquiring, of getting things right. And we who teach these things must address ourselves to our students' freedom, their capacity to see that they can be different, that things can be different. With this in mind, we can somehow trust that, if we have taught them how to search and let them catch some gleam of the untraveled, they will find their own ways, as we have done, and begin teaching themselves, pursuing their own possibilities.

Not only am I convinced that this cognitive, perceptual, affective, imaginative undertaking we call aesthetic education can alter the atmosphere in schools. I am convinced it must become central if our schools are to become truly educative, stimulating, and challenging in the way most of us want them to be. I believe that opening windows and doors for persons, releasing them to use their imaginations and their minds and their perceptual capacities, may save lives as well as change them. There is a terrible passivity and carelessness to be overcome: feelings of malaise, hopelessness, powerlessness. The arts will not resolve the fearful social problems facing us today; they will not lessen the evils and the brutalities afflicting the modern world. But they will provide a sense of alternatives to those of us who can see and hear; they will enhance the consciousness of possibility if we learn how to attend. And this itself may make a difference if more and more people are awakened, if they are freed to move through openings and develop a sense that things can indeed be otherwise than they are, somehow better than they are.

Listen to the last few lines of Elizabeth Bishop's poem "The Monument" (1997, pp. 23–25), about a mysterious monument like several boxes with "petals of board," built against a strange sea, "an artifact of wood," perhaps solid, perhaps hollow.

> *The bones of the artist-prince may be inside*
> *or far away on even drier soil.*
> *But roughly but adequately it can shelter*
> *what is within (which after all*
> *cannot have been intended to be seen).*
> *It is the beginning of a painting,*
> *a piece of sculpture, or poem, or monument,*
> *and all of wood. Watch it closely.*

Watch closely while you are here. Listen closely. There will be unpredictable openings, mysterious beginnings. It will be up to you.

Making the Petrified World Speak, Sing, and, Perhaps, Dance

(1982)

What is art? It is a transformation of the commonplace, one writer tells us. It opens windows in the actual, says another, permitting us to see alternative realities. Art is serious and beneficial, remarks another, a game played against chaos and death. Yes, comments still another, but art breaks open a dimension inaccessible to other experience. The languages and images we find in art "make perceptible, visible, and audible that which is no longer, or not yet, perceived, said, and heard in everyday life" (Marcuse, 1977/1978, p. 72). Indeed, art may make the petrified world speak, sing, perhaps dance.

There is no firm definition here, but we do not need one. What we need is a recognition of the ways in which encounters with paintings, dance performances, musical works, plays, and the rest open up new experiential possibilities—or might open them up if we become informed enough and aware enough to notice what there is to be noticed, to attend in such a fashion that art forms actually come alive. This Institute has to do with possibilities and, yes, allowing works of art to come alive. We are interested, you see, in enabling persons to multiply their perspectives, extend their visions, strive for new ways of apprehending the complex world. There is a poem by Wallace Stevens that often helps me communicate what this means. Surely, you know that poetry, like other kinds of art, offers ways of seeing, ways of feeling beyond the reach of ordinary discursive prose. This is from Stevens's "Six Significant Landscapes" (1982, p. 75):

> Rationalists, wearing square hats,
> Think, in square rooms,

Looking at the floor,
Looking at the ceiling.
They confine themselves
To right-angled triangles.
If they tried rhomboids,
Cones, waving ellipses—
As, for example, the ellipse of the half-moon—
Rationalists would wear sombreros.

Square, linear forms; floors, ceiling, confinement. Then, suddenly, a breaking through to new shapes and that startling glimpse of the half-moon and the image of sombreros, with all that sombreros connote, particularly with the square hats set aside. Of course there has to be work done in square rooms, but that should not be all there is.

We want to accentuate reality and to bring persons in contact with the many ways there are or might be of being alive. We want, if you like, to expand the range of literacy: offering the young new ways of symbolizing, new ways of structuring their experience, so they can see more, hear more, make more connections, embark on new and unfamiliar adventures into meaning. Yes, of course we know that verbal and numerate literacy is required in a culture like ours; and many people are beginning to see the need for computer literacy, various kinds of technical literacy, political or civic literacy. But, in addition, there is aesthetic literacy, of an importance equal to that of the others: the power to perceive and to respond to aesthetic qualities; the capacity to attend to paintings, dance performances, musical pieces—to engage with them in such a fashion that they actually do emerge in experience in their fullness, vividness, vitality.

There is an interplay here at the Institute between workshop and performance and exhibition. We are convinced, indeed we have learned, that experience with making kinetic patterns in dance enables persons to perceive such patterns on the stage, not only with their eyes and minds but with their muscles and nerves. We have learned that notating a piece of music, singing it, making ordered sounds with percussive instruments or bells or glasses make it more likely that people will learn to think musically, pay heed to textures, tonal values, themes. And there is always the importance of making discriminations, discerning relationships with the help of artists who live within the art forms concerned, who can enable you to see and hear in novel ways—if not through their eyes and ears, surely through your own. And then there is the part to be played by a philosopher-person—someone whose life is absorbed in teaching, trying to move others to wide-awakeness and reflectiveness, to learning to learn on their own initiatives; someone who has spent and continues to spend time trying to confront the questions that arise, that cannot but arise out of experiences with the several arts.

In fact, the ground of aesthetics or aesthetic thinking is in those questions, in those experiences. What is it that strikes sparks in my mind when I read that Stevens poem? How is that, having seen Balanchine's *Jewels* perhaps four times, I suddenly recognized that the dancers' movements were making me see the facets of particular jewels? How is it that, the more often I encounter a dance like that, or a painting like Monet's *Poplars*, or the Mozart *Divertimento*, the more I find to look at, listen to, resonate to? And how is it that we can never use up or exhaust a work of art—that, somehow or other, it always offers more?

My questions, you realize, are rather different from those a choreographer or a dancer or a painter or a musician or a stage director might ask about his/her particular art form. For one thing, I am especially interested in what happens or what might happen to the one who experiences the painting, the poem, the performance. For another, I am interested in finding out what can be done to enable diverse persons (children and adults) not only to attend in the way described, but to identify themselves, to choose themselves with respect to the aesthetic-artistic domain. How does an engagement with the drama or the dance feed into a person's lifelong quest for meaning, and the efforts to make sense? How does an awareness of the moon "as a ghostly galleon," the swirling moon in a Van Gogh painting, even Stevens's "ellipse of the half-moon" relate to or shed light on or enrich or make questionable the moon in eclipse a while ago—or the descriptions of it, the explanations? How does learning "what it feels like to live in music, move over and about in a painting, travel round and in between the masses of a sculpture, dwell in a poem" (Reid, 1969, p. 302) connect with or hold implications for other kinds of learning?

My part in all this, you see, is to provoke you to articulate what it all means to you as a person and as an educator. Also, it is to clarify some of the language used in the realm of aesthetics and the arts, to elucidate (if I can) such concepts as "aesthetic object," yes, and "work of art," "aesthetic experience," "quality," "aesthetic perception," "distance," "imagination," and even "beauty" and "organic unity." Now I have no desire to do this in order to make aestheticians out of you or to recruit you into the field of philosophy, although I surely would not try to keep you out if you wanted to come through the gate. I want to focus on the concepts or the ideas that might illuminate your actual experiences with the works of art you encounter here. That, after all, is the test. Does knowing more make you see more or listen more attentively? Does it give you a larger stock of knowledge to have at hand when you are ready to make your choices in your own classrooms? Let me make clear that I am not proposing that you teach aesthetics in those classrooms. Whatever questions I can provoke, whatever clarity I can make possible, whatever dialogue I can institute are intended to help *you* become more conscious, more reflective, more at ease in this domain. What I hope to see is a freer play of consciousness among you where the arts are concerned, a more informed awareness, a greater clarity about the role of the arts and the significance of the arts in your own lived life and in the work you choose to do in the school and in the world.

Now the word "aesthetic" refers to what we come to know directly and at first hand in an aesthetic experience, when we enter a kind of dialogue with a given work of art: the *Divertimento,* perhaps, *Hamlet, Peer Gynt, Pride and Prejudice, Moby-Dick, Giselle, Ballade,* the *Poplars,* Edward Hopper's *House by the Railroad,* De Chirico's *The Philosopher and the Poet* (a painting I happen to like particularly), the serene mask of a face made by the Ibo in Nigeria. We come to know it directly when we recognize the work in its concreteness, feel our way into it as an embodiment of meaning with its own reality. There is a pleasure, a particular kind of enjoyment associated with that, an enjoyment enhanced by our knowing to notice what there is to be noticed. By "what is to be noticed" I have in mind the textures of sound in the de Falla piece: the harpsichord, the woodwinds, the dark poetry of the cello; the enigmatic brown figure in the de Chirico painting, the empty blackboard, the white wall, the green sky beyond the door. As important is the realization of what may happen when feeling, sensing, perceiving, imagining inform the knowing process—and when knowing or cognition intensifies feeling, enlarges perceiving, releases imagining.

It is not enough to know that Manuel de Falla was a Spanish composer, influenced by Debussy, probably an impressionist musician-poet, and that he wrote one concerto for harpsichord and chamber ensemble. On the other hand, to have engaged with the concerto, to have tried to listen to its rhythms, its beats, its melody, its fragmentary sounds, is to begin to discover how mind and feeling, imagining and perceiving work together to disclose and reveal. So it is with coming to learn something about the structure of the work and perhaps a little about musical impressionism—and then listening to the work again. Some of you are already familiar with the liveliness and energy with which the mind—and, often, the entire organism—are activated when a work comes clearer and clearer in this way. Seamus Heaney, the Irish poet, has a nice metaphor that helps render what is involved (1995). He happens to be talking about poetry, but he might well be talking about any art form. He compares the poet with a diviner using a forked stick to discover well water, trying to make contact with what lies hidden—and having the ability to make palpable what he senses beneath the surface: in other words, to *tell* about what neither he nor anyone else can see or hear or even know. Heaney goes on to compare the reader (and he might well say the same about the listener or the beholder) with a diviner. The reader (or beholder) also makes something palpable by means of attending, something that releases hidden energies, that unlocks the structures of habit and sets the community strangely free.

To talk about aesthetic experience and aesthetic education, of course, is to presume that there exist certain objects and events that give rise to the distinctive experiences I have been trying to describe. Now it is indeed the case that you can have an aesthetic experience in the natural world, even on the streets of this city when you come to Lincoln Center in the morning. There are the angular shadows of the buildings, the hazy look of the towers downtown, the sometimes gray-blue light over the river, the green of leaves against stone, the occasional flash of the sun on a windowpane, the colors of the fruit on the Broadway fruit stands, the sound of a street violinist, the turn of a lithe body on a skateboard, the sun on a child's yellow hair. Now you know very well that, if you are primarily concerned with getting to Juilliard on time, keeping your eyes on the traffic, peering to see if the bus is coming, you are not going to pay heed to shadows or gray-blue light tones or the colors of apples and cherries and pears. The boy on the skateboard will be nothing but an obstacle. The yellow-haired child will be part of the crowd. It takes a kind of distancing, an uncoupling from your practical interests, your impinging concerns, to see what we sometimes describe as the qualities of things, to make out contours, shapes, angles, even to hear sound as sound. If you can uncouple in this fashion, if you are still for a moment, if you take the kind of stance that allows the river or the towers or the fruit stand to appear in what might be called an aesthetic space— one you would be bringing into being by your paying heed—you can indeed have an aesthetic experience with the world around. You might even have the sense of disclosure, the pleasure I have tried to describe.

What I think we ought to understand is that paintings, dances, musical works, poems, and the rest are deliberately made for the sake of such experience. They are sometimes called privileged objects for that reason. But if they are to come into existence for you as aesthetic objects or events, they also have to be attended to in a particular way. They do not open themselves automatically, anymore than do apples and cherries on a fruit stand; they have to be *achieved* as aesthetic objects, and that has everything to do with you. Take a Cézanne painting, for instance. Ninety years ago, an obsessive, troubled man named Paul Cézanne, working in a shadowy studio on a hillside in Aix-en-Provence, created pictures, numerous pictures of the nearby mountain, of the quarries, of the village streets or roofs. Because he was an artist, or at least acknowledged to be a considerable artist after his death, it is assumed that the pictures he made are to be classified as works of art, just as West 66th Street can be (theoretically) classified as a street distinctive for the shadows falling in a particular, measurable way at certain times of day.

My point is that, if the painting or the dance performance or the play is to exist as an aesthetic object or event for you, it has to be attended to in a particular way. You have to be fully present to it—to focus your attention on it and, again, to allow it to exist apart from your everydayness and your practical concerns. I do not mean that you, as a living person with your own biography, your own history, have to absent yourself. No, you have to be there in your personhood, encountering the work much in the way you encounter other persons. The proper way to encounter another person is to be open to them, to be ready to see new dimensions, new facets of the other, to recognize the possibility of some fresh perception or understanding, so you may know the other better, appreciate that person more variously. This is, actually, how we ordinarily treat each other as *persons*. We do not treat each other as case histories or instances of some psychological or sociological reality—not, that is, in *personal* encounters. Nor do we come up against each other as if the other were merely an inanimate object, incapable of reciprocation. There are analogues between this and encounters with works of art, especially in the readiness for fresh illumination, in the willingness to see something, to risk something unexpected and new.

The attention we offer, the rapt attention—taking time, being quiet— is very different from a practical, utilitarian, consumerist approach, one taken far too often in the presence of works of art. I am sure you know what I mean: the going to ballet because good, sophisticated, prosperous New Yorkers go to ballet so that, in some sense, they can tell themselves they have *had* the ballet, the way some people say they have *done* Paris. I am sure there are people who look at paintings and try to figure out what they cost or if they will fit over the living-room couch. Again, we do not want to use or to classify or to consume works of art. We want to encounter them and to realize, when doing so, that it is a free act. Only as a free act does an encounter have the possibility of becoming what we would call aesthetic.

There are some who make a distinction between the work of art (that which was made in time past by an Ibsen, say, or a Melville, or a Martha Graham, or a Cézanne, that exists "out there," whether or not anyone sees it or reads it or attends to it or watches it being performed) and the aesthetic object, the play or story or dance or painting perceived aesthetically. Aesthetic education is a process, in part, of educating persons into faithful perceiving. It is a means of empowering them to accomplish the task of perception from a unique standpoint, against the background of their own personal history. Perceiving involves a participation in what is being perceived; it is important to remember that. We perceive things as wholes, directly, immediately. We directly apprehend an African mask, or the de Chirico painting, or the Sokolow *Ballade* as it appears, as it is presented to us. If it seems interesting in and of itself, if we have an opportunity to encounter it more than once, we may find ourselves attending differently, paying heed to details. We may begin noticing colors in combination or contrast not noticed before, or the qualities of certain movements. We may perceive in such a fashion that what we perceive—colors, shapes, diagonals, thrusts— evokes unexpected feelings in us. We may find ourselves using words to point out various qualities: words like "warm," "restless," "peaceful," "hectic," "frenzied," "tender," "majestic." Becoming conscious of the whole again, a whole emerging now or coming to be, we may realize how much richer it is than when first perceived, how much richer our own intuitions are of what has occurred or been disclosed.

Not only is this likely to be true with respect to *Amadeus* and African masks and the dance called *The Steadfast Tin Soldier* and the remarkable piece by José Limón, *Unsung*. It is an experience accessible to us with every work of a particular density and resonance. But it must be said again that careful and active perceiving (of qualities of movement, textures of sound, nuances of color) is what releases imagination, makes possible syntheses and transformations. Were it not for imagination, we would not be able to move into *Schubert's Last Serenade* or allow for the presence of the great Franz Schubert in a New York City restaurant after a political demonstration on one of the city's piers. We would not be able to put ourselves in the place of Salieri in *Amadeus* or to believe in Mimi's death in *La Bohème*— or even to credit the boy's love for the alien creature in *E.T.* If we are unable to listen carefully enough to the Mozart quintet to allow our imaginations to weave the parts into an integral whole, we allow ourselves to exist in a place where unrelated sounds are being played, or where the music becomes a kind of liquid medium in which we allow ourselves to submerge.

It is not art appreciation with which I am concerned, certainly not affective education in the old, familiar sense. Art appreciation classes, as I recall them, meant being presented with a sampling of great paintings, say, told about their place in history, helped to recognize foregrounds and backgrounds, asked to write down the dates of the painters and the proper names of their styles. The object, more often than not, was to inspire a kind of reverence or awe. There they were—the Rembrandt, the Cézanne, the Picasso. There we were, ordinarily assigned three functions: to keep quiet, to take notes, and to admire. Presumably, that did something for us, improved us in some way, gave us a taste of the elite community where great works were appreciated and their pecuniary value understood. It had very little to do with the learning with which the school was fundamentally concerned; and it was not even integrally connected to the exploratory, or creative, or expressive activities happening in the art or music rooms, where actual works were seldom mentioned, seldom were seen, seldom were heard.

I am talking about another kind of commitment, one that provokes us to try to engage persons as imagining, thinking, feeling, perceiving, active beings, realizing that the more they know, the more they are likely to see and to hear. I am talking about being present, allowing personal energy to go out to works of art. I am talking about awareness of process and a realization that it is ongoing, that there is always something more. As I view it, there are implications here for all kinds of learning, if we value the sense of personal agency and the pursuit of possibility. And, indeed, that is what lies ahead for all of us: openings, adventures into meaning, the sense that there is always more.

Being Fully Present
to Works of Art
(1982)

Aesthetics, I have been trying to say, has to do with reflections upon our encounters with works of art. Thinking in the domain of aesthetics can only begin, in other words, with actual experiences. I tried to make the point that the object of an aesthetic experience (*Unsung*, perhaps, or Schubert's *Last Serenade*) must be seen as the object as lived, presented to consciousness, freed from the presuppositions of common sense and science. (Can you imagine someone protesting, while watching *Scooter Thomas Makes It to the Top of the World*, that people cannot come back from the dead?) It is important to realize that the stuff, the raw material out of which an object or event is made, be it sound or paint or the body in motion, has no intrinsic property that determines what might be called its arthood. There are those who say that an arrangement of colors and forms or a particular patterning of movement assumes the status of art if it functions successfully in an aesthetic field. Others make the point that any thing or quality, imaginary or real, with enough vividness and poignancy to make us appreciate it as given has the potential of functioning as a work of art. The crucial idea is this, I believe: to have in mind a context that includes what is generally thought to be an art object or event, and a living individual (or group of individuals) prepared to activate its aesthetic potential. I spoke earlier about the artist making the hidden palpable; I spoke of concretion, of concrete embodiments. I might speak of formed content, of transfigurations of the commonplace. I might speak as the Russian poet-novelist Boris Pasternak did about the ways in which the poet begins with the verbs and nouns of the world, transforms them into adjectives, and (by so doing) releases a whirlpool of qualities. I might speak of the artist's attending to qualities: of imagery, of symbolism, of expressiveness, of illusioned worlds.

You many recall Stevens's poem about the blue guitar, which may be imagination, or it may mean a certain mode of perceiving, of selecting, of saying. Surely, it remains a kind of mystery, but the important thing for us is that it may enable us to hear what we have never heard, make us (as Joseph Conrad said) feel and—above all—see. Conrad also said, distinguishing the artist from the thinker or the scientist, that the artist "appeals to that part of our being which is not dependent on wisdom: to that in us which is a gift and not an acquisition. . . .[The artist] speaks to our capacity for delight and wonder, to the sense of mystery surrounding our lives; to our sense of pity, and beauty, and pain; to the latent feeling of fellowship with all creation— to the subtle but invincible conviction of solidarity that knits together the loneliness of innumerable hearts" (1967, pp. 56–57). I know that has a Victorian ring, but there is something about it that moves me and makes me all the more dedicated to discovering the secret of aesthetic education—education for more discriminating appreciation and understanding of the arts. I want to stress the concept of educated *understanding* and distinguish it from the gaining of mere information and from pure analysis. Harry S. Broudy has another phrase: "enlightened cherishing" (Broudy, 1972), bringing together the notion of understanding and valuing and appreciation. And I cannot repeat often enough that the reason for informing awareness, for developing understanding is that our encounters with the arts will be richer for it, more vivid, more consequential in our lives.

John Dewey once wrote:

> Every one knows that it requires apprenticeship to see through a microscope or telescope, and to see a landscape as the geologist sees it. The idea that esthetic perception is an affair for odd moments is one reason for the backwardness of the arts among us. The eye and the visual apparatus may be intact; the object may be physically there, the cathedral of Notre Dame, or Rembrandt's portrait of Hendrik Stoeffel. In some bald sense, the latter may be "seen." They may be looked at, possibly recognized, and have their correct names attached. But for lack of continuous interaction between the total organism and the objects, they are not perceived, certainly not esthetically. (1980, pp. 53–54).

He said that the beholder or the listener has work to do, that the one who is "too lazy, idle, or indurated in convention to perform this work will not see or hear." I would underline that strange word, "indurated," because of the way it summons up visions of hardness, petrifaction, and constraint. Convention, taken-for-grantedness, routines: all these encase the perceiver. The informed awareness I have been speaking of involves a breaking through, a free play. Dewey was not only asking for a rejection of the routine and the automatic; he was asking that the same attention be paid to the arts as to reading and writing and arithmetic. He was suggesting that the old habit of seeing the aesthetic experience as something that comes naturally could not be defended. And, as always, he was objecting to the traditional dualistic separations—between feeling and perception, imagination and thought. He would also object, I am sure, to the odd separation we so often find between creative activity in art rooms and music rooms and education in perceiving, noticing, attending, paying heed. He would support our notion of educating persons through initiation into the *processes* of art-making. And he would agree on the importance of opening up spaces in the schools, channels of communication between those primarily interested in making and performing and those concerned about bringing actual works of art alive in experience.

Note the emphasis we placed upon the nature of the encounter between the living person and the work of art. He, too, saw the importance of the listener or the beholder breaking through habit structures in order to attend. This is not only the case where adults are concerned. It is clearly the case with children today, for all the fact that they possess a "natural" curiosity, a "natural" potential for a fantasy life. We need to take into account the constant "induration" imposed by the media, the taken-for-granted conventions of comics and sitcoms and science fiction movies. (I know the exceptions; I know that *E.T.* is supposed to be, in some ways, a celebration of childhood and the imaginative life. But I also know about repetitions and routines, and about the tendency to structure experience in accord with what television provides. And I know about passivity, as you do, and the constrictions being imposed on individual fantasy life. It is still necessary to empower children to invent their own extraterrestrial creatures, to play with words and shapes in their own authentic ways, to learn what it is to summon up illusioned worlds.)

Susanne Langer used to speak of perception as an opening of the subject into the object (Langer, 1957). We—or our students—are the subjects; the object, of course, is the dance or the painting or the sonata. Others have spoken about the ways in which aesthetic perceiving can redeem experience from its ordinary dislocations, fragmentations, and bare mechanisms, the ways in which it can restore order, structure, continuity. But all go on to speak of imagination as the mode of grasping, of reaching out, that allows what is perceived to be transformed. There is simply the importance of coming to see the qualities of movement, the shape of effort presented on the stage, of allowing our energies to go out to those leaps and plunges and thrusts, those jackknifing movements and crawling movements, to experience them (if we ourselves have moved) with our muscles and our nerves. And there is the importance of noticing the colors, the lights, the background; of listening to the beat of bare feet, watching the heads upturned, the hands clasped, the arms outstretched. Perceiving in this fashion, experiencing the dance kinaesthetically if we can, allowing our imaginations to transform what we see into a ceremony, perhaps, a ritual, an encounter with the gods, an event in our own lives, we have been as faithful as we can be—and probably come as close as we can come to achieving the work as an aesthetic object for ourselves.

But there is more, another phase of the imaginative activity: the savoring of what we have seen and heard in inner time, the elaboration of it, the seeping down. If we have attended authentically enough, broken sufficiently with the habitual and the conventional, we will find ourselves discovering dimensions of our own experience never quite suspected before we were present at this dance. We will find ourselves making connections, discerning meanings, or coming on new perspectives because of what we have beheld. We may find ourselves apprehending new dimensions of the Native American experience, of alienation, of circles of communion, of prayer, of transcendence through a kind of flight. Now I do not know if this happened to all of us or most of us on this particular occasion, but I am using it as an example. I want to assert that we cannot *make* such experiences take place; nor can we intrude when persons do become aware in this fashion. We cannot grade them on whether or not the phenomenon occurs. We need to try to invent situations that make it more likely that people will notice. All we can do is point, as well as we can, to the qualities we hope our students will see. All we can do is try to find (or invent) a language, perhaps a metaphorical language, to make it more likely for them to notice and share some of our perceptions—and then move on.

If we, the teachers, become capable of this kind of perceiving and imagining, if we become more aware of what actually happens to us in the high and resplendent moments when we feel we have achieved works of art, we are in a far better position to begin creating those conditions in classrooms in which energies and preferences can be released. We all realize by now that, where the arts are concerned, we must begin with experience, not with concepts. We must begin with blocks of "reality" first perceived globally, gradually revealing patterns, structures, details. I cannot stress often enough the importance of taking time and allowing for moments of stillness, of personal encounter, of coming to know. I think it is possible, when the time for dialogue arrives, to avoid concentration on how people *feel* about particular works. It is so much more fruitful to draw attention to what is actually seen and heard when students use their own powers, when they are *there*. As we, the teachers, think about developing our appropriate vocabularies, it may be helpful to turn to some of the good critics for clues. Some of them have the capacity, through language, to call attention to what would ordinarily not be noticed, to make dimensions of art forms somehow accessible, to open, to disclose. It is not our obligation, anymore than it is the critics', to determine the experience of the perceiver or the beholder. It is our obligation to open the way. I would recommend more reading of poetry for those concerned about language, the language that may indeed disclose. I think of Rilke on music: "O you the mutation / of feelings . . . into what?—: into audible landscape. / You stranger: music" (1996).

I think of an excerpt from William Carlos Williams's poem "The Dance" in *Pictures from Brueghel* (1988, pp. 407–408):

> *But only the dance is sure!*
> *make it your own.*
> *Who can tell*
> *what is to come of it?*

Let us remember that the awareness we seek must be an indwelling awareness, what has been called a "tacit awareness" (Polanyi, 1967). In the seminars, we are being introduced to certain concepts having to do with the elements of music or dance or drama. We are coming to know what pitch signifies, or rhythm, or melody, or articulation, as we work with sound and become used to attending to such elements. When we hear the Mozart *Divertimento,* however, for a second time, what we have come to know through that kind of attending should have become tacit. Such tacit awareness, below the surface of consciousness, ought to enable us to attend to the elements in the Mozart piece in *focal* awareness. There are cues, let us say, that become part of what is tacit, and they allow us to single out what is to be noticed the next time we are fortunate enough to hear the Mozart. To consider this is also to hold in mind the idea that the point of learning how to notice what there is to be noticed is not simply to master Mozart; it is to be empowered to go beyond—to Haydn, to Beethoven, to de Falla, to Stravinsky, to Charles Ives. We, as teachers, achieve what we hope to achieve (strangely enough) when our students leave us and make their choices in the open world, and oftentimes, we never know or can know what we have done. This may be particularly true of the arts. If, five years after this Summer Session, a young person who once attended school in District 11 is discovered in an audience for new music somewhere, or standing in line for a modern dance performance, some teacher somewhere can affirm success. But that is the risk and uncertainty of teaching. Who can ever know?

Now it must be noted that there are no guarantees. Also, we need to remember that very young children, for instance, are unlikely to grasp the notion of qualities or structures or even the concept of art *qua* art. There are developmental differences; there are experiential differences. But these should not discourage us from offering occasions for releasing as many young people as possible to see and to listen, to make and to play. It remains important to work for wide-awakeness, to help our students focus their attention, to provoke them to greater perceptual acuity. I am sure many of us try to arouse, to get young persons to pay heed to the green of the grass and the gray-blue light over the river. I am sure many of us try to move students to think of adjectives for the color of the grass and the shape of the clouds and the thumping sounds in the hall. We can empower them to realize that the naming of qualities is like the naming of colors, and to attend more sensitively to the qualities of things is to be freed from "induration," to become open to the arts. And, yes, we need ourselves to tell stories and allow the young to tell their stories, to draw them, to dance them, to shape some of the stuff of their lives. We want them to tap their image stores, to remain in touch with their memories. I believe that, when consciousness is opened to the appearances and to the sounds of things, when children are encouraged not simply to perform correctly, to demonstrate sets of skills or competencies, but to perceive and name dimensions of their lived worlds, they are far more likely to pose the questions in which authentic learning begins. I believe that if they can come to realize that there is always something—a color, a sound, a shape, an event, a moment of clarity—just beyond where they are, they are likely to exert the effort, to master the discipline that will enable them to reach beyond. That, to me, is what learning should be. That is moving toward possibility.

Situations involving the arts are always adventurous in some way, as we have learned, and the standard solutions almost always have to be set aside. Moreover, the beholder, yes, or the learner has to be there in person—confronting the art form, relying on his/her capacities, in some sense creating his/her meanings, constructing and reconstructing his/her world. We have to empower *individuals* to do this. We have to break, as much as we can, with the technical, the measurable, with the fearful ideas of effectiveness and efficiency. We have to make discovery possible again, and exploration, and the idea of standard. We have to launch ourselves and those others who are free to go on new adventures in sense-making. And, yes, we have to set many others free again, and one way to think of understanding freedom, you recall, is to think of it as the capacity to look at things as if they could be otherwise. The arts nurture that capacity, as the arts awaken to the process of living itself. But these are my particular views; everyone at the Institute is invited to develop their own, as they come to see and hear, as they begin to cherish what is disclosed—and decide to dust off any available sombrero so as to move through the open doors.

PART II

IMAGINATION AND TRANSFORMATION

The following lectures have to do with the significance of imagination—not only in being at the heart of aesthetic experience, but in giving rise on all sides to suggestions that it be central in education and scholarship. Imagination is the capacity to posit alternative realities. It makes possible the creation of "as-if" perspectives, perspectives that can be opened metaphorically and, oftentimes, through the exercise of empathy. Without the release of imagination, human beings may be trapped in literalism, in blind factuality. It is imagination that allows us to enter into fictional worlds, to bring paintings and sculptures into the domains of a lived experience, to transform bodies in motion into time-space meanings. It is imagination that discloses possibilities—personal and social as well as aesthetic. By imagining, we are enabled to look at things, to think about things as if they were otherwise.

Examples offered in these lectures, taken from encounters enjoyed at live moments during our Summer Session, suggest ways in which transformations occur when people break with what they simply assume or take for granted as given and unchangeable. Ordinary limits may be overcome; landscapes may be altered; windows may be opened to what might be, what ought to be. Pondering the lighting of what Emily Dickinson called "The Possible's slow fuse" (1960, p. 689), I cannot but think of introducing some sense of humane order into the startling new spaces now and then revealed by imagination. At once, knowing how young people yearn

for and seek out imaginative adventures, realizing how our history can
be frozen and our inquires crippled without the release of imagination,
I believe that all of those interested in the arts and in aesthetic education
ought to find opportunities to come together in order to find an honored
place for the imaginative—for the opening of possibilities—in our classrooms and in public spaces, wherever they exist.

Uncoupling from the Ordinary

(1987)

We have been talking recently about imaginative adventures into meaning. Meaning refers to connections made in experience as well as to the definition of certain terms. We use meanings in various ways: we mark off some of them as rational and practical; we fund them, structure them, and much of our teaching has to do with enabling the young to discover them. John Dewey made the point (in his *Experience and Nature*) that "the realm of meanings is wider than that of true-and-false meanings; it is more urgent and more and more fertile." Of course, some meanings have a claim to truth, he said; but truth does not have "monopolistic jurisdiction. Poetic meanings, moral meanings, a large part of the goods of life are matters of richness and freedom of meanings, rather than of truth" (1994, p. 332). For me, aesthetic education does not only have to do with heightened awareness and understanding of art forms. It ought to make possible, through direct encounters, openings to the "richness and freedom of meanings" of which Dewey spoke, meanings that can be encountered largely through the release of imagination and cognitive feeling, the kind of feeling that allows us to attend to a phrase in the *Brandenburg Concerto No. 2* or a passage in *Little Improvisations* as an embodiment of value. Indeed one of the things we are going to learn and, perhaps, have already learned is that—for all the cognitive knowledge we need to grasp, say, of the structures of music— without acquaintance through feeling, the music is so much dead wood. And so it is with the other art forms. What would *Antigone* mean if we only *knew* that Anouilh adapted it from the Sophoclean tragedy, if we only *knew* that it was responsive to the postwar world of 1944, if we only *knew* that it provides a dramatic illusion, an "as-if," an "unreal world"? Of course we have to know these things in order to make sense of the text before us and the enactment on the stage. But would it mean what it means if a whole range of feelings were not evoked in us when Antigone says to Creon, "I am not here to understand *these* things. I am here because I said *no* to you" (1973,

p. 52)? Or, when the Chorus says, "Well, Antigone is calm tonight. She has played her part" (p. 71)?

What we are about is the making possible of an intelligent enjoyment, or grasping, or apprehension that includes all the different aspects of consciousness: cognitive, affective, perceptual, yes, and conative—having to do with making an effort, exerting energy, reaching beyond. What we are about is a complex form of apprehension or meaning-making that can lead, should lead, to a deeper appreciation of the shared natural and human world—and probably to more enjoyment of it. Nelson Goodman has a way of saying it that also makes sense to me. He stresses the importance of taking time, of "reading" the painting as well as the poem, of attending with care to the language of dance, and he views the aesthetic experience, as we do, as dynamic rather than static. It involves, he writes, "making delicate discriminations and discerning subtle relationships, identifying symbol systems . . . interpreting works and reorganizing the world in terms of works and works in terms of the world. Much of our experience and many of our skills are brought to bear and may be transformed by the encounter. The aesthetic 'attitude' is restless, searching, testing—is less attitude than action: creation and re-creation" (1988, p. 241).

When you hear that, I suspect, it is somewhat easier to see the connection between exploratory action through a medium, a language, and experiences with works of art that "speak" in that language. You do not need to be convinced that aesthetic education has to do with process and not with products. One of the great differences between aesthetic education and what used to be called art appreciation is, in fact, the difference between a process-oriented and a product-oriented undertaking. I used to feel as if I were being ushered into a marvelous department store—with shelves for Renaissance painting, counters for impressionist works, special alcoves for Beethoven and Brahms. I was being taught to consume, I think, but not to be present, feelingfully, passionately, authentically present to works that might be brought continually to life by an attentive and yearning human consciousness. Brought to life, always to new life—because each work, each enactment, each representation is in a sense always new. That is why we cannot predetermine what will happen, or package it, or test for results. It is always an adventure, reaching toward the unpredictable, reaching toward possibility.

And that brings me to the questions of choice and transformation where all this is concerned. I realize as well as you that the heart of this experience, the exciting and surprising and fulfilling dimension of it, is the experience teachers can have with teaching artists. There is where you are being initiated, discovering what it is to be inside a work of music or a dance or a theatrical scene. It is there where you are discovering possibilities in your own body, your own being, that you never suspected because you never were given the opportunity to realize them. And I know as well that many of you are having experiences with the meaning-making that accompanies direct acquaintance with, say, *Magritte, Magritte,* or a Martha Graham tape, or actors offering diverse interpretations of Creon's words or Antigone's, or the sound world opened by a percussive beat. And some of you may be feeling already how poor a life can be when it is confined to only one reality, only one kind of meaning.

You are aware that the point of these remarkable experiences is to enable you to attend differently to works of art, to engage imaginatively, to recognize the significance of illusioned worlds, created worlds brought into being by movement, sound, dialogue, color and line. You know something now about energy expended in time and space and what it can create. You know something about the perceptual elements in the several art forms. You know enough not to run on the stage, as the poor fireman did, to save Desdemona. That is because you have come to realize, probably more than before, that you have to bracket out or put into parentheses the mundane, commonsense world when you watch a princess masquerade as a harlequin, tap your feet in response to *Rags 'n Things,* listen to George Crumb's *Madrigals.* It is, I think, a deliberate act—to uncouple from the ordinary, from the grocery list in your pocket, the parking ticket that may be waiting, the humidity outside, even from the judgments you think you ought to be making, the posture you ought to be taking because you are at a music school. You are learning more, I am sure, about what it is to move deliberately into what can be called an aesthetic space, where the familiar becomes unfamiliar, where all sorts of things become revealed that the cotton wool of habit has for so long obscured. This capacity to distance, to move into an alternative space by using your imagination does not mean, of course, uncoupling from your own personal history. When you are attending to the lift in the ballet, or the guard writing the letter for Antigone in what is supposed to be a shadowy prison cell, these are visions *for you*—made by persons for you as a person, since it is only a person with a past who can engage with a work of art. We do not bring with us, however, or we ought not, the rationally analyzed account of our pasts that are our personal and social histories.

If we are looking at a Utrillo rendering of a Parisian street, for example, when we dwell on its resemblance to streets we ourselves walked down, or to a photograph we took or someone else did, or on Utrillo's problems with his mother, or on his predilection for walls, closed buildings, streets moving out of sight, we are likely to lose the painting. All that material must be kept away, as it were, for the moment. What we know ought to be allowed to feed into our focal awareness. But if it is on the tip of our tongues, as it were, if it renders Utrillo's painting a commentary or an example or a reflection, we lose the occasion for an aesthetic experience. In a way, encountering a work—like a Utrillo, or an Anouilh, or a David Parsons—is like encountering another person: engaging in a kind of interested reciprocity, exchanging, replying, giving back uniquely one to the other. But there must be an interest; there must be a raptness of attention. There must be a presentness, a being there.

The problem for us is to internalize what we have learned, to resonate to it and to the works offered for our attention, and then to effect—slowly, perhaps—a kind of transformation. I mean this. In working with teaching artists, you may have been moved and impressed, as you should be, not only by their talents and their mastery of their craft and their looks and their teaching capacities, but by their membership in what strikes many of us as a privileged community—the community of art. For many of you, it is a humbling experience, even as it is a liberating one. You pay heed to the repertoires of your teaching artists, and many of you want, above everything else, to adopt those repertoires, make them your own, and replay what happened in the Summer Session in your classroom back at school. Here is where the transformation or the translation or the transliteration comes in. I keep reminding people (myself, as well as some of you) that teachers have their own crafts, their own repertoires, their own modes of artistry, even though they cannot call themselves practicing artists. But, like the choreographers and directors and musicians and visual artists you work with here, you also have a life project, a way of being in the world through which and by means of which you define yourself as a person. That project is teaching, and if you are like me, it is a lifelong quest, a lifelong project. Like the artists, we are always in process, always exploring our texts, our raw materials, always seeking ways of reaching others and moving others to come alive, to think about their thinking, to create meanings, to transform their lived worlds.

What happens here, I think, what ought to happen is not simply a planning for the school year, not simply pondering new curricula (important though all this is). There is something else: a reaching out on your part, an authentic reaching out to become different. I mean different in the sense of having more languages at hand for expressing what you have to say. I mean different in the sense of knowing what it is to let your imagination play, to look at things as if they could be otherwise, to open windows in the ordinary and banal. Dewey once linked the idea of freedom to becoming different in this way—to seeing new options in the field opening before you, new possibilities for being. Yes, there are particular things you can teach in your own way, which is not precisely your teaching artist's way: you can teach, you can make contagious the delights and dangers of imagination; you can say—in words the young will understand—what it means to move into another space sometimes, to address the self to a created world. You can communicate some of the seriousness of art—in its creation and in its pre-sentness—and indicate the ways in which the meanings it releases can enrich and deepen and not detract from the truth-meanings, the scientific mean-ings, the moral meanings in an increasingly complex world.

Also, and I think this is of the first importance, you can do more than most of us do to bring the young sensually and perceptually alive. I am sure some of you know Rudolf Arnheim and the important work he has done on visual literacy and the relationship between perception and thought. For him, visual perception grasps generalities, patterns the world, lays the groundwork for concept formation. He wants to see art recognized in edu-cation as visual form and visual form as the principal medium of produc-tive thinking. He calls on us to cultivate the ability to see visual shapes as images of the patterns of forces that underlie our existence—the function-ing of minds, of bodies or machines, the structure of societies or ideas. Of course we know that a continuing presence of art forms can enhance visual perception, but we also know (and too seldom act upon the idea) that we can, in our developing role as aesthetic educator, cultivate and stimulate the sensory life, the embodied life, the perceptual life of the young if we our-selves are open and adventurous enough to notice what is there to be noticed, to listen, to see.

There are times in my own life when, half deliberately, I take a kind of restless action to uncouple from the familiar in the midst of ordinary life, just in order to see. Like most people, I think, I go through the world, even the variegated, resonant, dramatic, multi-shaded world of New York City, without seeing or hearing it. Caught in reverie, perhaps, or in the lazy unsee-ing of everydayness, I almost forget that I have eyes and ears. I plunge ahead—my eye on the goal, as it were, my office, my kitchen—just to get there, and I am perceptually dead. Sometimes, though, something jolts me awake. Something catches my attention—perhaps the look of a red sun over the river at the far end of a city street that is like a canyon, with buildings forming the walls of the canyon. Indeed, looking down that way one late afternoon, I realized that I could see not only the sky over the river and the trees and even the vague shape of a ship; I could see negative space—the formed space of the sky between and among the buildings, something I never knew how to see before I learned something about Cubist paintings.

In any case, I did uncouple. I did notice. And by doing that, I moved into an aesthetic space—and noticed more about the texture of the buildings, the strange darkness of the street turned into canyon, even the peculiar granite-gray of the New York street. I was having, you will admit, a kind of aesthetic experience in the natural world. I think it is important; I think it is something we can make accessible for young persons. And then we can make clearer to them that works of art are privileged objects—deliberately created to evoke the experience, to make possible the pleasure discovered in the moment of awareness in the natural world.

For some reason (well, perhaps it is not so mysterious) I think of that old poem by Rupert Brooke—"The Great Lover" (1977, pp. 134–136)—which so wonderfully lists some of the sensuous joys of ordinary life.

> *These I have loved:*
> > *White plates and cups, clean-gleaming,*
> *Ringed with blue lines; and feathery, faery dust;*
> *Wet roofs, beneath the lamp-light; the strong crusts*
> *Of friendly bread; and many-tasting food;*
> *And radiant raindrops couching in cool flowers;*
> *And flowers themselves, that sway through sunny hours,*
> *Dreaming of moths that drink them under the moon;*
> *Then, the cool kindliness of sheets, that soon*
> *Smooth away trouble; and the rough male kiss*
> *Of blankets; grainy wood; live hair that is*
> *Shining and free; blue-massing clouds; the keen*
> *Unpassioned beauty of a great machine.*

I think we have to become lovers in that fashion—and critics as well, and the kinds of teachers who are awakening to the world and will continue to awaken in our own fashion, with our own idiom. Become different, if you like, contagiously different; we will be aesthetic educators empowered to move in that "urgent and more fertile" realm of meanings Dewey described (1994, p. 332), a realm infused with passion, fringed with joy.

Fragments Made into Designs: Perceptions and Emergent Patterns

(1987)

I have been talking of meanings, yes, and perceptions, and feelings, all to the end of moving you to ponder what aesthetic education signifies and how you as teachers can make it real. I believe that many of you have already experienced transformations in your lived worlds. You have begun to rediscover what it is *actively* to perceive the works presented and the world around. That means that you have discovered the central importance of attending to feeling-tones and vivid qualities—colors, shapes, melodic sounds—that are ordinarily unheeded in everyday life. You have come to understand, perhaps as never before, that perceiving is not simply a way of recognizing sensations. It is an active, participant way of engaging with the visible and the audible—a way of patterning, ordering, producing wholeness in a manner never suspected outside the domains of the arts. Think of the way fragmented, discrete movements come together into kinetic designs in your seminars, how you suddenly behold a particular dance as a pattern, a whole. Think of how percussive noises (glassy surfaces, keys, metallic bells, pieces of wood striking against each other) are unexpectedly heard as having a sequence, a structure, sometimes a theme. You have come not simply to hear and see but to interpret, to hear sounds *as* a rhythmic pulsation, to see lines and shapes *as* sensuous form, to attend to an actor's staggering walk *as* a saying, or perhaps a cry of despair.

I think of Nietzsche suddenly, writing that "gray, cold eyes" do not know the value of things. He meant eyes looking from a distance, from outside, without feeling, without interest, without curiosity or concern. He meant eyes that simply glance, that do not perceive—eyes that are blind to the possibilities of things. The more we can actively and interestedly perceive, you see, the wider becomes the field on which our imaginations can work. It is imagination that enables us to reach beyond, to open up those possibilities. Imagination invents, you realize; it discloses alternative realities. Think, for example, of those strokes of paint on the backdrop in *Antigone*—creating an empty space and then a prison cell. If it were not for imagination, we would not be able to form such mental images of what-is-not where actual existence is concerned. Our minds would lack the power to mold experience into something new.

Paul Cézanne said once that our eyes can see the front of a painting, while imagination curves to the other side. The poet Hart Crane wrote of the kind of "curving" he associated with what he called reflections: those that enabled people to see such relationships as that between "a *drum* and a *street lamp*—*via* the *unmentioned* throbbing of the heart and nerves of a distraught man" (1926, p. 37). Yes, if you like, imagining has to do with metaphor-making, discovering unexpected resemblances, making connections between the inner and the outer. Some say it has to do with appreciating the known and the unknown simultaneously, as perhaps we might appreciate the look of age in Rembrandt's *Portrait of an Old Man* and something about the human condition, something unknown about oncoming death. Wallace Stevens, looking from another vantage point, said imagination is the "power that enables us to perceive the normal in the abnormal, the opposite of chaos in chaos" (1951, p. 153). It is what he called the "motive for metaphor," a desire to identify the human mind with what goes on outside it or, perhaps, as Wordsworth put it, to realize we create what we perceive.

Northrop Frye has spoken of the "educated imagination" (1964), and one of the things we are discovering here, I think, is how imagination can be educated through informed encounters with the several arts. It must be clear by now that some of the paintings you have seen, the music you have heard, the dance performances and the plays you have watched (and, yes, have personally explored) have stimulated the perceiving I spoke of just before. They have done so in part because they have tapped some of the deepest sources of your interest. You have found yourselves grasping a Monet landscape, perhaps, or a Hopper street scene, or a pas de deux, or a movement in the *Brandenburg Concerto No. 2* in its full qualitative richness, and this should have provided you occasion after occasion for your imagination to work.

There are moments, different phases in the working of imagination, and, in the contexts of aesthetic education, it is important to hold these in mind. You know that you (and, in time, your students) have to learn to achieve some degree of detachment or distance to grasp *Antigone,* say, or the Pilobo-lus *Bonsai* or Reich's *Clapping Music* in its complexity. If you become so totally involved in *Antigone* or so emotionally identified with the heroine (or her sister, or a guard) that you cannot imaginatively grasp the interplay of themes or the ways in which the characters play off against each other, you may miss having an experience with the drama as work of art. If you cannot stand off and perceive the kinetic design in *Bonsai* or catch the rhyth-mic patterns in *Clapping Music,* you will not be able to realize it in your own consciousness, and this is something that can be taught. But the focus-ing phase, the ordering and distancing phase is not the only dimension of awareness. To say it somewhat differently: we need to weave circles of quiet-ness, of attentiveness about ourselves at first—to be detached enough to grasp what is happening and at once to let our energies pour into what is there. Our experience has to fill up, to rise, as it were, like a wave, to reach what Dewey called a moment of consummation. Then there comes the elab-oration, the discovery of the new, the unfamiliar, that which our imagina-tion has disclosed for each of us personally in the lived, visible, and sound-ing world. And I would repeat that the more we know, the more we can perceive in each work; the more we perceive, the more we can imagine; the more we imagine, the more possibilities will open for us—possibilities of meaning, of vision, of alternative realities.

As an educator, I am convinced that to ignore experiences like these, to limit learners to single modes of seeing and interpreting, may be to frustrate their individual pursuits of meaning and, in consequence, their desires to come to know and learn. Today, as we well know, it may entail the imposi-tion of a predefined conception of the "given," in these days a largely tech-nical rendering of the world. One of the important things we can do through aesthetic education, I am sure, is to enable our students to recognize the ways in which their experience can be expanded through the entertainment of asso-ciations and alternative possibilities. This means remembering at every turn that imagination is also one of the powers of the mind, allowing for the sense "that there is always *more* to experience and *more in* what we experience than we can predict" (Warnock, 1978, p. 202). Is it not likely that this might move students to wonder, move beyond?

Hannah Arendt once said that education is the point "at which we decide whether we love the world enough to assume responsibility for it" and that it is "where we decide whether we love our children enough not to expel them from our world and leave them to their own devices, nor to strike from their hands their chance of undertaking something new" (1968, p. 196). Even to ponder what it signifies to "love the world," I think, is to move into domains where poets ordinarily venture—and painters and playwrights and musicians. To think of the young undertaking something new is to think of engaging them in quests for possibility. I remember the poet Rilke writing to the "young poet" about inconsiderable things that must be loved, and about how they become "big and beyond measuring." And then he reminded his young poet how important it was "to be patient toward all that is unsolved in your heart and to try to love the *questions themselves* like locked rooms and like books that are written in a very foreign tongue. Do not now seek the answers, that cannot be given you because you would not be able to live them. And the point is, to live everything. *Live* the questions now. Perhaps you will then gradually, without noticing it, live along some distant day into the answer" (1934/1993, p. 35).

To me, this is the mood to be created by the beginnings we make possible through aesthetic education, when paintings, musical works, dance performances, and the rest can conjure up so many experiential possibilities and open so many questions—questions that must be loved. It is not a matter of making people "better" in this fashion, nor of initiating them into some Cézanne community where individuals are supposed to be more sensitive and in some manner more "civilized." For me, it is a question of doing what can be done to enable as many young people as possible to crack the old forbidding codes, to break through the artificial barriers that for so long have excluded so many from engaging in aware fashion with the arts. The idea is to challenge an unquestioning passivity, consumerist attitudes, or the kind of carelessness and indolence that move all of us to take the easy, the conventional paths. If we and our students can somehow find ways of choosing ourselves as imaginative beings risking presentness to works of art, risking questioning, new spaces will be carved out in experience. There will be moments of "freedom and presence" seldom seen in schools. There will be, as there were for Emily Brontë, articulate passions that refuse to be domesticated; there will be adversary images to enforced social practices, and such images often release to learn. I cannot help but think of the famous critic Kenneth Burke reminding us, "When in Rome, do as the Greeks" (1953, p. 119), and that may be part of the risk. Or perhaps I might quote the great anthropologist, Lévi-Strauss, saying that aesthetic enjoyment:

> is made up of a multiplicity of excitements and moments of repose, of expectations disappointed or fulfilled beyond anticipation—a multiplicity resulting from the challenges made by the work and from the contradictory feeling it arouses that the tests it is subjecting us to are impossible, at the same time as it prepares to provide us with the marvelously unpredictable means of coping with them. (1964/1969, p. 15)

There are always new questions and new beginnings, always untapped possibilities and elements of the unpredictable. I think, like me, you are eager to share with your students the experiences of new disclosures, new horizons. I know that, whenever I read or see or listen to something as familiar to me as *Romeo and Juliet* or *Death of a Salesman,* or the *Brandenburg Concertos,* or Alvin Ailey's *Revelations,* or Cézanne's still life with the pepper bottle, I am likely to discover some dimension, some shape or sound or glint of light or meaning I do not remember having found before. There have been works (Philip Glass's music, for example) that I have not originally "liked" and, after hearing over and over, after learning more about noticing what there was to be noticed, that I have come to relish for some wholly unanticipated breakthrough of a horizon of sound or form. Each time, new resonances are awakened, new connections disclosed. And I am made aware again of the uses of imagination and its place in helping me stay alive to the world—and to the locked rooms and the books in very foreign tongues. I also want to keep living the questions. It is imagination that offers me a vision of what may be.

You have discovered what can happen when you move inside the language of dance and are enabled to attend to dance performances as a body-mind open in entirely unexpected ways to the stirrings and dynamics of your lived and mobile world. You have found out what can happen when you are freed to set and improvise a scene, or play with dialogue in relation to gesture, or consider the choices made when persons come together to bring into being a theatrical work. You recognize now how the knowledge and understanding you gain through such explorations become a kind of "indwelling" knowledge and understanding that direct your attention and illuminate your awareness when you confront a finished work of art. But I have been saying that, significant as this is, it is not all and must not be all. We want to release capacities, energies, ways of being in the world that are ordinarily suppressed. We want to do so to empower you who are teachers by extending the scope of your awareness, enhancing your consciousness, offering moments of wonder and moments of joy. But we want to do so also because we believe that the openings you will make possible in your own classrooms will enhance the education of those we like to think of as persons, not simply human resources, persons who need to be critically alive in a deceiving and seductive world, persons who will love the questions and will continue trying to open the windows to discover what is beyond.

I remember, in my own experience, being fascinated by words when I was young, collecting them, listing them, trying to put them together in my own small poems and rhymes and (later) in imperfect little stories. Having wondered, having tried, I looked at actual poetry and tales with a fascination I would not have otherwise felt. I wondered how Emily Dickinson discovered the power of a simple sentence like "I'm Nobody!" And of those tiny questions: "Who are you? / Are you—Nobody—Too?" (1960, p. 133). And I tried to understand why such simple language evoked so many feelings in me when I read. I am sure the same wonder, the same curiosity, the same interest made me resonate to those hushed soldiers' voices at the beginning of *Hamlet,* to that spare "Call me Ishmael" at the start of Melville's *Moby-Dick.* (And then he writes, you may remember, "Some years ago—never mind how long precisely—having little or no money in my purse, and nothing particular to interest me on shore, I thought I would sail about a little and see the watery part of the world" [1979, p. 2].) Even today, removed as I certainly was and am from a crew on a whaling ship, I still get a chill at the sound of that. (And I do not know why.) Quite recently, I got a somewhat similar chill from the first line in Alice Walker's *The Color Purple:* "Dear God, I am fourteen years old. I have always been a good girl" (1982, p. 11). But I understand that chill a little better.

You all have memories like that, and, like me, you could tell your own stories about a personal presentness to subject matter and to works of art—something significant in all domains, but something we too rarely see. I am talking, too, about a kind of responsibility when it comes to making an effort, about the feeling of personal agency that develops when you realize how much is due to your own attending and your own achieving when a work of art takes on its true life as an aesthetic object and begins to exist, as it were, in human time. I am referring as well to the remarkable realization that we can never exhaust or use up any work of art—that every time you see a Monet or hear a Mozart quartet or watch a Balanchine dance performance, there is always more than could have been predicted, more to explore. You must feel that to be of pedagogical value, as I do. Indeed, I find the experiences made possible by aesthetic education to be examples for all learning—this active involvement on the part of the learner, the beholder, the listener, the reader. And it is hard for me to believe that spaces for this will not some day be provided, even in "effective" schools, technically oriented schools, academically rigorous schools.

I want to believe that we—and the administrators and school board members who work with us—came into education originally with the same visions, the same dreams. They were dreams about children growing, pursuing their freedoms, discovering meanings, finding their own voices, even as we prepared them to make their way and do their work and play their required parts in the world. And that makes me confident we can infect those around us with our obsessions when it comes to imagination and the opening of spaces. We can do that, we who are to be aesthetic educators in addition to what we are already, even as we work to maintain the strength of our society. We can do it openly and proudly, rising over the "tides of mediocrity," taking risks, reaching always toward what we and our students ought to be.

We Who Are Teachers Know
That Imagination Has
This Multiple Power . . .
(1990)

I have been talking about the ways in which works of art are realized in experience, how they may be brought alive by a particular kind of attending: the kind of attending being nurtured here as you move from workshop to performances, and enter into dialogue with each other and with various created worlds. You are more sharply conscious by now of the ways in which aesthetic qualities come into being in relation to your body and your mind.

Think of Doris Humphrey's *Day on Earth*, in which ordinary actions are made into extraordinary ones, in which everyday gestures are transmuted into dance. We are enabled, by means of these transformations, to come in touch in a fresh way with the palpitant life of generations: the child leaving, the mother bereft, the day passing. Looking at those bodies in movement, engaging with the images invented and remade, we may understand better how what is enacted on a stage can become an object of particular experiences of our own. That means it becomes an aesthetic object for *us*, for you and me. Learning something about Humphrey's use of space, direction, contraction, we might realize the manner in which qualities distinctive of that dance come into resonant being *through* their appearing to those of us able to perceive in a certain way. By qualities, I mean here texture, force, quickness, buoyancy—aspects realized only when they are attended to, grasped by an awakened consciousness. Compare your experience of that dance performance, when realized, with a chance experience on the street: a mother saying good-bye to a small daughter, a family holding hands and moving off into the distance. You might stop for a moment and take a look, especially when you feel peculiar—alive and attentive to things (as you often do when you are here). There is a difference, however, between what you experience here and what you happen on in the street. It has to do in part with what a choreographer *selects out* of the appearing world to bring forth—and, if you like, the ways in which we feel ourselves into the images on the stage, into what Humphrey shaped and set moving, what she transmuted into kinetic metaphor, what she expressed.

It is fundamentally similar to what happens when we look at the rendering of the unreal, yet profoundly recognizable universe called *Alice in Wonderland*. Remember the qualities that emerged for you as you made the polite bedazzled Alice, the King and Queen of Hearts, Tweedle Dum and Tweedle Dee objects of your experience, not simply images out there in objective space. Remember the Mad Hatter's hat, the hands pressing down on Alice's head, the table with those oddly appearing and disappearing little landscapes, the professorial gowns—and the duality, the ambiguity, indeed the darkness of the childish Victorian dream.

When present to such works, we experience a distinctive kind of relationship, not solely with them but with the others attending around us, each in their own way. I am so aware of what it signifies to encounter a performance or an exhibition with others—feeling the attentiveness of the others, sharing in it, even as I strive to see with my own eyes, hear with my own ears. There is a complex conversation going on each time, a transaction that draws us, in our community, both into the work and beyond what seem to be its limits. The more we are able to perceive, the wider and richer becomes the landscape on which our imagination and our feelings can work. Even now, remembering back—this time as a philosopher—I hear those language games in my ears, those puzzles and twists of logic, and I recall Alice saying she might write about it some day. Then it all becomes larger for me, as new openings in my experience are reached.

With that in mind, I want to place particular stress on imagination, that cognitive capacity that is too often ignored in educational talk and, yet, is so fundamental to learning, to being in the world. Dewey spoke of it once as the capacity to look at things as if they could be otherwise. In *Art as Experience,* he wrote that it is "a *way* of seeing and feeling things as they compose an integral whole. It is the large and generous blending of interests at the point where the mind comes in contact with the world. When old and familiar things are made new in experience, there is imagination. When the new is created, the far and strange become the most natural inevitable things in the world. There is always some measure of adventure in the meeting of mind and universe, and this adventure is, in its measure, imagination" (1980, p. 267).

I would emphasize as well the capacity imagination gives us to move into the "as-if"—to move beyond the actual into invented worlds, to do so within our experience. To enter a created world, an invented world, is to find new perspectives opening on our lived worlds, the often taken-for-granted realities of everyday. You have experienced some of those perspectives as opened by the rabbit hole, the tea party, the croquet game, as I have. (All I have to do is feel again the cool analytic British language and contrast it to that dizzying drop downward, and I see aspects of my own odd world anew.) We will all discover vistas opened by the familiar, and at the same time unfamiliar, tale of *Romeo and Juliet,* and their impulsive sudden adolescent love at another time when life seemed cheap and nothing seemed sure and there was violence in streets framed by public rituals. Speaking of vistas and imagination, I want to offer a tiny poem by Galway Kinnell called "Prayer" (1985, p. 19), which—if you can indeed release yourself into the unreal world even it creates—also offers a new vantage point on what is.

> *Whatever happens. Whatever*
> what is *is is what*
> I *want. Only that. But that.*

At a time of boredom, disenchantment, and passivity, few concerns seem as important to me as the concern for imagination, especially as that capacity can be released by encounters with the arts, and on whose release encounters with the arts depend.

For Mary Warnock, the imagination is necessary if we are to apply thoughts or concepts to things in their particularity; but it is also imagination, as Wordsworth said, that enables us to see "into the life of things," to engage with images in their depth. "The belief," writes Warnock,

> that there is more in our experience of the world than can possibly meet the unreflecting eye, that our experience is significant for us and worth the attempt to understand it . . . this kind of belief may be called the feeling of infinity. It is a sense . . . that there is always *more* to experience and *more in* what we experience than we can predict. Without some such sense, even at the quite human level of there being something which deeply absorbs our interest, human life becomes not actually futile or pointless, but experienced as if it were. It becomes, that is to say, boring. In my opinion, it is the main purpose of education to give people the opportunity of not ever being, in this sense, bored; of not ever succumbing to a feeling of futility, or to the belief that they have

come to an end of what is worth having. It may be that some people do not need education to save them from this; my claim is only that, if education has a justification, this salvation for those who do need it must be its justification. (1978, pp. 202–203)

Surely, it is not difficult to find relevance in what Warnock says for what we all hope to achieve in our classrooms and, indeed, for ourselves. We all want, I think, to open our students to what Wallace Stevens's guitar player has in mind in that wonderful poem, "The Man with the Blue Guitar," when he tells his listeners: "Things as they are / Are changed upon the blue guitar" (1982, p. 165). He does not mean they are magically altered or falsified. He means they appear differently; they appear in the light of possibility. He warns those who are listening, however, that this can never happen unless they break with fixities, with petrifaction. It cannot happen unless they try to find their own voices, their own visions, and try to break through the crusts of conformity and thoughtlessness. Near the end, he says to those who insist that he play things as they are: "You are yourself. / The blue guitar surprises you" (p. 183).

And, indeed, we who are teachers know that imagination has this multiple power: to create orders, to provoke authentic vision, and to surprise. For Stevens, the imagination enables us to perceive the normal in the abnormal, the opposite of chaos in chaos. It becomes, for him, the very source of meaningfulness. Like Dewey, he believed it implied something other than the habitual, the humdrum, the repetitive. It opened to what was new. If you think back to the ways in which some of the music you have heard here, some of the dance you have watched here, some of the drama you have seen here have glowed for a while in your consciousness, opened clearings here and there, you may begin to rediscover the significance of imagination when it comes to learning, and when it comes to the opening of art works and their transformation into something that is each of yours.

Coleridge used to write of the synthetic and magical power he called imagination, its ability to reconcile discordant qualities, the sense of novelty and freshness it brought to old and familiar objects and scenes. I am quite sure that some of us have found this out for ourselves at various moments during Summer Session. The linking of imagination to adventure and to opening spaces cannot but appeal to those of us interested in awakening the young to alternative possibilities in their lives. But, like ourselves, they have to keep relearning to look at the world. I find the importance of this to be more evident with every Summer Session I attend. I learn again in some fashion how to look and listen. I see the shadows on the sidewalk anew, the shifting reflections on the glass windows, I hear the voices in their multiple dialects. I begin inhabiting a world somewhat like Walt Whitman's, I sometimes think, with the endless details, the catalogues, the new patterns becoming visible at every turn. I notice, I pay heed, I become indignant now and then. I am part of it. I can no longer withdraw. Suddenly I notice, as Whitman did (in "Crossing Brooklyn Ferry"), the river and the "scallop-edged waves," the "big steam-tug closely flank'd on each side by the barges," the "flicker of black contrasted with wild red and yellow light over the tops of houses, and down into the cleft of streets" (1982, pp. 308–310) where all the shapes rise—of factories, railroads, sleepers on the bridges, the workmen, the prisoners. It opens for me. It becomes visible and audible. The curtains have parted once again.

Curtains part and, as Virginia Woolf said, bring the "severed parts together" (1985). Imagination makes metaphors, opens us to what Woolf called "moments of being" at the very heart of multiplicity and confusion and noise. Cynthia Ozick in *Metaphor and Memory*, tells of being asked to speak to some physicians who were unable to see the connection between their patients' vulnerability and the doctors' own unacknowledged susceptibility, their human frailty, if you will. "The writer," wrote Ozick, "an imaginer by trade, will suggest a course of connecting, of entering into the tremulous spirit of the helpless, the fearful, the apart. In short, the writer will demonstrate the contagion of passion and compassion that is known in medicine as 'empathy,' and in art as insight" (1989, p. 266). She is reminding us of what imagination can do as it creates relationships, institutes orders, and of what art can do as it awakens mutuality while it opens worlds.

Art expands visions, even as it challenges the taken-for-granted, as long as more and more persons lend their lives to works of art and bring them into being in their own experience. It is clear enough that the languages and symbol systems of the arts differ from one another and probably cannot be translated into one another.

All this means breaking with confinement, looking from an increasing number of vantage points—realizing that the world is always incomplete. I hope you will think back on your own experiences of joy and liberation and even grief—the experiences evoked by what you have encountered in the domains of art. You have made them possible by looking through the windows of the actual and the banal and the boring. Because that, as you well know, is where it must begin.

I cannot resist ending with an excerpt from Poem VIII of Adrienne Rich's "Twenty-One Love Poems" in *The Dream of a Common Language* (1978, p. 31):

> *The rules break like a thermometer,*
> *quicksilver spills across the charted systems,*
> *we're out in a country that has no language*
> *no laws, we're chasing the raven and the wren*
> *through gorges unexplored since dawn*
> *whatever we do together is pure invention*
> *the maps they gave us were out of date.*

Caught in the systems, we may indeed need to invent together, to remake and renew the common world.

Complex Intuitions in the Perceiver Make Content . . . Denser and More Provocative

(1990)

We have talked about openings in experience and new perspectives. I have tried to move you to think about imagination and what it means to realize works of art by attending to them in certain ways. You are certainly aware by now how this kind of attending is clarified and enhanced by the explorations your teaching artists make possible. Some of us, in our previous encounters with *Romeo and Juliet,* may have scarcely paid heed to the choreography of dueling, or to the changing look of the moon, or to the mingling of the down-to-earth and the hoping against hope in the poetry of the child Juliet. This time, we may—finding ourselves unexpectedly caught—have heard, have seen, as if for the first time.

I am aware of some of you sharing a recognition of such an awakening. You may not have seen what I saw this time; but that is not the point. You surely were more conscious of the play in its concreteness and variety; and you must have realized, as I did, that the richer and the more complex were the intuitions aroused in you, the denser and more provocative became the content of the play. With our bodies and minds working together, we felt more than we would have otherwise. This is very different from having emotions *about* the sad love affair of two adolescents in Verona, victimized by adult strife. It is a way of understanding, grasping through feeling—much enhanced by our capacity to know what is in the work, to hear the language, the tones of voice, to respond to movement, to resonate to light and darkness, to engage with that inconstant moon.

Denis Donoghue has written about the sense in which the arts are useless, in that they will not cure a toothache or relieve that great pain after

86

which, as Emily Dickinson wrote, "a formal feeling comes" (1960, p. 162). But then he talks about the sense in which they are momentous because of the way they provide for spaces in which we can live in freedom. He sees a connection between the main texts of our lives, those negotiated mainly by convention and routine and habit, and the margins in which the arts exist. Think of it as a page, he writes. "If the entire page were taken up with the text, we would have to live according to its conventional rhythms, even in our leisure hours" (1983, p. 129). But, as we are trying to insist at the Institute, the entire page does not have to be taken up with the everyday, with keeping things going; it does not have to be taken up with the text that requires us merely to coincide with our ordinary selves. The text, the main text, may provide the stuff on which the arts can work; but the margin highlights and frames the text, offers perspectives that keep us from forever coinciding with our ordinary selves, that allow us to see and deal with even the ordinary differently, that offer alternative ways of viewing and listening to and being in the world.

I was reading a chapter on education in a book by Martin Buber (*Between Man and Man*) the other day, and I found some sentences describing a children's choir in Prague, which released the previously silent "to a life of freely moving persons, rejoicing in their achievement, formable and forming, who know how to shape sights and sounds in multiform patterns and also how to sing out their risen souls wildly and gloriously; more, how a community of achievement, proclaimed in glance and response, has been welded together out of dull immured solitary creatures" (1978, p. 86). Buber had what he called a life of creativity in mind, and also a capacity for participation and partaking. He said that all human beings desire to make things, and what children desire most of all is their share in the becoming of things. Through their own intensively experienced actions, something arises that was not there before. This notion of participant experience—and sharing in the becoming of things—comes very close to what we mean by aesthetic education.

Surely, it applies to our efforts to help persons understand what it is to shape musical sounds in various patterns so they can hear better when it comes to Chopin or Robert Dennis or an oratorio or a chorale. An achievement, as Buber said, that is "formable and forming" (1978, p. 86) is what allows for the kinds of listening, the kinds of perceiving so important in this Institute. Again, think what it is to understand the shaping of sound, the making of patterns in space, the practice of mime from the *inside,* and how that relates to the idea of sharing in the becoming of things. Not only does this feed into encounters with increasingly diverse modes of art; it can feed into what we now know are very particular explorations of meaning.

Think of the meaning concentrated in the figure of Juliet straining over the balcony edge, or that in the aged Krapp hunched at his tape machine, or that in the battered shape of the Victoria Marks dancer huddled for a moment on the floor. Gathered in the image of Juliet's body, or Krapp's, or the dancer's, or (in another dimension) in the figure of Picasso's *Woman Ironing*, with its harsh lines and angles, its gray-brown atmosphere, the meanings speak to us directly. Transacting with distinctive media—dramatic dialogue, gesture, the body in crumbled motion, paint on canvas—these meanings take on a significance other than that gained in different ways of knowing. They differ, too, from what is gained in what Donoghue calls the main text. But do they not enlarge and deepen the life of meaning—in part by making it newly present to us as feeling, perceiving, thinking, imagining beings?

It may be that the intensity of the encounter is due to a recognition that art expresses meanings while the sciences and social sciences state them, and we are simply in a different relation to meanings when we are experiencing something rather than heeding a guidebook or a signpost, or a manual, describing a phenomenon or giving us directions for making it appear. A guidebook, for example, can give us the details relating to the great blue window in Chartres Cathedral even as it tells us where to find it. *The New Yorker* can tell us about and direct us toward the latest Shakespeare play in the park, or the Guare play at Lincoln Center Theater. We all know the difference between reading about the blue window before reaching it and feeling transfixed before its glow and imagery, between reading the description of the new version of *The Taming of the Shrew* and actually participating in it—physically and imaginatively.

Not only do we want to keep the aesthetic adventures into meaning visible and potent in the schools, along with the other ways there are of making or achieving or discovering meanings. We want to keep enhancing them with some understanding of contexts—movements, styles, traditions—and connections among diverse works at different modes of history. For one thing, we know very well that none of us comes to any work of art devoid of context or with what has been called a totally "innocent eye." Even when we come to *East of the Sun and West of the Moon*, many of us view it against memories of various kinds of enchantment (yes, and disenchantment), of frog princes and disguises and quests and journeys and (perhaps) transformative change. It may well be that the newcomer children from different cultures themselves grew up with versions of that story, whether there is a great bear or a troll queen or some other archetype, some other image that continues to live somewhere in imagination. Trying to arouse the young to attend, we may make it possible for them in their plurality to incorporate what they see and hear into their own distinctive repertories. We may create situations in which new experiences we provide can accommodate to children's funded meanings; it may be that the meanings themselves may be transformed. Dewey wrote that imagination was the gateway through which meanings derived from earlier experiences could find their way into present-day enactments. He said that present-day enactments become human and conscious to the degree they are extended by meanings and values drawn from what is absent and present only imaginatively. When that happens, the past itself can be remade, even as the present becomes more luminous. Again, I would remind you of how engagement in the arts can work to free past encounters to feed in this enriching way into the present. Think of how *The Adventures of Huckleberry Finn,* or *Little Women,* or "Bartleby the Scrivener," or *Hansel and Gretel,* or *The Prodigal Son,* or Martha Graham's *Appalachian Spring* can tap memories and stored meanings—and how, when those meanings do move through the gateway of imagination, they can illuminate the present.

We can think, at the same time, of how meanings are enhanced through the expansion of our sense of history, of relationality in time. We want to keep multiplying the perspectives through which works of art are viewed, and one way of doing this is to help people perceive them in time. It is enlightening, surely, to see Victoria Marks's choreography not only in the contemporary context, but against the background of Doris Humphrey's choreography and Balanchine's, even as it is important and sometimes startling to see Humphrey and Balanchine dances with the emerging shapes of a Victoria Marks dance in mind. So it is when we look back, say, from impressionist paintings to Turner's renderings of rain and mist and speed, or when we discover (as Ellsworth Kelly has enabled us to do) Picasso's responding to the architect Gaudi, Kelly's own responding to Giacometti and Braque and Cézanne. Everything depends, of course, on our attending—our being there in person to do our own informed readings of what presents itself to us. Again, the more multiple the perspectives, the more meanings accumulate. There are new connections to be seen, new openings, always new possibilities.

In my own case, I was struck this time by the randomness of the violence at Shakespeare's moment, by the shattering of medieval shelters and certainties, by the emergence of what I can only see as the modern world. I am sure my particular responses to this city, my personal seeking for some norm of justice and decency, my worries about those who suffer in our society from a lack of care affected what I selected out of *Romeo and Juliet* this time—

in text and in enactment. When Juliet lamented that "heaven should practise stratagems / Upon so soft a subject as myself!" I could not but summon
up the many adolescent girls, soft little girls, who feel themselves cheated
(who are indeed cheated) if not by heaven, by their world. The play made
me envisage once more the way in which injustices can occur even in the
lives of the innocent, and the absolute absence of guarantees. Feeling that,
I paid even more intense attention. Feeling that, I think I was moved as seldom before to go in search of some kind of meaning in the Elizabethan world
and in our world, to try to find a way to combat meaninglessness with some
sort of action, some sort of caring. I kept thinking of Camus' *The Plague*
(1971) and the affirmation there that, in times of pestilence, one should
always take the side of the victims.

I do not mean, I do not think I mean I was trying to rewrite the play.
I am simply suggesting how an engagement, a being present as oneself, with
one's own story, one's own memories, one's own sense of outrage, can open
up pathways in one's mind that may actually have been long closed. Because
I was attending so intensely and with such modern eyes, for instance, I was
struck as I had never been by Romeo's comment after Mercutio receives
his fatal wound and blames Romeo, you remember, for that final blow.
"O sweet Juliet," Romeo muses, "Thy beauty hath made me effeminate, /
And in my temper soften'd valour's steel." In that mood, infected (we might
say) not only by male macho values but by sexist ones, he takes his sword
and fells Tybalt, thereby calling down the fearful tragedy that dooms him
and Juliet as well. So it is not, as the critics have said for so long, the strife
of great families that brought on the tragedy, not that strife alone. It has to
do with posturing images of manhood, with feelings about women and
effeminacy. And that made me think about Virginia Woolf—not only her
description of men in their uniforms primping before the mirror, but her talk
of "Shakespeare's sister" who died young and never wrote a word. "Drawing her life from the lives of the unknown who were her forerunners, as her
brother did before her, she will be born" (1989, p. 114). If we prepare for
her, she may find it possible to live, wrote Woolf; and, by the end of the
drama, in the cold of the tomb, I am left with networks of new feelings and
ideas, even as I am absolutely present when Montague and Capulet repent,
and the Prince says "Go, hence to have more talk of these sad things."

I am sure you feel with me that works like these—and many others—are
inexhaustible, at least for those willing to attend adventurously. Eager for
new visions, for dynamic experiences, we know we have to confront the issue
many of us read about in Sunday's *New York Times*. It is the issue of "quality," perhaps of standards in our choosing. It is the issue of multiplicity

and what the author, Michael Brenson, calls "esthetic emotion." He writes—putting, I think, a huge responsibility on us who are teachers, "this is not an either-or age. It is possible to believe in the value of esthetic emotion while listening to those who question it. It is possible to believe in the tradition of Western art while paying attention to art that might call that tradition into question. It is possible to believe in the logic and imagination of form ... and still be curious about art that may come and go and amount to no more than a single political insight or an eloquent tantrum" (1990, July 22, p. 27).

We are charged with making the kinds of judgments we may never have tried to make before in a society dominated in a thousand ways by media and popular culture, strained by multiculturalism, haunted by fundamentalism. Some of us will struggle to defend what we love and work to make it contagious in our classrooms, even as we work for reflective awareness and for the kind of attending that may transform lives. Others of us will at once pay heed to such words as those of Ming Cho Lee, the great stage designer who was here at the Institute's beginnings. "This is only the beginning," he wrote to the *Times,* "and if we don't fight with all our commitment and passion, we will have a diminished and corroded democracy." You have lived your own beginnings here, many of you. There will be work ahead, yes, and joy. Elizabeth Bishop began a poem called "Conversation" with these lines, and I think I might close this way: "The tumult in the heart / keeps asking questions" (1997, p. 76). Keep asking, and keep wondering. It will keep you alive.

Charting Our Own Ways Toward Meaning in Various Works of Art

(1995)

Perhaps strangely, I choose to begin with the opening of *Hamlet* when the sentinels on the castle platform at Elsinore are uneasily asking each other to identify themselves. "Who's there?" asks Bernardo. "Nay, answer me," says Francisco: "stand, and unfold yourself." "Long live the king!" says Bernardo. Francisco, still uncertain, says, "Bernardo?" And, in some relief, Bernardo answers, "He." There is something about that exchange that makes me think of the beginning of an encounter with a work of art—Sam Shepard's *True West*, a British landscape painting, a Pilobolus dance, Samuel Barber's *Summer Music for Wind Quintet*. We cannot know. We cannot even know ourselves or what we will feel and discover when the lights go on and the action starts, when we make out the road moving off behind the trees. A space, a kind of empty imaginative space opens before us in our experience. Things are initially vague, as hard to decipher perhaps as the faces in that murky night at Elsinore. It is only when we begin attending, singling out the details, the particulars, that the space begins to fill, and we begin charting our way somehow, "reading" what we are watching or listening to, grasping it, making it ours.

There are other examples of what I have in mind, one from a novel we are reading called *The English Patient* (Ondaatje, 1997), in part about a mysterious pilot who fell from the sky with his helmet on fire over the African desert in the Second World War. He is picked up by nomads, bedouins, carried through the sand, and brought to a hospital in Pisa. At last he is taken to an abandoned hospital in a villa near Florence, where he is cared for by one young nurse when the hospital staff evacuates the ruin at the end of the

war. I find things in that novel that truly give rise to events in my consciousness, that change me as potent metaphors will. The pilot, in his childhood, inhabited a landscape of trout streams and birdcalls, which he recalls
as a "fully named world." Carried through the desert, his eyes are covered;
he cannot recognize the signs. But there is more. Deserts, for me, especially
African deserts, are empty spaces of whiteness, totally unnamed. In this
book, the desert is gradually named; it becomes "the fertile lands of Cyre-
naica, the salt marshes of El Agheila" (1997, p. 36). There are hidden towns,
the sounds of musical instruments. There are winds with names, a town
called El Taj; there are Goran tribes who crush a food made out of colo-
cynth. There are oases, names for a long unnameable world.

I said that I find in that story a metaphor, comparing things that are on
the surface dissimilar: the desert suddenly becoming filled up with settlements
and colors and moving nomads and dancing boys and figures in burnooses—
and the experience of those of us who find our lives being changed by active
encounters with the arts. *True West,* for me, is another example of what can
happen when a play becomes the object of a reflective consciousness, when
it is rendered meaningful by an active noticing, an offering of attention.
Like the rest of you, I am sure, I was brought up with movies about cow-
boys and Indians called "westerns"; my present experience is replete with
images emerging from California—of earthquakes, riots, O. J. Simpson,
Sunset Boulevard—the current West, presented as the "true" West to many
of us these days. There is something like a desert in that array of images and
what Lee in the play so haltingly calls "cliché"; a fictitiousness took it over
long ago. I reach back into the history I recall, trying to recapture (what?)
the real West of the settlements and the terrible journeys and the escapes from
the dust bowl and the Golden Gate or the Golden Mountain, made of arti-
fices and, too often, false dreams. And then, like the rest of you, I engage
with this play (I must say, not for the first time); I play the experience of seeing the staged world against the experience of the textual world I found in
the printed book, which I suppose I read in part as a work of literature.
Maybe for that reason the connections I made (as my imagination went to
work weaving designs, making connections, creating new patterns) were
with *The Great Gatsby* (Fitzgerald, 1995) and the search for the green light,
the quest corrupted by the "foul dust of the eastern air." And I thought of
the Langston Hughes poem "Harlem" and the dream dying like "a raisin in
the sun" (1959). And then I remembered (partly because I teach these things)
the presence of the wilderness in the American mind, the wild places, the
places that had to be defended against by the building of a stockade or the
building of a school or the building of small windowless log cabins where

people could huddle in the fear of wind-blown space and buffalos and strangers rushing by on horses, trying to reclaim the land. And out of all this and other memories, other associations, I became in some way participant in the action of *True West* with that desert (be it called Dakota or the Mojave or Tornado or even Alaska) out there beyond the elevators Austin is charged with riding, and the computer and the toasters and the six-packs and the plants that die in their particular foul dust if someone doesn't remember the cold water and keep them alive.

Then, with the two brothers battling, sublimating brotherly love in violence (as Americans so often do), battling over whose version of the West is "true," is salable, is convincing, can be made into a movie (although not a film), we confront a terrible question about expressing, about articulation, about art itself. Lee has lived in the desert, has had an "intimate relation" with the wilderness supposedly—but Lee has no language for telling about it. It is all fakery and wheezing and curses and (yes) clichés. Austin, on the other hand, is the writer soaked in popular culture and bourgeois ordinariness. How can he render the truth out there where his father, toothless by now, alcoholic, has run to escape? Who can say it? Where is the "true West"? What is the connection between art and truth? When, at the end, the two brothers, instead of killing each other, seem to merge, to become one—dark and large against the big sky, they may (as they stagger together toward the Mojave) embody the contradictory, always problematic "truth" about the West and about America and about the American quest. We do not know. It cannot be resolved. The questions beat and thud and hang there. And the spaces of our experience become fuller and more complex and richer and more full of contradiction. We breathe harder, perhaps, and this may be the intelligibility Dewey had in mind—as well as the source of questions, the questions with which searching and learning begin. Surely an experience like this is a way of countering the anaesthetic, the routine, the humdrum. It is not only the hour and a half spent with the play—it is what is summoned up, what is incited to come alive and connect.

That is what I meant by talk of possibility, of the unexpected surging up in experience. You and I could say kindred things about our encounter with Pilobolus or your work with shapes you never thought a human body could take, with designs made by human limbs and shoulders and heads—until the very presence of the human body changes, shedding off all fixity, becoming itself a process, something changing, something becoming in space and time. I think I have mentioned a vision before a painting, this one described by Jean-Paul Sartre while writing about how we all perceive things against the backgrounds of our own experience, about how things seem to open up from the vantage points of where we stand, from our lived situations. "If the painter presents us with a field or a vase of flowers," he wrote, "his paintings are windows which are open on the whole world. We follow the red path which is buried among other wheat fields, under other clouds which empty into the sea, and we extend to infinity, to the other end of the world, the deep finality which supports the existence of the field and the earth. So that, through the various objects which it produces, the creative act aims at a total renewal of the world" (1949, p. 57).

If this is true of the art of painting—of form and space and color, it is also true of music, which could be called the art of time. I think of the interplay of tonalities in Samuel Barber's piece, for instance, and the openings that are the counterpoints. There is something, in any case, about a woodwind conversation for me that ends, like many conversations, with more to say, with a sense of something—some sound, some frequency beyond. It may be that way too with dance, as in the many movements of the *Peach Flower Landscape,* with that early image of the flowing stream, with the male figure fishing, perhaps playing the flute, perhaps rowing, carrying us along on a kind of gentle current—among the farmers, in the forest, into ritual—and the stream again, never stopping, leaving us with flow and becoming. But then a dance is never a fixed object. It is an art bound to performance, and performance is always an occasion of experience. Something happens before us—whether we are watching a Balanchine ballet or an Ailey work or a Martha Graham. For Merce Cunningham: "When I dance, it means: this is what I am doing. . . . This is not feeling *about* something, this is a whipping of the mind and body into an action that is so intense, that, for the brief moment involved, the mind and body are one. . . . It is the connection with the immediacy of the action, the single instant that gives the feeling of . . . freedom" (1955/1997, p. 86). He is talking about the kind of occasion that actualizes, that produces an immediate presence binding choreographer, dancers, audience, and music into a synthesis, a continuous whole. It is a process of body engagement—a process that establishes a world through the body's moving presence. There is no summation in this play of powers, no end-point. Movement, a stream, a process—moving always beyond, filling the empty space, yet not filling it because the stream flows on, and there is always more.

So much of our gesturing, our thinking, even our understanding is made to seem *about* something. This stress on process, on movement, on the union of the mind and body seems to be of importance, certainly to our personal lives, as it is to the lives of those we teach. I always want to recommend a session of dancing before the young people take to their computers—even as I want to enable young people to try to express through movement sometimes how they feel, what they desire, what they understand. It is another language, another way of naming, another way of overcoming the emptiness. It may be the consequence of a mode of intelligence; it may not. But it has to do with our marking our spaces in time, generating the spaces, the medium of perceptual experience through movement. And there are connections, continuities, at once different from but similar to those I experienced in responding to *True West*. There are continuities within our bodies, with other bodies, with the environment, even with the cosmos. We can reach beyond through dance or through encounters with dance—imagining, feeling ourselves moving beyond, moving to wider and wider spaces—taking part, someone says, in "cosmic control of the world."

I want to end this lecture by talking about the sense in which what we try to do through aesthetic education is to move persons to their own creativity by means of active and participant encounters with works of art. Again, much has to do with participants' willingness to lend the works their lives—to achieve the works as meaningful by participants' own informed interpretations. Yes, indeed, people can be helped to create by means of media: young and old flower when given opportunities to inscribe images, to express their feelings in some significant language, to explore musical instruments and the sounds they make available for singing and saying in their own ways. They find new energies, surely, when they discover modes of making patterns with their own bodies in movement. They find new energies as well in making a design, in solving the problems of form and color, in trying to make present an imagined end. The capacity to create in these ways has much to do with an ardent, aware being in the world, as it does with opening people of many ages to the creative work of those we call artists, who have refined their craft—who cannot *but* write or paint or compose or choreograph in order to reach others as they impose their own orders upon the void.

I want to say that participant engagements with works of art can themselves be creative experiences, especially if prepared for as you are prepared in the workshops. Creation does not imply a making something out of nothing. It has to do with reshaping, renewing the materials at hand, very often the materials of our own lives, our experiences, our memories. I believe many of you share with me the remarkable discovery that dimensions of your lives, your life histories, your past may be disclosed, may be highlighted by what you read and hear and encounter in the way of the arts. As Rilke said in one of his poems, they call to us: "You must change your life" (1940/1974,

p. 93). And the rest? We and those we teach are moved, as in few other circumstances, to pose the difficult questions and to choose. I want to end with
a poem by Mark Strand called "Keeping Things Whole" (1980, p. 10),
because it is about moving ahead to fill the empty spaces, moving to keep
things whole.

> *In a field*
> *I am the absence*
> *of field.*
> *This is*
> *always the case.*
> *Wherever I am*
> *I am what is missing.*
>
> *When I walk*
> *I part the air*
> *and always*
> *the air moves in*
> *to fill the spaces*
> *where my body's been.*
>
> *We all have reasons*
> *for moving.*
> *I move*
> *To keep things whole.*

The Vibrancy and Tremolos of the Arts for the Person and the Community

(1996)

Last week, trying to articulate a greeting at the start of our Summer Session, I touched upon the significance of the arts in personal lives as well as in the life of the democratic community. I also suggested at what is involved in provoking diverse young people to engage in the active learning required by aesthetic education. And, indeed, you will admit that each person has to be personally present and alive to what is happening, if she or he is to achieve a work as meaningful in her or his own lived context. Attentive, aware, a person will come in touch with a play, a text, a painting, a musical performance, a dance piece in a mood of wonder, curiosity, often of questioning. To be sunk in habitual routines, to be merely passive is, we well know, to miss an opportunity for awakening. But we as teachers take the chances the young do when we try to enable them to defamiliarize their familiar situations—to take another look at them, to break through the crust, to reflect on things as if they could be otherwise. How, after all, do we know what "otherwise" might entail? And when we break through the crust of the conventionalized, what is on the other side?

My concern today is to suggest that our very asking is likely to sound empty if we ourselves do not think back on what experiences like this have meant—and mean—in our own lives. Also, I doubt if we would be able to invent the kinds of pedagogies needed for aesthetic education if we did not take the time to ponder what the arts have signified for us, not only as teachers, but as distinctive human beings trying to make sense of our lives. We are "condemned," one thinker says, to make meanings, to devise projects that make some imprint, to identify some purpose in our strivings and our undertakings. John Dewey wrote once that the self does not pre-exist. It is "something in continuous formation through choice of action" (1966, p. 351). (Stop and think, for a moment, what choosing to come here in the summer has to do with the forming of your self.) We cannot but be reminded by words like these that, like the learners in our classrooms, we exist in time and, like those learners, are on our way somewhere. Like them, we are in process, asked to chart our direction, to choose ourselves day by day. Reflective and diverse encounters with works of art, some of us believe, may well release and energize us for this kind of choosing, if only because they free us from the banal and repetitive. They cannot but open new perspectives on the natural and human worlds around us. We are made conscious, sometimes abruptly, of alternative modes of being alive, of relating to others, of becoming what we are not yet.

I am eager for you to reflect on what this means for you. Are lost memories aroused? Do you find connections between themes in your autobiography and what you have begun listening for in *The Trout Quintet?* Does some dimension of your consciousness come abruptly alive through your encounter with the movement of Martha Graham's *Lamentation?* Does the heretofore inexpressible find expression—and do you, on some level, for the first time understand?

Again, I want to turn to a particular poem to make my point, a poem that is conceived to be a work of art. Again, it is by a poet, Charles Simic, widely recognized as one of our great ones, and it offers us what I take to be a series of rather startling metaphors. Indeed, the poem itself may come as a surprise, and if it does, that seems to me to be a good thing in our context. It is called "Club Midnight" (1996, p. 66).

> *Are you the sole owner of a seedy night club?*
>
> *Are you its sole customer, sole bartender,*
> *Sole waiter prowling around the empty tables?*
>
> *Do you put on wee-hour girlie shows*
> *With dead stars of black and white films?*
>
> *Is your office upstairs over the neon lights,*
> *Or down deep in the dank rat cellar?*
>
> *Are bearded Russian thinkers your silent partners?*
> *Do you have a doorman by the name of Dostoyevsky?*
>
> *Is Fu Manchu coming tonight?*
> *Is Miss Emily Dickinson?*

Do you happen to have an immortal soul?
Do you have a sneaky suspicion that you have none?

Is that why you throw a white pair of dice,
In the dark, long after the joint closes?

Yes, you are perceived to be alone, but you realize, once you think about it, that seedy night clubs like this exist in cities, not in a vacuum, and within context, traditions—traditions shaped by the movies and the obsessions of the past, by the pull between the neon lights upstairs and the cellar, the underground, "down deep." And weren't there strange bearded thinkers who constructed the world that way, and not Dostoyevsky alone? (The doorman named Dostoyevsky, in fact, reminds me of old movies and the Russians who fled to Paris from the revolution.) And, suddenly, the element of popular culture, if you like, enters in the person of Fu Manchu—fictional, a stereotype, followed (with such respect) by "Miss Emily Dickinson"; think what seeing them together may set loose in your imagination. Then the club widens, expands, as do so many works of art, from the seedy night club to the cosmos, because it is in the light of the cosmos that we ask whether we have immortal souls, and throw the dice, and make that old, old wager with God.

There are other ways, many other ways of reading that poem, I realize, but I want to suggest a sense in which it offers us a paradigm of what works of art may challenge us to do. They open passages in our experience; they confront us with unlikely pairings and connections; they remove the guideposts; oftentimes, I think, they move us to choose—or at least to bet on the roll of the dice. As remarkably, I think, they begin in a kind of groundedness in the ordinary (the "seedy" this time, with neon lights and rats downstairs) and move us to reach out, to transmute, to transform.

It takes work as well as a kind of courage to engage with a work like this, or with *Lamentation* or with *Medea* or with "Bartleby the Scrivener" or with Beethoven's last quartets or with Picasso's wringing those magical and outrageous changes in the portraits of women, beloved for a time and discarded, moved from quiet realms of beauty to constricting spaces of ferocity. It is not, as we are often reminded, a matter of recognition, or putting the right label on the work, or murmuring "interesting" and moving on. Why *not* merely notice for a moment? What do we lose when we move on, say, in The Museum of Modern Art? What do we lose when we read a poem like the one I just read and think of it as merely cheap, merely modern, far removed from the lofty shapes of the classical, not making us grander because we took the time? How do we answer questions like that for ourselves?

I think of another related question and wonder how we would answer it. Does this exist in the same world as T. S. Eliot's *Four Quartets*? Would not it have been much more exalting for us to have read even one of those exquisite, worldly-wise quartets of which we can be sure—sure, at least of their aesthetic quality? You may recall Eliot writing of learning to get the better of words:

> *For the thing one no longer has to say, or the way in which*
> *One is no longer disposed to say it. And so each venture*
> *Is a new beginning, a raid on the inarticulate.*
>   (1952, p. 128)

There are, we know, many ways of launching raids "on the inarticulate," and we are asked to honor those we never recognized before. But the questions remain. How does Simic compare with Langston Hughes or Rita Dove or Jimmy Baca—or, yes, Eliot—when it comes to relevance for our time? If something is not, at least on first appearance, relevant to our lives (as "Club Midnight" may not appear to be, at least at first), how and why do we gradually construct it as meaningful and relevant? And if we claim our encounter with it as giving rise to an aesthetic experience after all, what do we mean?

I am most interested, of course, in metaphor and its role in the spells cast by works of art (or the revelations made, or the disclosures attained). We are surrounded by metaphors in the performances we have attended here at the Institute. Think of Martha Graham's visual metaphors (the linking of the moving folds of drapery to an unspeakable grief). Think of the metaphorical sparks springing forth from that broken jug, or the continually renewed metaphor of the rocks opening and the sound of the words "Open, Sesame." We all have some idea of how metaphors open our views of the world. They do so in part by enabling us to understand something by likening it to something else. (Recall the dancer's moving draperies again.) When Wallace Stevens likens imagination to what he calls "a blue guitar / you do not play things as they are" (1982, p. 165), he is enabling his reader to grasp the ways in which imagination breaks with fixed boundaries and definitions, the ways in which it opens to the unexpected. "The blue guitar surprises you" (p. 183), he writes, and of course it does, since what it discovers is never predictable. And, obviously, we are able to reach from the empty dance floor to the inscrutable because there is something that connects the problematic loneliness in that seedy club to the mystery of the human condition itself.

The signal point about a metaphor relates to the point we try to make about aesthetic education: the meaning lies in the transformation it brings about in the perceiver, the participant, lending one's life to a work. It performs what might be called an existential function in that "it provokes a change in the way we view things, it brings about a transformation in our thinking." (I cannot but recall, when I say that, the number of Summer Session participants who say—when they think back upon their summers here—that the experiences have changed their lives. And I should like to say that that immeasurable affirmation may be the test.) The power of "Open, Sesame" in *Ali Baba,* of the split crockery with the gaping hole in *The Broken Jug,* of the sounds of instruments mingling with the voices in *John Somebody,* of the poetic metaphor angrily challenged by the old aunt in the film *The Postman,* of such images as "sweet chariot" in old spirituals: all these are realized when they bring about changes in attitude, direction, and—at length—understanding. And that is how we find out how metaphors mean.

As important, perhaps in these days particularly, is the connection between metaphor and empathy. By empathy, I do not mean the intuitive ability to become one with another; I mean the capacity to see through another's eyes, to grasp the world as it looks and sounds and feels from the vantage point of another. Cynthia Ozick has said that it is through and by means of metaphorical concentration that doctors can imagine what it is to be their patients. "Those at the center," she writes, "can imagine what it is to be outside" (1989, p. 283). How can we not think of *Seven Guitars* or *Bring in da Noise; Bring in da Funk* or Toni Morrison's *Jazz* or the Nai-Ni Chen dancers or Leslie Silko's novel about Native Americans, *Ceremony,* to be reminded of how conscious engagement with works of art activates, if you like, our metaphoricality, or makes the concentration Ozick mentions possible? She goes on to say that, by means of metaphor, "The strong can imagine the weak. Illuminated lives can imagine the dark. Poets in their twilight can imagine the borders of stellar fire. We strangers can imagine the familiar hearts of strangers" (p. 283). Is not that what many of us hope to bring about in classrooms, as our worlds expand?

This reminds me of something else Ozick points out. She describes metaphor as a "shocking extension of the unknown into our most intimate, most feeling, most private selves" (p. 282). The unknown. Remember the desert stretching out beyond the confined kitchen in Sam Shepard's *True West,* the desert as metaphor for the unknown, for what cannot be captured in ordinary or in artful words. Remember the ocean surrounding the island in *The Tempest.* Remember in *A Delicate Balance* the people who come to seek refuge in their friends' house because they are inexplicably afraid, afflicted by a terror or a plague. Again, it is a matter of extension, of expansion, of breaking with the conventional, the anaesthetic, going beyond.

It takes metaphor, too, to transform memory into a principle of continuity in experience. I think that, like me, many of you are able to reach back and find out (especially when you shape your narratives, tell your stories) how understandings made possible by art experiences enabled you to identify the themes, to articulate the hidden movements in your lives. I remember the beginning of Melville's *Moby-Dick* and the meanings that radiated from Ishmael's talk of a "damp, drizzly November in my soul" (1979, p. 2). I remember the impact of Mrs. Ramsay's dinner party in *To the Lighthouse,* of Laura's candles in *The Glass Menagerie,* of Matisse's *The Dancers,* of the Shirley Temple dolls in *The Bluest Eye,* of the shapes discovered by Pilobolus, of those diagrams and geometric figures in Wallace Stevens's poem—and, suddenly, "the ellipse of the half moon." All of them helped me bring to the surface stirrings, desires working below the surface, and translate them into images, into ideas. And I want to believe that can be true of young people too, as we move to release their voices, to overcome the silences, to awaken them to naming and to choosing and to life.

If we can infuse our classroom speaking with metaphor, if we can make available and accessible a diversity of art forms, we know we are on the way to that kind of awakening. We are on the way to overcoming the many modes of illiteracy, of inarticulateness. But we cannot accomplish this by talking *about* works of art or arguing the centrality of the artistic-aesthetic in a fully human life. As we learn here at the Institute, works of art do not necessarily or automatically give rise to what we think of as aesthetic experiences. Not only do we have to learn to attend, to lend our lives to the works before us; we must, as I have said repeatedly, learn how to notice what there is to be noticed in the *Trout Quintet,* in *The Broken Jug,* in *Appalachian Spring,* how to respond to the qualities in particular works, how to engage as living, incomplete human beings in search of connection, in search of ourselves. The poet Rilke, writing about an encounter with a work of art (the "Torso of an Archaic Apollo") wrote that—in its presence—"there is no place / that does not see you. You must change your life" (1940/1974, p. 93). Change, yes, and teach, and awaken. And throw the dice, if we have to, gambling on their making sense.

The Open Questions in Classroom Dialogues

(1996)

You have heard me often; you have lived through the experiences made possible here; and many of you, according to what you have said to some of us, have felt your lives to have been transformed. To think why, to ponder the nature of your engagements with the works made available to you may well clarify your encounters, may help you name the perspectives opened in your experience, the connections made, the meanings disclosed. At once, you know much more than you might have known about the relation between what you have done in your workshops and what you have been able to see and hear and feel. How did you come to notice the variation techniques in *The Trout Quintet,* and how did that mode of noticing affect your enjoyment of the piece? How did your recognition of the role of the director in bringing *The Broken Jug* to concrete comic life affect your view of theatrical reality and the manner in which you bring it alive? How did you experience the conflict in Martha Graham's *Errand into the Maze?* What does it mean to you to realize that the conflict may be in Ariadne's own mind, that she must conquer her own yoked fear? How did you react to *John Somebody?* Did it push back the horizons of sound for you, alter what "music" signifies? If you could not respond, why do you think that was? Would it have helped to have worked with a teaching artist or worked longer with one? Why?

Obviously, I am suggesting that the more you can reflect upon what happened to you in the course of Summer Session, the more you can engage in dialogue about it, the more empowered you are to devise situations in which students can engage with what is made present to them. Of course you will not instruct them on what they are supposed to see or hear, even though you will help them notice, help them attend. You will be confronting the problem that arises in all instances of constructivist teaching. How do you prepare the way for the making of meanings—knowing that not anything goes or should go? What do you do to make it more likely for youngsters to have what you understand to be aesthetic experiences? How can you find out if they have had them? What is the point of aesthetic education if its consequences can never be precisely defined? Much, as you realize, depends on what you have discovered when you have reflected on your own experiences, on the importance of the arts—or some of the arts—in your lives. I have talked about the significance of metaphor and how it can only be understood in terms of the difference it makes in a person's experience. Again, think of that yoked male figure in the Graham dance. Think of the "blue guitar," the moon as a "ghostly galleon," the idea of invisibility in *Invisible Man* (Ellison, 1994). Did such figures make you see more, feel something new, discover some meaning you had never thought of before? Some of you may engage your students in dialogue that stems from questions like these. To render them more aware of their own awareness, more likely to reflect back on what they have perceived may well enhance their particular experiences with, say, *Ali Baba* or the Urban Bush Women or Pilobolus or Thelonious Monk. Perhaps some of you may encourage students to "speak" the language of movement when they respond to some of these or the language of visual imagery. I think we recognize, from our own experience, the difference it makes to articulate what we have disclosed, to create new relationships with those around by sharing or by looking through another's eyes.

The self-awareness I am calling for, the communal self-awareness, needs to be tapped, I think, in relation to two issues I would like to raise before we conclude. One has to do with the connection between what we do here at the Institute and popular culture, and the impact of what might be called mass culture upon those we teach. The other has to do with some of the moral issues raised by works of art and the questions into which they may feed.

Not many years ago, a program of this sort would be conceived as one in which youngsters in various ways disadvantaged were initiated into at least the anteroom of the elite's domicile. In an almost philanthropic mood, the tastemakers, the people in power, the defenders of what they called "high art" permitted strangers to gaze from afar—receptively and in a kind of awe—at some great paintings, or to listen to classical music, or to attend to plays marking the great tradition. The arts (or what were called the arts) existed in a separate enclave. When that happens, wrote John Dewey, when works of art "are separated from both conditions of origin and operation in experience, a wall is built around them that renders almost opaque their general significance, with which esthetic theory deals. Art is remitted to a separate realm, where it is cut off from that association with the materials and aims of every other form of human effort, undergoing, and achievement" (1980, p. 3). John Berger, writing about the visual arts, years later, talked about the "bogus religiosity which now surrounds original works of art," and about how the arts were so often relegated to a separate preserve, made part of the culture of the ruling class (1977). Like Dewey, who was committed to restoring some continuity between the arts and ordinary human experience, Berger wrote about the way the language of images, for example, confers a new kind of power when we use it "to define our experiences more precisely in areas where words are inadequate." And that was the point—for Berger, for Dewey, for ourselves—to find in the languages of the arts a means of clarifying our experiences, not only personal experience, "but also the essential historical experience of our relation to the past: that is to say the experience of seeking to give meaning to our lives, of trying to understand the history of which we can become the active agents" (1977, p. 33).

Not only does that mean doing away with the preserves and the private enclaves. It means expanding our notions of what the domain of the arts includes. It means breaking down the old dichotomies, the separations between "high" and "low" art, between the arts and popular culture, even between the arts and those forms with their roots in folk or ethnic histories. Some of you may have read the recent *New York Times* article about John Rockwell, the director of what is described as a "cross-pollinating, multi-arts festival" about to open here at Lincoln Center. Rockwell—critic, cultural historian, cultural correspondent of the *New York Times*—"developed an omnivorous, pan-stylistic curiosity that made it possible for him to write comfortably about the music of Meat Loaf as well as fin-de-siècle Viennese opera. Like the Blues Brothers, he jokes, he is on a mission from God: to argue that cultivated art forms should revitalize themselves by opening up to popular influences" (Malitz, 1996, July 14, p. 1). Obviously, of course, the sociological subgroups who prefer that Viennese opera music remain intact think of Rockwell as guilty of "musical Maoism." He is doing something, I think most of you will agree, that is of enormous importance for teachers in a school system throbbing with newcomers, with youngsters coming to us from all sorts of musical traditions, from diverse traditions of theater and puppetry and magical tales and story-telling, from different histories of painting and engraving and shaping—from different and distinctive modes of leaving imprints on the walls of the world. It is important and dizzying in potential complexity—because we can no longer ask the authoritative tastemaker, we can no longer turn to predetermined standards or to norms like fixed stars in the sky to tell us if the Urban Bush Women's work is really dance or if *John Somebody* can be classified as music or whether Thelonious Monk belongs on the same program as Franz Schubert. We can only reflect back, as I suggested before, on events brought about by differing encounters with art works in our own lives, engage as many people as possible in open-ended dialogues, and try to find the best reasons we can—communally, perhaps—for saying "we prefer" or "we choose."

It is of interest to find John Dewey, when he is objecting to the whole idea of keeping art on a remote pedestal, pointing out that the arts which have the "most vitality for the average person are things he does not take to be arts" (1980, p. 5). This was in the 1930s, and Dewey's examples were the movies, jazz, comic strips, and newspaper accounts of love-nests, murders, and the exploits of bandits. Because what was generally thought of as art was relegated to museums and other preserves (or, too often, to the making of valentines and ashtrays in schools) "the unconquerable impulse toward experiences enjoyable in themselves finds such outlet as the daily environment provides." Then Dewey went on to say that "because of their remoteness, the objects acknowledged by the cultivated to be works of fine art seem anemic to the mass of people" (1980, p. 6). What he called "esthetic hunger," in consequence, was often satisfied by the cheap and vulgar. He not only wanted to acknowledge the integrity of the many art forms that were outside museums and concert halls; I think he realized, as we do, how much had to do with enabling all kinds of people to crack the codes kept secret by those in power, and how much had to do with taking participatory and critical approaches to whatever was made available. He was eager to recover, he kept saying, "the continuity of esthetic experience with normal processes of living" (1980, p. 10). That meant removing arts from their pedestals and equipping all kinds of people to engage with them, to lend them their lives. And it meant enlarging the domain of the arts so that all kinds of silenced voices could be heard, all kinds of once discarded imagery be attended to and, at the very least, explored.

If he were living now, he would celebrate the remarkable presence of a Wynton Marsalis, whose jazz works were being welcomed into the spaces of musical art before Marsalis became so important at Lincoln Center. We might add Thelonious Monk and Duke Ellington and Ella Fitzgerald and Billie Holiday to the list, and we would open the doors to the gospel music and the spirituals arising out of the sufferings and rebellions of time past. We have the startling example of *Bring in da Noise; Bring in da Funk,* that transmutation of African American history since the days of the Middle Passage into movement and all sorts of unexpected sound, unexpected syncopation. A work like that demands the kind of personal and communal presentness we strive for here. It demands the kind of informed noticing, the pouring in of diverse energies, the "readings" from the vantage points we welcome here. We have the wedding of rock and opera in the amalgam of new music with *La Bohème* in the musical called *Rent*. We have come to take poster art seriously and a range of photographic images and graffiti marks as never before. We are familiar now with the critical discoveries of film as art (and the films that fall outside of whatever boundaries we can identify as a community). We have witnessed the magical shaping and reshaping of the patterns of street life and the pulsations of the city in something as finely wrought as the work of the Urban Bush Women which, not very long ago, would never be imagined on a stage recently inhabited by a Martha Graham dancer. Bringing such works into the company of Schubert and van Kleist and Tennessee Williams and Arthur Miller and Terrence McNally not only expands the spaces of our experience, extending the possibility of experiences that are enjoyable, as Dewey said, "in themselves." It also calls upon us to see differently, to attend differently, to engage actively with often problematic, sometimes uncategorized forms—to adventure in new realities, new worlds—while toppling the old pedestals and freeing the traditional arts to live and breathe in a figurative open air.

I have suggested before that, in the kind of world in which imagination is alive, people have the capacity to look through one another's eyes, to take one another's perspective upon the world. When I think of the moral issues raised, say, by issues of violence in the works we study (as, for instance, in *Ali Baba* or in the novel *The Bird Artist,* or in *Macbeth* or in *Crime and Punishment* or in films about the holocaust), I think again of what engagements with works of art allow us to confront in our own experience that we would not otherwise confront. In part it is a matter of bringing to the surface forces, stirrings, desires we often cannot name. In part it is a matter of creating dialogical situations in which persons, caring for one another, able to look through one another's eyes, talk about what they are discovering together about themselves, about the world, about what is and what might be. For me, the moral concern begins with that kind of connectedness, with reciprocity, with the imagination needed to experience empathy. It is enhanced and deepened by what some of us call the ethical imagination, which I want to believe can be released by encounters with the arts. For one writer, Richard Kearney, it is time for a new kind of imagination to emerge—"an imagination schooled in the truth that the self cannot be 'centred' on itself; an imagination fully aware that meaning does not originate within the narrow chambers of its own subjectivity but emerges as a response to the *other*" (1988, p. 387). And the response? It is the response of feeling in a face-to-face relation—the kind of response that says "here I am." ("When a naked face cries 'where are you?', we do not ask for identity papers. We reply, first and foremost, 'here I am' " [p. 362].) I think we have learned something through our shared encounters about what it means to be with another "face to face." I believe that our imaginations have been released enough to extend to the ethical—to confront, to deepen, to be more responsible in the world.

I have reminded you often of that blue guitar, and I choose to end, once again, with that evocation—addressed to all of you.

> *You as you are? You are yourself.*
> *The blue guitar surprises you.*
> (Stevens, 1982, p. 183)

Surprises, yes, and discloses—perhaps to the way things ought to be.

This Is a Place from Which to Perceive the Unexplored . . .

(1997)

Welcoming you all, I was trying to communicate some notion or some reminder of what we mean by aesthetic education. "Aesthetic" is simply an adjective used to identify a mode of education intended to make possible informed, aware participation in works of art. It is, as most of you realize, not the kind of undertaking geared to the transmission of pieces of knowledge or specific skills to passive learners. It involves active learning and the making of meaning. Learners are thought of and treated as human beings on the way, in quest of understanding and direction, in search of projects by means of which they may create their own identities. Those of us who "do" aesthetic education, those of us who try to find spaces for it in problematic schools, are sensitive to the multiple life stories young people are carrying with them into our classrooms. We are sensitive to the multiple voices that need to be heard, the multiple vantage points from which the young look at an often uncaring world. At once, we are aware of what are thought of as multiple intelligences, as diverse symbol systems and languages for interpreting what presents itself as reality. And we are particularly conscious of the importance of imagination, so often omitted from education reports: imagination that enables us to challenge the fixed and the taken-for-granted, that allows us to open windows in the actual and disclose visions of what might be. It may be our interest in imagination, as much as our interest in active learning, that makes us so eager to encourage a sense of agency among those with whom we work. By that I mean consciousness of the power to choose and to act on what is chosen. I mean a willingness to take initiatives, to pose critical questions, to play an authentic part in ongoing dialogues—to embark, whenever opportunities arise, on new beginnings. This means that we desire, through aesthetic education, not only to foster continually deepening understanding of the several arts, but to empower teachers, students, parents—all those involved with the care and nurture of the young—to act upon their freedom in the world they share with others. That means resisting determinism, apathy, indifference, carelessness, and the numbness or the anaesthesia that seems to affect so many people's lives. Dewey once said that the opposite of "aesthetic" is indeed "anaesthetic." In relation to that, we might think of aesthetic education as education for wide-awakeness—for a more active, responsible, ardent mode of pursuing our human quests.

In the workshops available to you here, you can learn more about the languages of art, not in the hope that you can be transformed into a chamber-music player, or a dancer, or an actor, but so you will have at hand a greater range of means of expression, ways of saying what ordinary spoken language can rarely capture or convey. I think of John Dewey again, saying that the voice of the artist or the freeing of the artist is a precondition for the creation of informed public opinion. That is because, Dewey said, our conscious life of opinion and judgment often proceeds on a superficial and trivial plane. "But their lives," he said, "reach a deeper level. The function of art has always been to break through the crust of conventionalized and routine consciousness." He spoke of common things ("a flower, a gleam of moonlight, the song of a bird") as means with which "the deeper levels of life are touched so that they spring up as desire and thought. This process is art. Poetry, the drama, the novel are proofs that the problem of presentation is not insoluble. Artists have always been the real purveyors of news, for it is not the outward happening in itself which is new, but the kindling by it of emotion, perception, and appreciation" (1988, p. 184). In some fashion, that almost describes what some of us find in the workshops. When we do find it, we find ourselves far more present to the works of art being offered here. For some of us, this ought to be made contagious in our classrooms.

I cannot say with absolute authority how aesthetic experiences come about or how we know when other people are having aesthetic experiences. I do know that they begin in an encounter, a very particular encounter. I can try to describe it by saying there are two poles, as in the case of our coming in the presence of Meredith Monk's *Facing North*. At one pole, there is the remarkable performance piece, which cannot be characterized as only a dance performance, or a musical performance, or a piece of theater. Indeed, we may be more likely to have an aesthetic experience if the work is *not* categorized in advance. There is another pole: the subjectivity or the consciousness of the perceiver, with all of one's feelings, memories, likes and dislikes, past experiences with the arts. Present to the piece, looking at it from the sidelines, we and the performance compose an aesthetic situation. In order to be there, really to be there, we must, as existentialists put it, "bracket out" our ordinary concerns—our grocery lists, our ballet tickets, our baby-sitters, our parking places. We are, along with those around, looking at what is happening, listening to what is happening in a very special way. We are not taking the role of a program developer, a school-board member pre-occupied with cost, a building and grounds worker keeping his eye on his wristwatch, watching the way the space is being used. Rather, we are pay-ing heed to the qualities made visible in the cold setting, the wintry clothes with their evocations of the steppes, the unpredictable movements of legs and arms. And perhaps (and this is always memorable for me) the vocal music, which we cannot really call singing *or* traditional music. We listen to it, or I should say, I listen to those sounding syllables without the kinds of meaning expected from a continuum of song. Listening after a time, I find myself understanding in some mysterious fashion, as if something inex-pressible in the languages familiar to me is trying to find articulation.

My point is that the meaning of the work (for me) emerges from a spe-cial kind of transaction between my embodied consciousness, my memories, my feelings and what is being enacted on the stage. The meaning does not inhere in what is on the stage, or in Meredith Monk's intention, or in the work's particular history. It emerges as I allow myself to be in a kind of con-versation with the work. It comes into existence in some invisible space between myself and the stage—some event that never happened in the world before. The same can be said about the qualities possessed by the work to which we are attending. The qualities that mark the work—the old seren-ity, the strangeness, the wintry atmosphere, the unadorned gestures, the air of innocence, the softness against ice: all these might not exist except in rela-tion to my body and mind. Ideally, dialogue will follow our being present. We will tell those around what each of us saw, felt, noticed—and keep refer-ring back to the work we saw and felt. Perhaps we will find that the work, *Facing North,* is more complex, more many-sided, more expressive of the depths than we ever suspected. Perhaps we will find that it is simpler and more romantic than we guessed. Whatever the differences, I will still insist that the work-as-grasped is what has become an object of my experience, has fulfilled itself somehow, has created new connections in my experience, and therefore can be called a work of art.

But how do I know? What if my students ask me grudgingly why I try to convince them that something incapable of turning them on can play a role as work of art? I think I have to say what Dewey said at the beginning of *Art as Experience:* "In common conception, the work of art is often identified with the building, book, painting, or statue in its existence apart from human experience. Since the actual work of art is what the product does with and in experience, the result is not favorable to understanding" (1980, p. 3). He went on to criticize those who would separate art objects from their conditions of origin and their operation in experience. His task, as he saw it, was "to restore continuity between the refined and intensified forms of experience that are works of art and the everyday events, doings, and sufferings that are universally recognized to constitute experience."

It is not just a question of liking or disliking; nor is it a question of turning on or not turning on. We have to take account of the diversity in our classrooms. We have to think of those with such different cultural traditions that it is difficult for them to grasp the very concept of art. For many, the masks and sculptures and vases and carvings we collect and speak of as instances of art are to be regarded as religious or ceremonial objects. They are not set forth to be regarded behind glass as unique and precious objects; nor are they usually considered as the products of individual artists, speaking through their own symbol systems to individual perceivers capable of recreating the objects they encounter by ordering the elements that compose them or reordering them into an expressive whole. On occasion, it is as if the objects themselves beg to be treated as cultural products—like folk dances, perhaps, like the flamenco, like Native American quilts, like the wall painting in Egyptian tombs.

All we can try to do is to involve the stranger in situations of noticing and, yes, situations of expressing, situations where there are media to be explored, technical problems like those the artist may have faced. We can try to help her pay particular heed to aspects, say, of a painting—to look at the crows flying over Van Gogh's wheat field, to ask why they were placed in such an unusual pattern; to look at the color field paintings of Jules Olitski and ask about experience with color, the significance of colors. How do you think of that deep red with the sense of open sky behind? How is loneliness portrayed in Hopper's city paintings? What do those large Serra constructions make you feel? What of the Virgin in her many manifestations? What of the photographs of a colonized Africa, taken to justify ongoing control? And what of the pearls glinting in the light in that Vermeer painting? There are ways to make a work that is felt to be alien an object of a stranger's experience, but there is no way of making him enjoy the experience and go in search of levels of meaning. All there may be are dialogue, curiosity, good will, and ongoing efforts to translate one mode of seeing and making into another. Even without powerful aesthetic experience, there is still something worthwhile in exposing the young to the works we treasure or what certain inhabitants of our world name as worth treasuring, and there is something worthwhile in the inclusion throughout the curriculum of various forms of art. Surely, all this must be accompanied by teachers' own search for understanding of the work of other cultures. We hope to hear dialogues about what different individuals love—as persons and as members—even as we convey the wonders and the mysteries we have found in the art objects and performances we have come to love. Many of us are willing by now, as we affirm pluralism and multiplicity, to offer to our own "strangers" the things we care for and try to understand (with young people's help) what these others love and pray to and dance to and esteem.

Talk of strangers and of differences makes me turn for a moment to Edward Said in the closing paragraph of *Culture and Imperialism.* "No one today is purely *one* thing. Labels like Indian, or woman, or Muslim, or American are not more than starting-points, which if followed into actual experience for only a moment are quickly left behind." No one, he insists, is only or exclusively white or black, or Western, or Asian. "No one can deny the persisting continuities of long traditions, sustained habitations, national languages, and cultural geographies, but there seems no reason except fear and prejudice to keep insisting on their separation and distinctiveness, as if that were all human life was about. Survival in fact is about the connections between things; in Eliot's phrase, reality cannot be deprived of the 'other echoes [that] inhabit the garden.'" To think about others concretely and not just about ourselves is more rewarding. "But this also means not trying to rule others, not trying to classify them or put them in hierarchies, above all, not constantly reiterating how 'our' culture [or our country] is number one" (Said, 1993, p. 336).

To speak of possibilities, as Said does, to end with talk of connections and with a line from a poem inevitably leads me back to what we are doing. I believe that authentic and reflective involvement with works of art (or the works of art with the potential to become objects of our experience) can sustain and vitalize the becoming Said describes. Also, I believe that encounters with the arts do indeed make for connections in experience, for patterns and new orders never imagined before. In some way, the arts are always oriented to the unexplored, and so is the move away from separateness Said describes. Fascinated by the unexplored, I choose to conclude with something that still stirs me deeply and makes me still yearn to pursue possibility. It is taken from a *New York Times* Op-Ed article written about two years ago by a great poet named Philip Levine (1995, October 29, p. E13). It begins with a recollection of a course in Romantic poetry offered in a Detroit community college for factory workers about fifty years ago. Levine, who was an automobile laborer at that time, wrote about being hooked by John Keats's "On First Looking into Chapman's Homer" to such a degree he felt it "on his pulse." The very idea of an auto worker discovering Keats for himself in the twentieth century, lending the young poet's work some of a poet-to-be's life, and thereby bringing it into the world again, offers us a marvelous metaphor, I believe.

The speaker in the Keats poem says that he felt like:

> *. . . some watcher of the skies*
> *When a new planet swims into his ken;*
> *Or like stout Cortez when with eagle eyes*
> *He star'd at the Pacific—and all his men*
> *Look'd at each other with a wild surmise—*
> *Silent, upon a peak in Darien.*
>
> (1975, p. 9)

There are levels, nuances in Keats's poem: the speaker is recounting his experience with a classic text, connecting Homer with another young poet's startled discovery that finds expression in the rendering of a new planet and the Pacific Ocean viewed for the first time. It does not matter that Keats erred in placing Cortez at the Pacific shore. What is important is the seeing, made possible by a release of the imagination—a "wild surmise," the men in their silence turning to look at one another, perhaps to know those around in ways never experienced before.

What Keats may bequeath to us even now is a metaphor of possibility, involving people in whatever community they choose as theirs, now silenced by surprise and wonder at the distances, the strangeness. Behind the hill lies the dreadfully familiar world, in this case a world of routine, hierarchies, and submission to orders and the taken-for-granted. From the peak, there can be seen the provocatively unfamiliar, and there is neither predicting nor testing nor measuring what opens to each one's "wild surmise." We are standing again, most of us, on unfamiliar shores, reaching toward fullness, for ardor, for possibility.

This is a place from which to see the unexplored, to come together as we reach the peak, to think of things as if they could be otherwise.

Thinking of Things as if
They Could Be Otherwise:
The Arts and Intimations
of a Better Social Order
(1997)

I began last week with talk of imagination and the relation between the release of imagination and the pursuit of identity. I was trying to call attention to the breakthroughs that occur, to the upsurges of the unexpected we may experience at certain moments of engagement with works of art. Most of us can summon up such moments. They may be associated with a scene in a play (*Twelfth Night,* perhaps, *Death of a Salesman, A Doll's House*), with a movement in a string quintet, with some lines in a poem ("a wild surmise"; "They said 'you have a blue guitar, / You do not play things as they are'"), with the startling images of an Irish town, as in *Angela's Ashes,* if not *A Portrait of the Artist as a Young Man*. We experience a sense of surprise oftentimes, an acute sense that things may look otherwise, feel otherwise, *be* otherwise than we have assumed—and suddenly the world seems new, with possibilities still to be explored.

It seems obvious to me that shocks of awareness of that sort can be of great significance for learning in a world so characterized by routines, by a kind of drab everydayness. I quoted Mary Warnock saying that the greatest obstacle to the kind of education we seek is boredom. Boredom comes, she says, when people feel they have come to the end of what is worth having. Numbers of you have commented on the empty eyes of some of the children in your schools, and I think we know what Mary Warnock means. I believe that too many people (including young people in many of our schools) resemble the citizens Albert Camus described in *The Plague*:

"The truth is that everyone is bored, and devotes himself to cultivating habits." Then he went on to say that these habits were not peculiar to the town of Oran: "really all our contemporaries are much the same. Certainly nothing is commoner nowadays than to see people working from morn till night and then proceeding to fritter away at card-tables, in cafés and in small-talk what time is left for living." (Before thrusting this aside as a moral judgment, I think we are each bound to ask what he meant—and, more important, what *we* mean—by living.) In any case, he followed this by saying that there do still exist "towns and countries where people have now and then an inkling of something different" (Camus, 1971, p. 4).

That "inkling" is what I want to talk about. I want to suggest that works of art have a potential for evoking an intimation of a better order of things. I mean, of course, a consciousness of possibility. You all know, however, that works of art do not spontaneously give rise to such a potential, that it only exists *as* a potential if there is a consciousness ready to respond to it. What we do here, by means of what we call aesthetic education, is to empower persons (alone or in a community) to know enough to notice what there is to be noticed when participating imaginatively in *Krapp's Last Tape*, let us say. The same applies to the dances of the Urban Bush Women, or the odd shifts and rearrangements in Cunningham's *Scramble*. It is not a matter of watching from a distance. Once caught up in the life of our workshops, we learn what active perceptual participation means, as we learn more about the substance of the art form and the dimensions of the experienced world. Engaging along with others, attending to the qualities of the works at hand (the unsteady, uneven rhythms of Krapp's restless pacing; the sensuality, the whisper of the magical in the storyteller; the shades and nuances of bebop in the Monk pieces), exploring for ourselves sound and movement, color against color, voice against voice, we may well find ourselves transformed.

And then we have to ask, in our reflective phase: How did it happen? What does it mean? What was there about that combination of tones that pushed back the ordinary horizons of sound? What does Cunningham mean when he says, "I think of dance as a constant transformation of life itself (1985, p. 84)"? Can we say that about our projects, our searches for ourselves? What does it mean to say that a dance, or a piece of music, or a short story only becomes a work of art when it becomes an object of our experience? And when it does, how does it radiate through our transactions with the world? For John Dewey, the task of those who choose to write about the arts is to restore continuity between the refined and intensified forms of experience that are works of art and the everyday events, doings, and sufferings that are universally recognized to constitute experience.

In many respects, that is what we are trying to do here. We know that the capacity for responding to metaphor has to be cultivated, just as does the capacity to respond to an "as-if," to a created and alternative reality. A metaphor may, in Virginia Woolf's terms, bring the "severed parts together" (1985). We have just been studying Woolf's *To The Lighthouse* (1990) in my workshop; the bringing unlike things together through the metaphors of window and lighthouse reoriented much of our way of addressing the world. The window, you may recall, summons up a wealth of meanings associated with domesticity, family care and connection, flickering perceptions of order and disorder and death too complex to fit into a rational category. It exists in tension with the lighthouse—a principle of order, of direction, a shape of stern resolution standing there to be achieved. To view them as feminine and masculine symbols is to drain them of the significance within and outside the book—a significance due to the almost endless possibilities that a many-sided search for order, for harmony, opens in our consciousness. Without metaphor, it would be difficult to explain the transformations brought about by imagination. "It is through imagination," writes G. B. Madison, "the realm of pure possibility that we freely make ourselves to be who or what we are, that we creatively and imaginatively become who we are, while in the process preserving the freedom and possibility to be yet otherwise than what we have become and merely are" (1988, p. 191).

I would stress more than does Madison the idea of the self in process, and I would be wary of the term "pure possibility"; but the notion of a realm of possibility with relevance for all those we teach and whom we hope to liberate some day connects, for me, with what we do here at the Institute. And it makes me want to re-imagine the purposes of education here and in the schools around: to invent situations in which young people are enabled to freely make of themselves who or what they are, that they "become creatively what they are," and that means, in part, an infusion of their teaching-learning situations with opportunities to engage continually (yes, and knowledgeably) with works of art. I remember Dewey writing that only personal responses involving imagination can lead to real understanding even of what are called "facts." Then: "The engagement of the imagination is the only thing that makes any activity more than mechanical." It was a matter of recognizing the role of "imaginative vision," a capacity we believe can be released and nurtured through active learning of the arts.

It is always important to keep in mind the importance of attending, and the recognition that the more we know, the more we see and hear and notice and even feel. I want to speak about opening spaces in our classrooms, more and more spaces where people can appear as who they are and not *what* they are, spaces for action on the part of all of those involved. Hannah

Arendt made very clear that action, in contrast to behavior, means taking an initiative, embarking on a beginning, setting something in motion. I am eager to say and say again how much this has to do with the kinds of aesthetic discoveries and experiences some of us are living through—and the effect it can have on the spaces we open, how much it has to do with encouraging a sense of agency on the part of teachers and learners both.

Concerned as I am with going beyond the schoolroom space into the larger spaces where we look for communities-in-the-making, for (in other words) democracy, I want to talk for a moment about the meanings of what we are doing for the larger community. I find pointers in the work, among others, of the poet Adrienne Rich. Very much troubled, as are many of us, by the carelessness and the desperation in our society, she spoke of the different kinds of dread being suffered by people. She had in mind such human beings as welfare mothers, the unemployed, the neglected children and old people, the victims of violence, and she said, when interviewed by Bill Moyers, that she thought "more and more people feel uncared for; feel that their lives are not only unvalued but meaningless; feel that though they may care for their lives, no one else will; feel that the only way that they can protect their survival and interests is by the gun. I'm afraid that many people feel an enormous desperation which plays into the propaganda of hate." When asked how she could reconcile such bitterness with the affirmations in her poems, she said something of great significance, I think, for our understanding of art and the possibilities they open for us. "I think that poetry speaks beyond that, to something different, and that's why it can bring those parts of us together that are both in dread and which have the surviving sense of a possible happiness, and a possible collectivity, a possible community, a loss of isolation" (Grubin, 1995). I believe that possibility is inherent or at least potential in many works of art—including Merce Cunningham's work and Thelonious Monk's and Meredith Monk's. Part of our obligation, after all, is to find out what can be done in our lives with young people to lessen the dread, to resist the undervaluing of their lives.

Some of us, reading children's poetry, looking at their journals, know the forms that dread and feeling uncared-for can take. Without calling the arts remedial or in some manner therapeutic, we still can introduce those works to which the young respond and pay heed to the bringing together of those parts of us which exist in dread and those which have the surviving sense of "a possible happiness, collectivity, community, a loss of isolation." I think of Mike Rose's book *Possible Lives* and his telling of schools that indeed "speak beyond to something different." Rose hopes for a day when kids will recall rich experiences such as taking a tour with New York City's chief engineer through the city's water tunnels, where they all realized how important water was for the life of the city. "And then," the students would reflect, "we read poetry together, and I never thought engineering and poetry could be connected." Rose concluded by saying how much he believed in people making a future for themselves. "We want," he said, "to open kids up to all the possibilities of learning and do it with a variety of people who have widely different perspectives on things" (Rose, 1995, p. 215).

Many of those who speak for imagination, possibility, the kindling of hope, and engagement with the arts are sounding chords great artists of the past have sounded repeatedly—the musicians (Bach, Beethoven, Mahler— everyone has their own list), the painters (Cézanne, Rothko, Van Gogh, Mary Cassatt), writers like Dostoyevsky, Melville, Toni Morrison, Doctorow. They are chords, themes that remind us of the need to acknowledge the darkness and, working against that darkness, to conjecture, to design, to protest, to imagine, to transform. I ponder (who can escape pondering) the violations of children we hear about almost every day, and I have to turn, not to the *New York Times* or the social work or even the philosophy journals, but to an artist, in this case Dostoyevsky, to provide words for the questions throbbing in us all. There is a scene in *The Brothers Karamazov* in which Ivan Karamazov is talking to his brother Alyosha about the tormenting of children. People who torture children may behave benevolently to other human beings, "like cultivated and humane Europeans; but they are very fond of tormenting children, even fond of children themselves in that sense. It's just their defencelessness that tempts the tormentor." And you may remember that Ivan then says that with his "pitiful, earthly, Euclidean understanding," all he knows is "that there is suffering and that there are none guilty; that cause follows effect . . . that everything finds its level— but that's only Euclidean nonsense, I know that, and I can't consent to live by it!" He keeps asking: "What am I to do about [the children]? . . . Listen! If all must suffer to pay for the eternal harmony, what have children to do with it, tell me, please?" And then he says, "I don't want harmony. From love for humanity I don't want it. I would rather be left with the unavenged suffering . . . and unsatisfied indignation, *even if I were wrong.* Besides, too high a price is asked for harmony; it's beyond our means to pay so much to enter on it. And so I hasten to give back my entrance ticket. . . . And that I am doing" (Dostoyevsky, 1879–1880/1945, p. 302). He is refusing, he says, to accept happiness on the foundation of the suffering of children—of even one tiny victim, "crying unavenged tears." Think about some of the children in this city; read Dostoyevsky—and ask yourself about the uses of the imaginative vision. It seems so clear to me that it is indeed art that brings the parts of us, perhaps even the parts of our community, together.

For Jean-Paul Sartre, a paragraph like that appeals to our freedom, or to our indignation. Certainly, it must nudge us out of somnolence and move us somehow to choose to act, to engage in a beginning. At the very least, Dostoyevsky is doing more than asking us to write letters of protest or join picket lines. He is arousing us from a kind of slumber, once we come to him through an act of imagination. As an artist, he is making us feel the demand in the face of a child, acting in a way that affirms the feeling, "I choose to be here for you." All of us, reaching into our past, can recall ways of encountering the human condition through the arts: Jacob Lawrence's "Migration" series, those renderings of African Americans moving up from the South in the 1920s, as Toni Morrison's characters do, hoping to find dreams come true in the chill of Chicago and New York. There are Edward Hopper's solitary figures in hotel rooms, luncheonettes, etched by direct light and the sparest of lines, speaking a visual language that comes before words. We need to keep reminding ourselves of the part played by imagination, as we continue learning to attend, learning to notice, learning to see. And somehow this makes me think back to John Keats again, saying, "I will call the world a School, instituted for the purpose of teaching little children to read. Do you not see how necessary a world of pains and trouble is to school an intelligence and make it a Soul?" (Walsh, 1959, pp. 109–110) Perhaps that can feed into the making of our purposes, too.

Thinking about, yearning for an extension of what we are doing into the public space, where we hope to see a community-in-the-making, I choose to return to Adrienne Rich for still another beginning, another reminder. It is called "In Those Years" (1995, p. 4).

> *In those years, people will say, we lost track*
> *of the meaning of* we, *of* you
> *we found ourselves*
> *reduced to* I
> *and the whole thing became*
> *silly, ironic, terrible:*
> *we were trying to live a personal life*
> *and, yes, that was the only life*
> *we could bear witness to*
> *But the great dark birds of history screamed and plunged*
> *into our personal weather*
> *They were headed somewhere else but their beaks and pinions*
>   *drove*
> *along the shore, through the rags of fog*
> *where we stood, saying* I

Resistance to Mere Things:
Art and the Reach of
Intellectual Possibility

(2000)

My concern last time was for beginnings and the opening of new perspectives in experience. The arts, I was trying to say, always confront us with new beginnings since they are, each in its own way, inexhaustible. There is always more to be felt, seen, heard, yes, and understood. "You never reach bottom," as the poet Rita Dove put it. And that takes me to some ideas having to do with imagination, what Wordsworth called that "visionary power." In the poem called "The Prelude," about the growth of the poet's mind, he described the vague sense of "possible sublimity"—of something wonderful that will some day happen—experienced by many of us when we were young. As we grow, he said, as our capacities develop, we continue to feel that "whatsoever point they gain" (meaning no matter how adult we may become), "they still / Have something to pursue" (1984, p. 400). Emily Dickinson, as some of you recall, wrote that imagination lights "The Possible's slow fuse" (1960, p. 689). A philosopher, G. B. Madison, says that "it is through the imagination, the realm of pure possibility that we freely make ourselves to be who or what we are, that we creatively and imaginatively become who we are, while in the process preserving the freedom and possibility to be yet otherwise than what we have become and merely are" (1988, p. 191).

Our interest here at the Institute is in the connection between imagination (the ability to "look at things as if they could be otherwise," to become aware of alternatives to the given, the ordinary course of things) and the several arts. Or, more particularly, between the release of imagination and the capacity, not only to notice what there is to be noticed in a given work of art, but to learn something about its construction, its shaping, and the skills required to make it what we call a work of art. Our view of aesthetic education is largely based on the belief that the more we can come to understand, say, the patterns of movement in *The Goldberg Variations,* the kinetic designs in space, the reciprocity between bodies in motion and the music, the more our imagination is likely to be activated. And when that happens, as you know by now, the dance performance (or the play, or the musical piece) is transformed (by your agency) into an event in your consciousness. Some degree of the possible may be attained, although there is (as I keep repeating) always, always more.

More and more images become visible; more and more meanings emerge for us; our lived world, our shared world becomes strangely more intelligible. There is no *naming* of the possible that is sought. It is a matter of our transcending ourselves, moving beyond what is merely given. I think now of what this present encounter with *Julius Caesar,* experienced with our current awarenesses of tyranny, mass hysteria, what human beings are capable of, the way it horrifies and moves and makes me want to fix things somehow. The open questions left in me by *The Scarlet Letter* and *The Awakening* moved me (and I am sure many of you) beyond conventional compliance with traditional treatments of women; *Invisible Man* pushed aside all sorts of curtains where oppression and humiliation were concerned; Martha Graham's solo dance called *Lamentation* still makes me feel more and see more, going far beyond words where the loneliness of loss, of grief is concerned. Again, opening to art forms, enabled to enter them by the work we do with our teaching artists, by our own attending, helps us break what Dewey called "the crust of conventionalized and routine consciousness" (1988, p. 183). No, nothing is solved, and nothing is cured. But as teachers and, yes, as learners, we may be in the world differently—feeling ourselves in process, in quest, working together as seekers, as questioners in what we sometimes call the learning community.

Saying all that, arguing for a centrality of imagination in our classrooms, in our lives, I need to ponder, perhaps along with you, two issues having to do with imagination. One makes me feel a kind of desperation; the other, a kind of bemused wonder. The first has to do with the undeniable fact that imagination is not always benevolent. When we picture the Columbine killers with their black lipstick and black raincoats, or the so-called skinheads drawn to the symbols of fascism, we cannot deny the fact that they too have been and are in search of some alternative reality. There are, of course, those who say the word "imagination" should not be used to describe such aberrations. Indeed, I think it was Hannah Arendt who said imagination could not encompass Belsen or Auschwitz. But when I think of some of the horror films and the violent ones that appeal to some of our youth, offering them experiences they might consider much like aesthetic experiences, I believe we should think more often about the kinds of spaces we can open for dialogue, for shared reflection. We all know the spread of the market for rap music, including much too often what is called "gangsta rap" or varieties of sexist and homophobic material. At least we can try to open discussions on what the young seek as possibilities for themselves, and how the works that entice them express desires they share, hopes they cherish. Perhaps if we construct atmospheres that offer encounters with alternative forms—including works we conceive to be works of art, the dialogue may deepen and diversify, and the participants may think more attentively about their own thinking, their own desires, what they yearn for in the world. I know there are no easy answers when daily life seems to offer so little. At the very least, we may open doors.

The other issue we need, I believe, to consider is the great excitement about the Harry Potter books, similar to the heralding of *Star Wars* not so long ago. This is testimony to the eagerness of many young people for imaginative adventures. Wizardry, yes, magic, ingenious games, journeys outward from the dull and the unkind: the Harry Potter books absorb, initiate many into the delights of reading. They appear to work on many levels, bringing pleasure and fascination to old and young. Yes, they belong to a long tradition of story-telling and fairy stories and even myths; but they are new and even startling in the way they draw their readers into another world. Should we include them in our aesthetic education curricula? Do we see them as supplements to the wonderful children's books now in most libraries (at least where the school can afford them)? Can we use them as launching pads for experience with even more varied, more multilayered literary works? Do they appeal mainly to middle-class white children here and in England? Do we know? Ought we to find out? How do we answer, in any case, the accumulating questions about what ought to be categorized as art? Who has a right to impose, to publicize, to affirm that certain works change lives for the better, and others simply do not? How do we in aesthetic education deal with what is called "hype"? What about works of other cultures, in other languages? How can we tell, here or abroad, what the relation is between adulthood and childhood—no longer empty, no longer innocent, no longer immune to pain and the dark?

So much depends on our—the teachers'—own recognition that meanings must be achieved by those with a sense of agency; they do not preexist, to be dug up like nuggets of coal or even lumps of gold. This is as much the case with train platform number 9³/4 and the entry into the domains of wizardry or Harry Potter as it is with Ishmael's decision to go to sea at the start of *Moby-Dick,* or the graveyard scene at the end of *Swan Lake,* or Carmen's death outside the bullring, or the shapes and colors of Van Gogh's bedroom in the painting that haunts us all. Thinking about the restless search for meanings that keeps so many of us alive, I want to remind you how important it is to stay in touch with our own narratives, what we feel to be authentic in our addresses to the world around. It is so easy to give way to what is taken for granted as efficient and acceptable. It is so easy to set aside our particular modes of sense-making, our dreams of what ought to be. Trying to keep alive and visible what we associate with the arts and possibility in a not always friendly moment, we have consciously to resist some of the alien views (the views of the "other" many times) that silence our voices and blur our vision.

I want to turn to the poet Marge Piercy for a moment. Her work is often concerned, not so much with the dangers of conformity, but with the ways in which our dreams, perhaps our own true stories, can be secreted and repressed. In a poem called "The Provocation of the Dream," she explores the connections between our dreams and our identity. She explores the energies set free by a sense of potentiality. She says:

> *We are sleep walkers troubled by nightmare flashes.*
> *In locked wards, we closet our vision, renouncing.*
> *We turn love loud on the radio to shut off cries in the street.*
> *Ours is the sleep of objects given, sold, taken, discarded,*
> *a shuddering sleep whose half remembered dreams*
> *are cast on the neat lawn of the domestic morning,*
> *red blossoms torn by a high wind from a crab apple tree.*
> *Only when we break the mirror and climb into our vision,*
> *Only when we are the wind together streaming and singing,*
> *only in the dream we become with our bones for spears,*
> *we are real at last*
> *and wake.*
>
> (1989, p. 167)

Certainly she knows what it signifies to keep dreams awake in institutional settings with the spectres of measurement always around us and a uniform standard that discourages difference. What seems so remarkable about her poem is the movement from the recognition ("nightmare flashes," "cries in the street") to the fear that what *we* know *we* see and hear must be renounced, that somehow or other our vision is eccentric or mad. There follows so often the urge to deny what we say we heard and saw, and oftentimes, like the normal people in society, we turn for comfort to objects, to things. I have in mind the consumer goods we are supposed to dream about: new cars, kitchen equipment, jeans, Hilfiger jackets, Nike sneakers. If we are lucky, if (for example) we spend some time attending to a work of art, we may find ourselves recalling, recapturing the repressed vision. (Poems do that for me; music, for many others.) We may find ourselves becoming real when we come awake and no longer hide behind the consumer goods, the fixities, the things of the world. I am moved to say a little more about the swelling movement, like that of a rising wave, I associate with an imaginative encounter with, say, an Elizabeth Bishop poem, a Virginia Woolf novel, a Bach fugue. I want to try to convince you of something many of you have known and yet deny—that significant moments with a work you have come to know and cherish enhance understanding of many things, as it opens us to visions of unexpected possibility. Objects once bought, after all, close off possibility; works of art, never exhausted, open to the unpredictable, maybe even the sublime.

Of course we are frequently reminded that we who are teachers must be freed to consult what we truly know, and freed to select the projects by means of which we define ourselves. When we are compelled or lured to remain passive receivers of discrete parts of a curriculum, say, obliged to speak in a manner others determine and to follow some extrinsic logic, we become disempowered. We are no longer able to address students as diverse persons in quest of themselves, as who they really are, not what they are, not creatures condemned to live with the radio blaring and the windows shut. The point is to address them as beings in process and to do so as persons who themselves are incomplete, still imagining what we are not yet. Learning happens as the questions come in the context of conversation among persons (old and young) in search of themselves.

Recently I found something in one of John Dewey's works (*Philosophy and Civilization*) that holds implications for all of this and for what we are doing here. He was lamenting what he called "our lack of imagination in generating leading ideas. Because we are afraid of speculative ideas we do . . . an immense amount of dead, specialized work in the region of 'facts'. We forget that such facts are only data; that is, are only fragmentary, uncompleted meanings, and unless they are rounded into complete ideas—a work which can only be done . . . by a free imagination of intellectual possibilities—they are as helpless as are all maimed things and as repellent as are needlessly thwarted ones" (1931, p. 11). Surely some of you remember

Dickens's Mr. Gradgrind, in *Hard Times* (1996), trying to silence and shame the little girl brought up in the circus, the little girl with an aesthetic consciousness, with "Facts, Sissy, facts!" And I am sure, with the arts so often discouraged in the schools, with the technical made the governing force, many of those in authority are muttering the same demand today. In my own case, not so long ago, I was often accused of speaking in what was called "soft" or even "non-cognitive" language. I was often silenced by some saying, "I don't know what you are talking about." Often, too often, I repressed my dream—complying with those voices telling me to be sensible, to stay with the facts, to stop diverting myself with the arts.

Dewey's treatment of facts as dead things summons up a metaphor for me. I associate to the object world, to products rather than processes, to what is fixed and hard (indurated, as Dewey would say) in contrast to what leaps forward, what moves beyond. And then Toni Morrison's *The Bluest Eye* (1999) comes to mind. You may recall how the young Claudia tries to tell the story of Pecola Breedlove, an unloved little girl convinced by the world around that she is ugly and unloveable. Pecola dreams of looking like Shirley Temple with blue eyes, with the belief that the world will look different seen through such eyes. Moreover, people will love her, as they never would if she remains small and black, rejected by her mother, later (in a deadly moment) raped by her father Cholly, whose own tragic life could only be captured, says the narrator, in the sound of a clarinet.

In any event, the Shirley Temple dolls are despised by Claudia, the narrator, the more grown-ups keep proffering them as desirable. Claudia sees them as bone cold with pancake faces, unpleasant products adults kept foisting on the young, even the African American young. Those dolls evoke Dewey's facts, the repellent, the unmoveable. Claudia writes about the "Adults, older girls, shops, magazines, window signs—all the world had agreed that a blue-eyed, yellow-haired, pink-skinned doll was what every girl child treasured. 'Here,' they said, 'this is beautiful, and if you are on this day 'worthy' you may have it'" (Morrison, 1999, pp. 26–27). Note how imagination can be corrupted by what authorities (parents or teachers) insist is beautiful and good. Claudia thinks of destroying the dolls and succeeds in pulling out the eyeballs and the metal piece that was the source of the doll's bleating cries. The grown-ups were outraged, but Claudia could not say why she hated the doll so much. "But I did know that nobody ever asked me what I wanted for Christmas" (1999, p. 28). And then:

> Had any adult with the power to fulfill my desires taken me seriously and asked me what I wanted, they would have known that I did not want to have

anything to own, or to possess any object. I wanted rather to feel something on Christmas day. The real question would have been, "Dear Claudia, what experience would you like on Christmas?" I could have spoken up, "I want to sit on the low stool in Big Mama's kitchen with my lap full of lilacs and listen to Big Papa play his violin for me alone." The lowness of the stool made for my body, the security and warmth of Big Mama's kitchen, the smell of the lilacs, the sound of the music, and, since it would be good to have all my senses engaged, the taste of a peach, perhaps, afterward. (p. 28)

Claudia, I would say, can learn. She is the one who explained the story by saying no one could make clear why so many dreadful things happened to Pecola, why the marigolds never bloomed: "since *why* is difficult to handle, one must take refuge in *how*" (1999, p. 10). So the questions come, the maimed facts give way to unexpected openings, to probings of desire, to an understanding of what might promote life rather than reify it.

Of course I am also talking about the potency of works of art when they are grasped by personal experience—not solely novels, but all the forms of art—painting, sculpture, film, music, and, now that new roads are opening every day, I would include video art and the startling apertures through which we are being enabled to see. In all the arts today there is a movement to see encounters with the arts, not as distanced modes of awe or admiration, but as modes of participation, modes of engagement. In some fashion, as one attends, one lends the work one's life. Or one brings it into the world through a sometimes mysterious interpretive act in a space between oneself and the stage or the wall or the text.

I think of Jacob Lawrence's *Migration* series, with those figures lining the railroad stations in the South, or appearing abruptly on the barren streets of Chicago, and I feel myself gravitating from admiration of the line, the space, the color, to feelings of outrage, to indignation at what Lawrence has revealed about human power and human suffering. I remember how involved I become with those lonely figures in empty rooms and hallways in Hopper paintings, how I stared at the light, the spare emergent light, the shadows, the empty spaces that become full of loneliness and light. Perhaps Claudia's account of the experience she yearned for says something about what it signifies to become engaged with works of art—as a mind, a body, an imagination. I recall the door slamming at the end of *A Doll's House,* when Nora demands her right to seek her own humanity in the world outside. I think of the conclusion of Albert Camus' *The Plague* and the doctor talking about the need for some to be healers as the plague advances, retreats, and returns. I think of Edna Pontellier in *The Awakening,* finding her only release by swimming to her death at sea. And I reflect back on imagination and think how I want to connect our imaginative journeys, our efforts to look at things as if they were otherwise, with the struggle for social justice, for what Paulo Freire called "a lovelier world" (1994/1997). And still I realize, as I hope you also will realize, that without the understanding of the arts that can be gained through what we call aesthetic education, I would not be able to use my imagination as I choose to use it. I would not respond to the darkness rendered by so many artists. I would not feel the indignation that buoys me up, that is evoked by so many of the art experiences I have had, in which the human condition has appeared before my eyes—and the pathos of so many lives strikes against my heart.

I am not saying that the exercise of the imagination or active encounters with art forms (similar to a reflective engagement known as "reader response" theory with respect to literature) can make persons better or more critically conscious of their ability to change the world. Herbert Marcuse (1978) said that the arts do not change the world, but they can change the living beings who might change the world, and I suppose I do have that in mind when I ponder how to move people to questioning, how to awaken them, how to free them to respond not only to the human condition which we all share but to the injustices and the undeserved suffering and the violence and the violations—to respond and endeavor to repair.

I turn to Jean-Paul Sartre, talking with literature in mind and with (for me) relevance to the work of imagination and the lives of the several arts.

> And if I am given this world with its injustices, it is not so that I might contemplate them coldly, but that I might animate them with my indignation, that I might disclose them and create them with their nature as injustices, that is, as abuses to be suppressed. Thus, the writer's universe will only reveal itself in all its depth to the examination, the admiration, and the indignation of the reader; and the generous love is a promise to change, and the admiration is a promise to imitate; although literature is one thing and morality quite a different one, at the heart of the aesthetic imperative we discern the moral imperative. (1949, pp. 62–63)

He speaks of works of art as being gifts, generous gifts to those willing to attend, to lend their lives to them. They are, he says, acts of confidence in the freedom of human beings; and perceivers and readers and listeners, coming to the arts, trusting their imaginations, recognize this freedom and demand that it manifest itself. The work, Sartre goes on, can sometimes be defined as an imaginary presentation of the world insofar "as it demands human freedom." To respond to that demand (to free teachers and learners to find and use their own voices) is to teach for value and to reach beyond—

looking through the window at the half-moon. And that may be how values are created: in efforts to overcome deficiencies to heal, to repair, to transform. There must be the sense of a future and a decision to invent. And that may be one of the functions of the arts, in their beckoning, in their mystery. I turn to Elizabeth Bishop for a last word, which ought really to be a beginning. Here is the opening stanza of her translation of "January First" by Octavio Paz.

> *The year's doors open*
> *like those of language,*
> *toward the unknown.*
> *Last night you told me:*
> > *tomorrow*
> *we shall have to think up signs,*
> *sketch a landscape, fabricate a plan*
> *on the double page*
> *of day and paper.*
> *Tomorrow, we shall have to invent,*
> *once more,*
> *the reality of this world.*
>
> (1997, p. 273)

PART III

EXCELLENCE, STANDARDS, SCHOOL RENEWAL AND REFORM

We pay heed to the cacophony when standards are discussed, especially when a state board somewhere discusses the imposition of unitary standards or standards derived from advanced disciplinary frameworks. At once, the participants in such arguments know, as we know, the importance of living up to something thought to be good trombone-playing, the writing of good poetry, a well-played game of golf. We are moved when we watch somebody or hear somebody reach toward a notion of what one ought to be when it comes to a project that is prized, an art form that is loved.

Not only do we try to make visible the ways in which our teaching artists (and the artists who perform and exhibit) consciously live up to the standards or norms governing their communities—we try to communicate what it is to internalize a standard, a goal, even an ideal—and to feel a kind of personal obligatoriness when it comes to realizing it. We try to create situations in which the very culture encourages and rewards modes of striving—sometimes with the help of role models, sometimes through agreement among friends. All this, clearly, has to do with the choosing of projects, and, yes, the idea of excellence. Hannah Arendt has written that excellence means "appearing before others as the best one knows how to be." We who are teachers, authentically committed to enabling the young to become, know what this means and how hard this is to attain. In aesthetic education, classes can open the way to what seems secret or hidden. They can appeal to each person's sense of what might be, perhaps ought to be, as one reaches toward the horizon.

We know there are similarities between the way we look at encounters with the arts and what is thought of as a constructivist approach to learning: a search for meanings and the meaningful, a construction of those meanings in the light of the learner's experience, the demands of one's lived world. We know, as well, the ways in which reflective encounters with the arts add to the multiplicity of our realities, open roadways out of fields once closed in, open frequencies or sounds we never believed could be uttered on heaven or earth. We see ourselves in partnership when we think of educational renewal, but our part has to do with mystery and possibility, with loving questions that are unanswerable, with probing depths that are no longer closed. Our contribution to reform may be a suggestion for catching more frequent glimpses of the half-moon, more frequent movements with flamenco dancers, more heart-stopping dialogue with those who find themselves on stage. It is immeasurable, but it may signify a necessary professional development; it may be named "possibility."

From Discovery to Expression

(1985)

I have been talking much about blue guitars and the meanings of aesthetic education: how it has to do with enabling persons to decipher and to open themselves to diverse works of art. I have been trying to make clear that the noticing that is necessary, the rapt attending, the perceiving, are made increasingly likely by actual engagements with the media involved: bodies in motion, sound, language, paint, clay. Most of you know that the courtly movements of *The Moor's Pavane*—broken by the plunging, lunging gestures of suspicion, jealousy, and revenge—provide new and unexpected ways for modern persons to articulate what they feel, even what they know, and to do so in a language of movement, not a language of words. You have discovered how it feels to invent your own movements, to express your own energies in limited space and time, to work on different levels—and, at once, to respond to someone facing toward you, to make unexpected patterns and designs. Seeing *The Moor's Pavane*, with your own recollections of moving, of making, of effort, of shape, you cannot but notice particulars you could not have noticed before. You cannot but achieve a fidelity of perception; you cannot but feel your imagination set free to discover new possibilities in the drama of *Othello*, perhaps in the dramas of courtliness and manner, in human self-presentation, in the tension between culture and nature, in all sorts of things I cannot define.

And so it has been for some of you with Shakespeare's *The Winter's Tale*, which you are being empowered to experience through your own adventures in the materials of dramatic art: inventing scenes, improvising, finding dialogue for male/female or generational transactions, discovering gestures, uncovering paradoxes and disguises in yourself and others you may not have suspected before. Already, you who have seen the enacted play are aware of the craft involved in every aspect—the use of space, the positioning of the characters, the rapid movements and the slow ones, the shadings of voices, the facial expressions, the dance—and it is a kind of dance—

of language and gesture. Costumes white and black; flowers; water in a basin; steps going downwards to a prison; a basket with an imaginary infant; a man torn apart by an imaginary bear: you know it is illusion; you are constantly reminded it is illusion, theater, taking place on a stage. And yet, and yet, how do you explain the believability, the verisimilitude of that ending, when Hermione (now that the lost child, Perdita, is found) returns to warmth and life? Could there be anything more implausible, more dependent upon coincidence than the discovery of Perdita? And still, at the end, we believe, and the lived world has taken on a new intelligibility. In a certain fashion, we *know* more; we understand more. For most of us, I am convinced, that would not have occurred were it not for our workshops, our preparatory work—our aesthetic education.

I could say some of the same things about Tania Leon's *Permutation Seven* and the opening of new dimensions of sound, about moving into a Bartók sonata and beginning to think in very specific musical terms about fairy tales and drama. But my primary interest at the moment is in locating all this in the contexts of what is happening in American education today: the demand for common learnings, cultural literacy, and the like; the cry for excellence and higher standards of achievement; the emphasis on critical thinking in all classes, in all undertakings; the preoccupation with merit and mastery. I mentioned the margins last time, and the significance of the margins. But, like you, I am not content to argue for the arts as fringe subjects nor for aesthetic education as something rich and exciting for teachers (as it unquestionably is) but not as something integral to the concerns of the public school today.

I want to argue that it is integral, that a school committed to educating rather than training is somehow morally obligated to attend to the kinds of values realized here. I have, of course, the values of craftsmanship and style in mind among other things. At a moment of carelessness in our society, of a general shoddiness in many places, how many people bring conscience to bear on what they do? When I am asked to speak about excellence, I very often find my examples here among the teaching artists I have come to know. Yes, I talk about the knowledge a dancer has garnered, the knowledge of a certain range of skills and proficiencies, about his/her educated capacity to do what he/she has learned how to do. I talk about the bodily kinaesthetic intelligence dancers seem to have, involving a sense of timing and a sense of direction, a point of no return. There are other ways of describing it; and when it is linked, as it is here, to personal intelligence and linguistic intelligence, one cannot but be struck by the power of it, as one cannot but be troubled by the thought that the capacity, the knowledge described is not thought of as intelligence within the schools. Howard Gardner and others have reminded us that there are multiple intelligences, ranging beyond the logical linguistic, the mathematical and so on. Jerome Bruner has been writing about a mode of knowing he associates with story-telling, with narrative. Nelson Goodman, writing about ways of knowing the world, about world versions, stresses the *languages* of art (1988). We are being told, in other words, by all sorts of scholars that our focus is too narrow, that we are confining the young very often to a single or a one-dimensional reality, condemning them to what has been called a "poor life indeed."

Some of you remember my obsession with a stanza from a Wallace Stevens poem, and I am going to quote it again, because it says so marvelously what I have in mind (as poetry so often does).

> *Rationalists, wearing square hats,*
> *Think, in square rooms.*
>
> (1982, p. 75)

Of course there must be rationalists, mathematicians, logicians, and the rest, but there is no good reason for them, grounded human beings as they are, to confine themselves to "right-angled triangles." Nor is there any reason to confine those we teach to abstract concepts, numbers, factual statements— to techniques, competencies, skills. There are dimensions of the world (rhomboids, cones, waving ellipses) that will remain forever out of reach if the range of intelligences remains untapped, if passion is ignored, if imagination is unused. It is imagination that permits the move from cones to waving ellipses to "the ellipse of the half-moon" (Stevens, 1982, p. 75) to the vista beyond, the view out the window, to a reality yet to be known. And it is imagination that finds unexpected resemblances and contrasts—not only contrasts between square hats that are like mortarboards, the very symbols of dry academicism, and sombreros that belong to sunlit places and dreams, perhaps, and play—but odd connections between ellipses and sombreros, moonlight and sombreros, perhaps even scholarship and panache, scholarship and play. Whatever is summoned up, think how the space enlarges and the meanings accumulate. Does this have nothing to do with learning to learn? Might this not become another argument for making aesthetic education central in the schools?

I think of still another aspect of what we discover here that holds implications for, if you like, "excellent" education. I suppose it is crucial to our undertaking, but we may never make it evident enough. The more we know, we say, the more we perceive. That is one part of it. The more discipline we exert, the more care we take, the more freedom, the more delight we will enjoy. Those of you who have worked with the Shakespeare play or the Bartók piece or the Taylor dances do not have to be told about the mysterious relationship between knowing and perceiving. Seeing *The Winter's Tale* under ordinary circumstances, a person, especially a young son, might be slightly perplexed by the poetry and by the multitextured account of Leontes' jealousy and the reasons for it, inner and outer at once. Yes, he might grasp the story in some general way, might focus especially on the lost baby (since foundlings somehow play a part in most people's memories), the disguises, the father-son relationships. Consider, having come to know as much as you have by now, all the details you have been enabled to see and to hear, how much material has been provided to your imagination, how many possibilities have opened up for further thought—not solely about Shakespeare, but about marriage, children, friendship, self-deception, the passage of time. If we could communicate to more and more young persons that the point of mastering a degree of know-how, a set of knacks, an array of tools, is to be able to see more, to notice more, to make more sense of the actualities of life, would not that, in itself, make learning to learn take on a different tinge? If we could indicate to those we teach that hard work and hard thinking and craftsmanship are likely to open up whole areas of freedom of mind and of imagination, might that not contribute to the quest for what is being called "excellence"?

In many respects, I know, it is a matter of choice on the part of the learner, since, as we all know, we cannot *learn* anyone; we have somehow or other to create the kind of situations in which students will pose the kinds of questions, articulate the kind of curiosity or the kinds of wonder in which learning begins. Dewey used to talk about devising situations that released spontaneous preferences on the part of the young. I have already suggested the ways in which the presence of art forms, actively encountered, might enrich and diversify classroom life. Consider what it might mean to engage your children in the translation of their favorite fairy stories into plays. Or finding musical sounds, as Bartók did, to render experiences with walks in the woods, with flowers, with animals and birds. Or discovering a movement language for saying something about those animals and birds, or about family gatherings, or picnics, or about making repairs. We have found out (and surely you have found out) that actual—and lively—experiences with theatrical and musical and dance pieces, through their stimulating of perception and their freeing of imagination, suggest such activities for children to undertake.

As you well know, however, no one can have an art experience without freely choosing to weave a circle of attentiveness around one's self to pause, to be there in person before the painting, the dance performance, the concert, the play, the text. You can usher a child into a theater or museum, encourage, explain, tempt, support. But children must discover a sense of their own agency if the particular work of art is to come alive; they must make their own use of what has been taught; in fact, children must go beyond what has been learned—to do what might be called untaught things. In many ways, this may be called a paradigm case, since this is the way authentic learning always takes place: children go beyond what they have been taught and begin teaching themselves. In a moment when what Christopher Lasch calls "the minimal self" (1984, p. 59) is so common, when passive acceptance or conventional stimulation is more likely than autonomous response, this seems to me of great importance. We may, in fact, conceive the consciousness of agency to be essential for critical thinking and certainly for interpretive thinking, for deciphering the meanings of the world.

Recalling the number of young persons who feel they confront a predefined world, marked off and explained by others (usually others whom they do not know, and who do not have their interests at heart), I think of powerlessness and the ways in which the sense of powerlessness (unwarranted or not) stands in the way of learning. Sometimes it is due to felt oppressiveness, to victimization. Sometimes it is due to a terrible inarticulateness, like Miss Celie's at the start of Alice Walker's *The Color Purple* (1982), the kind of inarticulateness that makes it impossible for her to write "I am." Sometimes it is due to the feeling that an individual has no right to an opinion or a judgment, that what is "given" must be accepted on its own terms. And then, perhaps strangely, I associate to something Virginia Woolf wrote, published in that collection of her posthumous writings called *Moments of Being* (1985).

She is talking about how much of her life in childhood contained what she called "non-being," the feeling of being "embedded in a kind of nondescript cotton wool" (Woolf, 1985, p. 70). Nothing made any particular impression on her, she said. "Then, for no reason that I know about, there was a sudden violent shock; something happened so violently that I have remembered it all my life" (p. 71). Then she gives three instances of what that meant. One involved fighting with her brother and suddenly realizing how foolish it was to hurt another person. She dropped her fists and let him beat her. "I remember the feeling. It was a feeling of hopeless sadness. It was as if I became aware of something terrible; and of my own powerlessness.

I slunk off alone." Another involved looking at a flower bed and realizing that a flower was part of the earth, part earth, part flower. She put away the thought as one "likely to be very useful to me later." The third instance was overhearing her father say that a family friend had killed himself, and somehow connecting that with walking near an apple tree. "I could not pass it. . . . I seemed to be dragged down, hopelessly, into some pit of absolute despair." She calls all three "exceptional moments," two ending in despair, one in satisfaction (p. 71).

The difference between them, Woolf writes, arose from the fact that "I was quite unable to deal with the pain of discovering that people hurt each other, that a man I had seen had killed himself. The sense of horror held me powerless. But in the case of the flower I found a reason; and was thus able to deal with the sensation. I was not powerless. I was conscious—if only at a distance—that I should in time explain it" (pp. 71–72). And she says that the older one gets, the greater one's power to provide, through reason, the kind of explanation that "blunts the sledge-hammer force" of blows from without that leave one dominated, passive. The shocks in her adulthood were always valuable, she writes, supposing that "the shock-receiving capacity is what makes me a writer. I hazard the explanation that a shock is at once in my case followed by the desire to explain it" (p. 72).

I quote Virginia Woolf at such length because she makes so clear to me the connection between the feeling of powerlessness and the incapacity to understand. Also, I cannot but believe that the shock of awareness she describes, shock that becomes so valuable for her, is more likely for people whose attentiveness is enhanced by exposure to the arts. It is certainly true for me that novels and plays and films help me free myself from embeddedness in cotton wool. The disclosures I experience are not always pleasant; some of them afflict me with outrage, some with a kind of despair. But I agree with Virginia Woolf: they are almost always followed by a desire to explain. And I know that I have to take the responsibility for explaining, for learning enough, for honing the skills of inquiry, and (I would say again) looking at things as if they could be otherwise. It seems to me that this is what we want or should want for our young people at a moment when they are being charged with thoughtlessness, impassivity, and—yes—a lack of care.

I am not talking about the arts or aesthetic experiences as motivational. I am talking about an atmosphere that may be created by the teachers who are the focus of our institutes. Some of you, understandably, speak about the pressures, the interferences of review tests and the like. Some of you speak of parent resistance to anything that does not constitute what they perceive as basic literacy. Some of you speak of the so-called career ladders and of how people who have no sense of what the arts can mean are defining merit and mastery. Still others mention the Hatch amendment or other signs of political objection to anything but a conservative skills orientation. Your arguments need not be sentimental nor elitist; they need not focus on creativity or art criticism or even common learning; they need not beg any questions as to whether or not the arts lead to measurable improvements in reading.

Aesthetic education is a process, an open-ended process, that can become integral to any educational enterprise. It depends, as we well know, on the presentness and openness of teachers and learners, on the accessibility of certain kinds of materials, on the availability of performances and other works of art. It involves an intentional effort to move persons to more informed and more discriminating encounters with diverse art forms—and, yes, with the appearances of their lived worlds and the living beings inhabiting it. Opening perspectives as it ought to do, it enlarges the spaces—the perceptual, imaginative, and conceptual spaces—in which the young come in touch with and try to interpret their worlds. What we are doing is expanding the range of literacy, introducing people to what standards can mean and what discipline can mean, even as we introduce them to the symbol systems that define our culture, even as we are provoking them to move beyond, to realize untapped possibility.

I referred to Hannah Arendt when I began and to her notion of a "space of excellence." She had in mind a space, you remember, where people appear before one another as the best they know how to be. She wrote in other places about people in their plurality, in their distinctiveness, speaking in terms of who, not what, they are, embarking on continually new beginnings as they come together to create something in common among themselves. I believe that is what we are doing here, what you will be doing in your classrooms. "Education," Arendt said, "is the point at which we decide whether we love the world enough to assume responsibility for it and by the same token save it from that ruin which, except for renewal, except for the coming of the new and young, would be inevitable. And education, too, is where we decide whether we love our children enough not to expel them from our world and leave them to their own devices, nor to strike from their hands their chance of undertaking something new, something unforeseen by us, but to prepare them in advance for the task of renewing a common world" (1968, p. 196). In my view, what we do in this Institute is to empower people to love the world and, at once, by engaging the young in attending, in what has been called "enlightened cherishing," to open the path to renewals of all sorts. We can never expel those to whom we are disclosing Shakespeare and Grimm and Bartók and Limón—because these, after all, are among those who create our world. And the idea of undertaking something new, something unforeseen, summons up the sound of blue guitars once more. Near the end Stevens's guitar-player says, "Throw away the lights, the definitions, / And say of what you see in the dark" (1982, p. 183). You *can* see, you who are teachers. You will be nurturing the growth of persons in the presence of the arts. Is there an excellence greater than that?

The Wonders of Mystery, the Rejection of Commodification

(1994)

We began with questions—questions about art and the aesthetic experience, questions about reality and illusion, about traditions and diversity. You were asked to reflect upon some of your own encounters with works of art—to try to understand them and, in doing so, to discover why the arts are important in your life. Surely it is clear that, if they were not important to you (attending in "the first person"), you would not be able to communicate to those you teach the wonder, the challenge, the surprises waiting for them in the domain of the arts. And, yes, the mystery, that which goes beyond explanation. I think of the writer Denis Donoghue objecting to talk of art as a commodity with all the mystery removed (1983). He wants to reinstate mystery and distinguish it from mere bewilderment or mystification. He turns to Gabriel Marcel, who said, "A problem is something met which bars my passage. It is before me in its entirety. A mystery, on the other hand, is something in which I find myself caught up, and whose essence is therefore not to be before me in its entirety" (1935/1949, pp. 100–101). The point is that the artistic vision (whether Shakespearean or Mayan or French impressionist or southern Indian) deflects every attempt, as Donoghue says, "to pin it down by knowledge or define it in speech." And then I recall Wallace Stevens writing, "Throw away the lights, and the definitions, / And say of what you see in the dark" (1982, p. 183). Yes, there are adventures in meaning into which you want to usher those you teach—adventures in movement, sound, dialogue; but they are not adventures that come to comfortable ends. There is always, always more.

One of the questions you will carry with you has to do with how you can embody that kind of awareness in such a way as to enable the young to feel it, to yearn toward it. How, by being in your classroom as a person, can you translate into your own authentic practice some of what you have felt, explored, perceived, imagined—learned? Many of you have said how enlightening it is to recapture the experience of learning, of finding yourself in a place where you are a stranger, where—for a while—even the language in use is unknown. I hope you try to hold in mind what happened as you gradually came to know, how you learned to learn the language of Alvin Ailey, say, of the pre-Columbian myth-maker, of the dance called *Bharata Natyam*, of the dances from the commedia dell'arte, of American jazz, which you may have thought you knew until you were allowed to move inside. And I hope, as well, you recall the ways in which that learning affected your seeing and your listening—your noticing what was there to be noticed when the works were presented on the stage.

There are no recipes, as you well know, for translating all this into classroom practice; there are no generalized formulations that can be applied to the situation-specific occasions with which we deal as teachers. There are intuitions on which we try to rely, moments of improvisation, moments of tuning in to this student or that. There are conversations, instances of dialogue, collaborations with fellow teachers and teaching artists. There is the singling out of particular children or young people to help in the creation of an atmosphere. There is the effort to invent a situation in which there can be spaces for doing, spaces for attending, spaces for becoming.

And spaces for action. I think of Hannah Arendt, making the point that action, in contrast to behavior, means taking an initiative, beginning, setting something in motion. It is, she wrote, "in the nature of beginning that something new is started which cannot be expected from whatever may have happened before. This character of startling unexpectedness is inherent in all beginnings." Look back again on your experiences this summer, even the casual and the unfinished ones, and you may recognize what Arendt had in mind. Think of the dance movements in which you participated, the myths you have enacted, the scripts you have written, the texts and subtexts you have explored, the visual shapes you have made, the perspectives you have looked through (even when examining a cut-out of your own silhouette upon the floor), the boxes you have emptied and filled and foraged in, the voices that have taken you by surprise. As a teacher, I want to find out more and more about creating occasions for such experiences—and, I must say, not in the arts alone. I like to talk about moving from the predictable to the possible. The predictable is what is seen and measured from the outside (from the lab, or the administrative office, or the visiting observer); the possible is what is seen from the vantage point of the actor, the one with a sense of agency, the beginner. I like to believe (and I suspect many of you will agree) that our Summer Session, viewed from the perspective of the participants, is a realm of possibility. Think what it would mean if our classrooms, too, became such realms.

I have quoted Emily Dickinson before, writing that "The Possible's slow fuse is lit / By the Imagination" (1960, p. 689). All we need to do is to summon up the cognitive capacity called imagination to remind ourselves that experience always holds more than can be predicted. When I think of the youngsters I have met and heard about who view their futures in terms of roadblocks, closed doors, even early death, I become obsessive about communicating this idea—this sense of something beyond the actual, this consciousness of alternative possibility. In the midst of institutions too often governed by images of linearity, by calculative symbols, by talk of measurement, the young are made to feel that this is what the world is; this is objective reality as defined by authoritative others, excluding the vantage points of the young. Again, for some reason, I think of Wallace Stevens and a poem called "The Motive for Metaphor." He is describing what may be viewed as the objective world, the world set over us—against people like the young in schools.

> *Desiring the exhilarations of changes:*
> *The motive for metaphor, shrinking from*
> *The weight of primary noon,*
> *The A B C of being,*
>
> *The ruddy temper, the hammer*
> *Of red and blue, the hard sound—*
> *Steel against intimation—the sharp flash,*
> *The vital, arrogant, fatal, dominant X.*
>   (1982, p. 288)

Yes, somewhere they, like us, desire "the exhilarations of changes," and we would like to help them give that desire voice. And perhaps articulate for them that it *is* indeed a "motive for metaphor," for making new connections, for identifying with a world that seems so alien, for looking at things as if they could be otherwise. Again it is a matter of enabling them to open themselves to vistas of possibility—and to summon up visions of human agency, their own agency, that transcend correctness and the passing grade or the mere mastery of skills.

To have a feeling of agency is to recognize that the living being—the perceiver, the reader, the listener—has an active part in achieving a work of art as meaningful. When the school reformers talk, as they do, of active learning and of people telling their stories and of the sense of agency, I want to remind them of the ways in which the experiences we have here, the kind we want to make possible in our classrooms, may well be paradigmatic for the new schools we want to build.

We have learned here repeatedly that it is never enough to take a look, to label a particular work or simply to recognize it as something by Ailey, something by Cézanne, something by Shakespeare. It is never enough to attend to it as something *out there,* defined by official others, to be perceived, read, or heard as those others decide. At once, it is not enough to deal with it as impulse would have it—conventionally, as Dewey would say, stupidly, as Sartre would say. We want the works at hand, remember, to become objects of experience for those who come to them; and that takes a going-out of energy and a care, even a solicitude in noticing, in paying heed to nuance and to detail, and then ordering the parts perceived into a whole within experience—that is, at once, true to the work and something that never happened in the world before. In *Hamlet,* as we discovered once again, there are a thousand elements that have to be heeded—in the poetry, in the text and the sub-text, in the enactments, in the play within the play, in the relationships, in the nature of the court, in the impinging war, in the presence of England across the water, in the human condition as rendered in this work. We as teachers are obligated to enable our students to attend well, to pay heed, to notice what might not be noticed in a careless reading or inattentive watching. But then we have to open the spaces I tried to talk about before—the spaces for their meaning-making, for their interpretations—which are bound to be manifold. They must decide what Hamlet's relation to Gertrude is and was, whether Hamlet is really mad or a good play actor himself, whether Rosencrantz and Guildenstern honestly know what is happening, what friendship signifies—and betrayal—and the thought of suicide, what is actually rotten in the state of Denmark, how the state of Denmark is like the American state today. No, there are not as many *Hamlets* as there are spectators; but there are vast possibilities for interpretation, multiple adventures of meaning (depending on who is undertaking the adventure, and what risks they are willing to take).

Also, there is the community. One of the significant aspects of our adventure here is, I believe, our gradual consciousness of ourselves as members of a community. We come to share values here, and norms, and a sense of craft, and a feeling of what excellence is. We share all this as we somehow share our stories with one another, as we begin to recognize each other—in ways we all hope will happen in classrooms. I think of Ralph Ellison's narrator at the start of *Invisible Man* who says his invisibility is due to "a peculiar disposition of the eyes of those with whom I come in contact. A matter of the construction of their *inner* eyes, those eyes with which they look through their physical eyes upon reality" (1994, p. 3). We know enough about the racism and classism that impose invisibility upon so many and make the weaving of community so difficult. We know, too, that an absence of imagination is involved when that happens, the absence of an ability to see Ellison's narrator as a living human being. The seriousness of the existing condition in the eyes of those who look is shown when Ellison's narrator says it makes him doubt *if* he exists. "You wonder whether you aren't simply a phantom in other people's minds. Say a figure in a nightmare which the sleeper tries with all his strength to destroy. It's when you feel like this that, out of resentment, you begin to bump people back. And, let me confess, you feel that way most of the time. You ache with the need to convince yourself that you do exist in the real world, that you're a part of all the sound and anguish"(1994, p. 3). And he speaks desperately of how hard the effort is to get others to recognize you and how, without recognition, you can hardly be held responsible. Think what it would mean in our increasingly diverse classrooms for teachers to be enabled through Ellison's art to imagine what it signifies to be "invisible" and to realize at the same time that that person is kin to them. And to realize as well how such invisibility stands in the way of community, and how the arts enable persons to create their own visibility, to change their lives.

Think, too, what it would mean to enter Toni Morrison's character in *Beloved*, remembered for his struggle to describe how he felt about a particular woman. "She is a friend of my mind. She gather me, man. The pieces I am, she gather them and give them back to me all in the right order. It's good, you know, when you got a woman who is a friend of your mind" (1988, pp. 272–273). This may be another mode of imagining: becoming a friend of someone else's mind, with the wonderful power to return to that person a sense of wholeness. That may be because the imagination has the capacity, as Virginia Woolf said, "to bring the severed parts together," to integrate into the right order, to create wholes. Released as it is by encounters with works of art, it may well begin weaving the webs of relationship essential for the existence of community. Some of you may, even now, think back to your workshops and to the ways in which diverse people, people who were strangers a little while before, became—through their explanations of an art work—friends of each other's minds.

It is through imagination, G. B. Madison has said, or "the realm of pure possibility that we freely make ourselves to be who or what we are, that we creatively and imaginatively become who we are" (1988, p. 191). The becoming described is very much dependent on membership in a community of recognition and regard. Those who are labeled, fixed like butterflies in amber as deficient or alien, have little chance to feel they can "be yet otherwise" unless they are encouraged to seek their images, find their voices, inscribe their losses and their pain and their desires in journals, on canvasboards held up for others to see. Or, again, to be ushered into the spaces of art where, using eye and mind, they can be enabled to bring new visibility to the physical world, new melodies and resonances to the sounding world, new recognitions to the human world. Community cannot be produced through rational formulation or by edict. Like freedom, it has to be achieved by persons offered a space in which to discover what they recognize together, appreciate in common. It must be the space infused by the kind of awareness that enables those involved to imagine alternative possibilities for their own becoming, and their group's becoming—to refuse always the state of being complete.

From my point of view, that is the primary function of Lincoln Center Institute: to open spaces in which teachers can choose themselves, can pursue untapped possibility. Such a teacher—ardent and in pursuit, impatient to see the Picasso show at the Metropolitan, the David Salle show (and to read the interview with Salle in *The New Yorker*), to get a ticket for Pilobolus or Twyla Tharp, to read Doctorow's new book or Toni Morrison's Nobel Prize Address, to experience Tony Kushner's *The Millennium,* to taste the Renaissance at the Frick, and, perhaps, to try sketching herself or himself, to try a dance movement, to recite passages from Shakespeare's sonnets aloud, to take up the violin again, to connect being and becoming with adventures chosen for oneself in this domain of many windows—such a teacher is the kind who enters the classroom after an experience like Summer Session. And my belief is that the teacher open to the mystery, open to the wonder, open to the questions, is the one who can light the slow fuse of possibility even for the defeated ones, the bored ones, the deserted ones. There is room for them; we can make room for them in our community of recognition, wide-awakeness, caring, and regard.

Also, I hope—as I think many of you do—that you will become articulate about the meaning of all this for school restructuring and reform. Again, remember the language now in use for this new era of reform: active learning, critical questioning, narrative, meaning-making, authentic assessment, collaboration, community. We can give each term, each phrase a new and palpitant content by recalling what we have found for ourselves about activity and questioning and story and meaning and community. It is a matter of participation in the works at hand; it is a matter of engagement in the first person; it is a matter of reflectiveness and self-discovery and surprise. And, yes, it is a matter of sensitivity to diverse ways of being and knowing and art-making, to new ways of creating visibility. You will argue, I am sure, for more opportunities for school people to join the forever unfinished dialogue to which works of art give rise in their wonderful incompleteness, in their opening to indefinable possibilities. Again it is a matter of awakening imaginative capacities and of appealing to people's freedom. Free human beings can choose, can move beyond where they are, can ascend to places of which, in their ordinariness, they could have had no idea.

I am moved to end with some lines I used at the conclusion of another piece—lines worth repeating at an end that carries within it a new beginning. They come from "Furious Versions" by Li-Young Lee, who wrote a lovely book of poetry called *The City in Which I Love You*.

> *I wait for shapeliness*
> *limned, or dissolution.*
> *Is paradise due or narrowly missed*
> *until another thousand years?*
> *I wait*
> *in a blue hour*
> *and faraway noise of hammering,*
> *and on a page a poem begun, something*
> *about to be dispersed,*
> *something about to come into being.*
>   (1990, pp. 14–15)

He is making something; he is turned to the possible—as we are in this dislocating time. These may be blue hours for us as well. Something indeed is about to begin.

The Arts and the
Human Condition . . .
(1995)

Talking about imagination, perception, and the making of meanings at this Institute, I have a sense of community in the making: a community of wide-awakeness, exploration; a consciousness of what might be, what is not yet. We try, as you well know, to enable persons in their diversity to engage with plays, dance performances, music, visual art forms, and literary works actively, reflectively, and against the background of their own lived lives. Whether we are sharing in the comic improvisations of *The Number 14* or confronting the tensions and mystery of *True West,* we are refusing the anaesthetic in our experience, breaking with the routine. Whether we are moving from Carl Nielsen's or Samuel Barber's wind instrument sounds to a lovely unfamiliarity in the West African *kora,* or from the delicate shapes of the Peach Flower dance to the Pilobolus adventures in movement, we find ourselves making unexpected connections in our experiences, integrating what we have never before seen or heard or felt in quite the same way into the treasure trove of encounters we have been accumulating since early, early youth. Not everything we live through here is simple and joyous, of course. Some of it evokes uneasy and troubling questions, the kinds of questions that bring us in touch with the emotions that we have in common, that mark the human condition. The community we achieve, the dialogues we enter take shape *across* the differences, preventing those differences from tearing us apart, linking us in a desire to see more, feel more, understand more, listen more acutely, dip more passionately into life.

On reflecting, I think that that is why many of us are teachers. When we choose teaching as our life project, after all, we are creating identities for ourselves. John Dewey wrote once that "the self is not something ready-made, but something in continuous formation through choice of action"

(1966, p. 351). And then he connected the quality of selfhood with the interest taken in certain things, the desire to relate, to grasp, to *be*. Not only are we inventing ourselves by means of the choices we make with regard to our teaching; we are trying to devise situations in which young persons can authentically form themselves through meaningful choosing, through becoming different, through learning to learn. When I associate this process (which I also try to nurture) with what Dewey called "interest," I cannot but think of present-day articulations of what is needed in the schools. Some of us talk about school restructuring, others about school renewal. When we ponder what ought to be done in cities like this one, most of us think in terms of small schools, of coalitions and collaborations and communities.

There is stress, among those who speak of renewal, on "active learning," on what Deborah Meier calls "habits of mind" and "the power of ideas" (1995). Mike Rose, who has just written a book called *Possible Lives,* talks about what young people *can* do, about their potential for what Eleanor Duckworth describes as the having of "wonderful ideas" (1996). And, yes, there is talk—as there must be—about the construction of meanings and about conversation and story-telling and image-making. I am pleased to say that in Deborah Meier's new book, *The Power of Their Ideas* (1995), there is talk of opening spaces for the exercise of imagination by teachers as well as those they teach. Paulo Freire, the great Brazilian educator, talks in his new book called *Pedagogy of Hope* about the importance of imagination in anticipating "the lovelier world" to which we try to move our students to aspire (1997). Vivian Gussin Paley, in her book *Kwanzaa and Me,* writes about the importance of stories—about her "journey into black and white" which, like any other self-defining region, "must always involve storytelling, the children's, mine, and that of all the interested parties I meet along the way" (1995, p. 9).

I could go on with other books that focus upon possible schools as well as possible lives, but the point I want to make has to do with the relationship between these books and the movement they are representing and the arguments we are trying to devise on the focal significance of the arts and the aesthetic in public education. I want to say that the values we have espoused and explored here at Lincoln Center Institute are very like the values being pursued by the greatest school reformers and restructurers today: Linda Darling-Hammond, Theodore Sizer, Robert Moses with his work in algebra, Michelle Fine in her efforts to disclose the long-silenced voices in our schools, my friend Bill Ayers in the work he is doing with the so-called Chicago Reform, James Comer at Yale, Gloria Ladson Billings, Sara Lawrence-Lightfoot, Courtney Cazden, Herbert Kohl, Jonathan Kozol—

I could go on and on. I am not suggesting that all of them are including an emphasis on the arts and humanities in their writing, but I am suggesting that the efforts they are making to remake and renew public schools are, in numerous ways, of a piece with what we are trying to do at the Institute.

All of us, in one way or another, are recognizing the narrowness of a public discussion that concentrates on declining standards, lack of discipline, sexual practices, drugs, ignoring of the basics. It is miseducative to focus on measures of achievement and the models of effectiveness that preoccupy so many critics. Yes, of course, we have to recognize the social issues, the economic changes, the erosion of families and neighborhoods, the violence, the tawdriness, the vulgarity, the impact of the media. But we also have to attend to the possibilities in new ways of teaching, new ways of creating environments in classrooms, new ways of developing the sense of agency in children—and, yes, the sense of hope for something beyond what *is*. And that is where the efforts of the Institute overlap and relate to the efforts to remake schools, to alter testing practice, to rethink accountability, to equalize resources, to enable children to break through what they experience as the fixed frames of their lives.

Again, as we discover our own voices for convincing others about the enormous importance of art experiences for learning as well as being in the world, we need to go back as often as we can to recapture moments of awakening here at the Institute. We have often said that one of the great values the Institute provides for us is to discover what it feels like to learn, to learn something heretofore undiscovered, to learn something new. There are those who say that to engage with the arts is, very often, to recapture a lost spontaneity. That means, in one sense, to recapture the feeling of wonder at the strange, at the impinging world around—an attitude of questioning so soon covered over by commonsense acceptances, by discrete pieces of information, by all the ways of being immersed in the ordinary and the everyday. I have spoken before about a memory so many share: the memory of reading with a flashlight under the sheet when young. The more we thought of it as a guilty secret, the more momentous an experience it became. But it was at moments like that that I, at least, began to suspect how complicated the world was, how much I had to figure out if I were ever to grow up, how many questions there were, how much there was to learn. Sex was only one part of it; there were all the ways of being a wanderer, a stranger, a runaway—like Huck Finn and so many others, like Albert Camus' Meursault later on. There were all the puzzlements of growing up and choosing a career, especially if you were a little girl torn between becoming an opera singer or Amelia Earhart or Florence Nightingale or a version of Jo in *Little*

Women or (if the Gods really smiled) a movie star. I could say something similar about involvements with all the arts—about the ways in which they opened up an alternative reality, the ways in which they filled the empty places in experience, the ways in which they highlighted the mystery of what I did not know, the ways in which they moved me to pose the questions, the concrete questions in which learning (I am sure) begins.

Think of what an informed listening to jazz masters can mean: the opening to the great stories of Charlie Parker, of Miles Davis, the kind of experience exemplified for me by an image of a little boy looking at Wynton Marsalis playing a trumpet, looking up with a rapt expression on his face as all sorts of roads opened before him toward still unknown rhythms and riffs, toward ways of being. (I could feel him wondering what you had to learn to *be* Marsalis, to play Marsalis.) Think of finding out how to listen to the story of Orpheus and let the passages in that story pervade and make patterns in experience. Suddenly the fear of darkness takes on a shape; suddenly you feel your own power to say how it means to lose a wife that way— to pursue, to be deceived, to regain. What do you see? How does it mean to you? Of what does it remind you? Is there a story you want to tell, a tune you want to hum? That is what we teachers ask if we are good enough, if we have regard both for the child and the outreach of the art form. That is what it means to construct meaning, to make a world.

I am not talking of the arts as motivation, nor am I justifying experiences with the arts as means to the end of learning to read or to do math or to grasp the renderings of history. They may on occasion work that way, but my concern is with the ways in which informed encounters with art forms— preferably by means of initiation into the language of each form (as in the workshops here)—affect our being in the world. I shared my own experience with *True West* last time; I began to do so with regard to the novel *The English Patient, The Winter's Tale, The Tempest,* Edward Hopper's paintings, Jacob Lawrence's *Migration* series (at the Museum of Modern Art this past spring), *Love! Valour! Compassion!, Arcadia, The Postman,* Robert Wilson's *Hamlet,* Mahler's Eighth—I could go on, not to suggest that everyone must compile the same list but to say once more the ways in which each engagement, each moment of attending, each moment of careful noticing opens new perspectives for me, reveals new possibilities for living and being. And this is why I believe the arts and occasions for participation in a variety of art forms are so necessary to a fully lived life. And it is why I believe that denial of the arts—through budget cuts or narrow-mindedness or one-dimensionality of vision—represents a violation of children, a deprivation of the young.

When I speak of the young, I cannot but think of the diverse young in our schools, and, at once, I cannot but think of the disservice done many of them by what is often understood as multiculturalism. The cruelest thing we can do under such a rubric is to categorize young people, to know them by their category, whether we call it "Asian," "Hispanic, "African American." Some of you may recall Anna Deveare Smith's play, *Fires in the Mirror* (1993), her orchestration of voices responding to the riot in Crown Heights not too many years ago. She spoke about the "tension of identity" (p. xxxiv) in our country, how (on the surface) we see Crown Heights as a picture in Black and White. Looked at more closely, however, "One sees motion, and one hears multiple symphonies. The Black people didn't all come from one place, and neither do the Hasidim" (p. xxxvi). Like many of us, she argued against stereotypes, clichés. I would point out that the most dependable way of dealing with the problem is to treat what are conceived of as works of arts in other cultures as works of art, not cultural artifacts. I should like to see, for instance, the Haitian fairy tale *Owl in Love* made accessible everywhere as a possibility for experience, to be interpreted by those who hear (as a Mozart concerto is interpreted) against each one's lived life. These should not be anthropological experiences; they should be occasions for listening to a blue guitar, to imagination working in novel ways with materials not ordinarily well known. If listeners or spectators are enabled to hear more or see more in their own experiences, if (again) there are new perspectives to be opened, new visions to be had—that should be enough, and that should create an occasion for empathy, for imagining (as Cynthia Ozick writes) "the familiar heart of the stranger." Everything depends on metaphor, on attentive engagement with the arts if, again, we are to bring into being a community.

Last, I hope that, as we argue increasingly for a centrality of the arts in schools (discouragement despite) and link it to the arguments for school renewal, our voices will join those demanding continuing support of the arts and the humanities, through the endowments—if it is not too late, or even if it currently is. Why the arts rather than B-2 bombers, rather than marching bands at the Pentagon, rather than doing away with the budget deficit? Why the arts rather than submergence of everything into the conventional, the blandly acceptable, if not consumer goods? Each of us has to answer for herself or himself, because this is a moment of crisis in the arts, and we cannot leave Lincoln Center Institute with nothing to say.

I would end, again, with a poem called "Delta" by Adrienne Rich, displayed in the subway as one of the "Poetry in Motion" pieces:

If you have taken this rubble for my past
raking through it for fragments you could sell
know that I long ago moved on
deeper into the heart of the matter

If you think you can grasp me, think again:
my story flows in more than one direction
a delta springing from the riverbed
with its five fingers spread.
                                    (1989, p. 32)

You see, there is no stopping. Again, it is time to begin.

The Power of Incompleteness

(1997)

Mary-Louise Parker, interviewed by Sylviane Gold in Sunday's *New York Times* about her starring role in Paula Vogel's *How I Learned to Drive,* said about doing theater that "It's never completely complete. It can always be improved upon." Then, a little later: "It's still growing, it's evolving, it's getting better.... I'm not there yet; I'm *closer*" (Gold, 1997, July 13, p. 5). Not only was she saying something deeply important about art and artistry. What she said holds profound relevance for what we call "active learning" and feeds into our arguments for aesthetic education in the schools.

In my two previous talks, I put great emphasis upon the centrality of imagination—where encounters with the several arts are concerned, where sense-making in general is concerned. My point has been the connection between imagination and the opening of new perspectives, new possibilities in experience. There are, clearly, multiple ways of understanding what imagination signifies. "If American civilization does not eventuate in an imaginative formulation of itself, if it merely rearranges the figures already named and placed—in playing an inherited European game—that fact is itself the measure of the culture we have achieved" (Dewey, 1931, pp. 10–11). Other modes of talking about imagination have focused on the idea that the use of imagination (thinking in terms of what might be, what ought to be) makes people realize that experience holds far more than ever can be predicted. Also, it opens up a world of meanings; indeed, by means of the making of metaphors, imagination can reorient consciousness through its disclosure of patterns, relationships, shadows and lights and slivers of sound that are wholly unexpected, "new" in some wonderful fashion. Exercising imagination, the individual—looking into the faces of those around in what Keats called a "wild surmise"—is liable to come awake as seldom before, to call out, "I see, I hear, I feel, I *know.*"

This happens, however, mainly when there has been a sense of incompleteness, of something not yet attained. Think again of Mary-Louise Parker and so many of the teaching artists who have worked with us here. There has repeatedly been the recognition that a play, let us say, is always in the making in the minds of those involved. It seems evident enough that *Krapp's Last Tape* can never reach a conclusion for the actor: there are always new intonations, new facial expressions, new modes of shuffling or staggering or pacing, as more and more meanings unfold. If any of you were in a workshop concentrating on the Beckett piece, you remain aware that, no matter how often, how deeply you tried to plunge, you could never entirely realize the potential in that strange duet of tape and old man's voice: the cut of memory, the instants of poetry, the almost inexpressible desolation. And yet it was through the trying and the reaching that you felt yourself enter into the enactment, pour in your energy, bring it to life in your own experience. And, having brought it to life, many of you discovered dimensions of your own lived life, past and present, that you had never known.

Some of you can recall the encounter (almost a confrontation) with the flamenco dance, that startling interweaving of rhythm, movement, wailing song, swirling skirts, stamping feet, embodying—what?—passion and jealousy and flaunting and teasing and flirting and loving. Surely, you thought that if you could see it several times, having learned something about the flamenco tradition and its roots in Spanish culture, folk dance, ritual, and the rest, you would inevitably see more and more. We all learn, by means of aesthetic education, that the more we know, the more we explore, the more we see and hear and feel. If we can physicalize what we are learning, enter in it as embodied consciousnesses, there is even more to apprehend. Those of us who worked to capture the rhythm, the heel movements, the gestures of the fingers, were able to experience the dance as more than a spectacle, more than an acting out of a tradition. Certainly, that encounter went beyond the purely cognitive. What has been called the kinaesthetic intelligence was awakened, and the move beyond knowing to understanding had to be considerable. The same thing may be said about the Japanese drummers, with their remarkable choreography, their tapping of so many traditions, their almost infinite variety of rhythms (yes, and melodies) which pushed back accustomed frequencies and made some feel they were landing on a kind of auditory Mars. We discovered once more the difference between aesthetic education and the so-called art appreciation of old. There is no way most of us can envisage a distanced contemplation of the hues and angles of the dance, the largely formal elements that, for some, add up to flamenco. Nor can the disinterest that once was supposed to characterize the aesthetic attitude help us unconceal what is there for us, what is happening on the stage. We learn here to be participant and to participate against the consciousness and memory of our own lived lives, our own lived movements and love affairs (perhaps) and gender preoccupations and dreams. Doing so, reflecting on our doing so, asking ourselves what we expect from what are called works of art and what happens when we make them ours, we cannot but be transformed.

In my workshop, "Literature as Art," we read two novels that hardly seem to belong together in the same frame. They were Virginia Woolf's *To The Lighthouse* (1990) and Toni Morrison's *Sula* (1974). They are both, it is true, focally concerned with women; they both probe the happinesses and despairs of family life; they both are much affected by the accounts of context—academic, social, and class differences in one case; racial and economic in the other. I have spoken before about the inexhaustibility of works of art, and we certainly found, most of us, that we had had no idea what could be revealed each time we read those novels (and most of us had read them before). More than that, there was the dialogical relation that was formed as we talked about sections of each novel and lent each one our lives. We thought about writing our narratives as well and about the connection between our shaping our own life stories and these fictional shapings that made the "as-if" lives somehow more intelligible than our own. Then Ramona King came and helped us, as she said, "physicalize" certain parts of *Sula*, taking off from the section in which Sula, swinging a little boy named Chicken Little around by the hands, suddenly loses hold of his hands and (along with her friend Nel) watches him disappear beneath the surface of the nearby river—never floating to the top again. Ramona had us enact and, in some sense choreograph, what it meant to look, to stare in the realization that one should have intervened, could have intervened, and did not. The straining, the creation of bodily images, the putting on of blank and, at once, preoccupied expressions: all these inserted new meanings into the scene as each of us had constructed it. And there was a way in which the involvement with that scene led to a weaving and a meshing of most people's experiences of retreating, ignoring, being indifferent, refusing responsibility, and a reflection on what such phenomena signified for the rest of one's life. There was no evasion when it came to the context. It was clear enough that the characters in *Sula* live in a fearfully oppressive, racist society that deprives most of its inhabitants of the choices the privileged have at hand. Moreover, the people in that society look at God and death with a kind of vital expectation and resignation, even as they mouth their refusals to submit.

Treated as a document, something *not* a work of imagination, a work of art, *Sula* might become one of many social scientific documents on the fate of children in largely African American Midwestern towns. Or it might become a kind of case history, or an account of a pariah. We believe here at the Institute that it is crucially important to become as familiar as we conceivably can with the distinctive languages or the forms of art. This is a time when the questions regarding the arts are innumerable. There are many artists whose very works pose questions about the meaning of art: Nabokov, for instance, Magritte, John Cage. As I view it, the study of aesthetics actually begins with the questions we pose with respect to experiences we have had. What accounts for the feeling of transcendence some of us have in listening to the *Ode to Joy* or a Bach cantata? How, given the horror of a Greek tragedy like *Medea,* can we still feel in some manner energized, awake, renewed after engaging with it? What about the influence of Hollywood and the use of theatrical and special effects by individual artists to create what are called "fixed hallucinations"? Some of these were exhibited at the Whitney Museum's Biennial Exhibition this year along with Chris Burden's Pizza City and a representation of rooms in a mental hospital and a pile of pink bubble gum out of which visitors could sculpt their own shapes. How does it mean? How does it mean still to resonate to works like *Heart of Darkness* which we know are racist and colonialist—and which still have profound effects on our minds? What is the importance of the arts? How important is the mystery? Questions like these are what keep many of us alive and alert, uneasy, reaching for answers, hoping to know, realizing we can never know for sure. And they are the kinds of questions that challenge people to wonder, to learn to learn, so long as they are authentic questions provoked by concrete experiences with actual works of art.

What is central here at the Institute is the experience; but, at once, we are fully aware that the experience involves the presence of an aesthetic object, that it has something to do with the activity of feeling ourselves into aesthetic objects—paintings, dance performances, works of music, and the rest. Dewey talked always about the rhythm marking the interaction of live creatures with their surroundings, and he believed that the function of art is consciously to restore "the union of sense, need, impulse and action characteristic of the live creature" (1980). An occurrence like that, said Dewey in *Art as Experience,* is integrated and consummated in *"an* experience," the distinguishing mark of the aesthetic. Maurice Merleau-Ponty carried this somewhat further when he talked about the body as the field of perception and action and then went on to describe a movement from what we directly

perceive (a poplar tree, a child's face, the side of a mountain) further and
further outward to a totality, to the lived-in world itself (1962/1967). What
these thinkers have in common with one another and many other contemporary explorers of the arts is their interest in engagement with art objects
from lived vantage points. They are interested, as we are, in opening to new
possibilities of perception and imagination, in enabling the several arts—
when reflected on—to radiate through human experience, enabling persons
to live more intensely and with more eagerness and awareness in the always-
changing world.

The critic Denis Donoghue asks:

> Wouldn't it be better if the artistic impulse were fulfilled rather than humili-
> ated in the ordinary run of daily life; if our social arrangements were to take
> into account not only justice but beauty? The philosopher John Dewey once
> imagined a time when 'the collective life that was manifested in war, worship
> and the forum knew no division between what was characteristic of these
> places and operations, and the arts that brought colour, grace, and dignity into
> them.' According to such a vision, the arts didn't exist as separate interests,
> the spoils of power, money, and leisure, but as enhancements, indistinguish-
> able from the ordinary life they adorned. (1983, p. 11)

Dewey knew, as Donoghue knows, that—for this to happen—people have
to be knowledgeable about the arts and imaginative enough to explore new
avenues of perception, feeling, and thought. He undoubtedly also knew that
there would always be, there would have to be, a certain mystery associated
with the arts, if the arts were not to be commodified, not treated as the
sources of problems to be cleared up. To remove their mystery is to tame
the arts, to eliminate the tension that always exists between the arts and ordinary, conventional life. Most seriously of all, it is to remove their interrog-
ative power—that which springs from their persistent incompleteness, from
the questions to which they must give rise. I appreciate Donoghue's reminding us that the arts may be useless in the sense that they cannot cure
toothaches, but in another way they are momentous "because they provide
for spaces in which we can live in total freedom. Think of it as a page. The
main text is central, it is the text of need, of food and shelter, of daily preoccupations and jobs, keeping things going. This text is negotiated mostly
by convention, routine, habit, duty, we have very little choice in it. So long
as we are in this text, we merely coincide with our ordinary selves. If the
entire page were taken up with the text, we would have to live according to
its conventional rhythms, even in our leisure hours. . . . The arts are on the
margin, and it doesn't bother me to say that they are marginal. . . . It's enough

that the arts have a special care for those feelings and intuitions which otherwise are crowded out in our works and days. With the arts, people can make a space for themselves, and fill it with intimations of freedom and presence" (p. 129).

What I think we are trying to do at the Institute is to empower teachers to make the kinds of spaces for themselves where they can act on *their* freedom and choose themselves and their projects in response to what they see happening in the world. I always want to imagine teachers in quest, as Mary-Louise Parker is in quest—and, in addition, in quest of wider landscapes, wider visions of what makes sense, what ought to be. I would like to imagine them in a collaborative search with their students, even as they work to coach them in learning what they need to learn to keep moving on their way. It is a matter of posing questions on both sides and of loving the questions that merge with one another, questions about living in the world and creating communities and collectivities, caring for each other, making each other feel worthwhile. I would insist that it takes imagination to think this way, to pursue purposes in this way. I was interested in reading Theodore Sizer the other day, arguing against mindlessness and statistical thinking in education and teacher education, arguing for "intellectual places—yeasty, imaginative, self-consciously critical, balanced. Out of such places will the practical ideas for serious school reform arise, and in such places will talented prospective teachers choose to enroll." And when he speaks of school reform, he again talks of the need for teacher educators and educators in general to engage "more imaginatively, thoughtfully, and resourcefully" in the task of building a modern educational system.

Spaces, presences, awareness, and the life of imagination: these are the wonders of our Institute, and these are what hold the promise of nurturing humane and alive education, even in these times. We are marvelously incomplete. We move. I choose to end (or perhaps begin) with some words by the poet Mark Strand:

> *"Keeping Things Whole"*
>
> *In a field*
> *I am the absence*
> *of field.*
> *This is*
> *always the case.*
> *Wherever I am*
> *I am what is missing.*

When I walk
I part the air
and always
the air moves in
to fill the spaces
where my body's been.

We all have reasons
for moving.
I move
to keep things whole.

                                          (1980, p. 10)

So much is up to you: the keeping things whole; the envisioning possibility; the passion—the reflective passion—for the arts. And the awakening of children.

Partnerships and the Search for a Common Language

(1998)

Much has changed since our beginnings, when we were bound to argue against the neglect of the arts in education, the belief that they nurtured only affective and intuitive capacities, and the widely held conviction that they were frivolous subjects, fringe subjects, irrelevant in a competency-based school. They appeared to have little or anything to do, in fact, with the obligation to educate the young (often called "human resources") for an emerging technological society, one committed to gaining military as well as economic primacy in the world.

In this day of arts partnerships and a range of reform movements, the arts have found a new centrality in educational discussions. More and more frequently, art education is being linked to aesthetic education—or efforts like ours to make possible reflective, discriminating encounters with all the languages of art. Museums, theaters, concert halls, neighbor-art groups: all in various ways are moving into relationships with public schools. Literacy programs are opening to the arts; artists' alliances and other organizations are interested in finding out what they can do in public schools and even, now and then, higher education.

When I think of partnerships, whatever form they take, I cannot think of institutions in collaboration. Rather, I think of individual persons—teachers, artists, arts administrators, art supervisors, parents. Primarily, I think of teachers, because so much depends upon them. From my point of view, teachers have never had so much responsibility where the development of authentic arts programs and practices is concerned. You are the people who have to be the generators of change, significant and humane change.

I have been asked many times lately to speak about a common language, a language that will enable all those involved to communicate with one another without losing "in translation" the concerns, the values, the meanings that define each undertaking, that give it its distinctiveness. That has made me associate to the title of a collection of Adrienne Rich's poetry: *The Dream of a Common Language*. To conceive of it as dream, of course, is to imagine it as something still out of reach. I like to think of those of us participating in this Summer Session as dreamers in Adrienne Rich's sense. Also, I like to think of the multiple activities here as giving rise to dialogues about, to thinking about what a common language might mean. If it is the case, for example, that the languages of art cannot be translated into one another, how would you find a common language that articulates something fundamental to all of them without reducing any one of them to a uniform symbol system? How would you find the kind of language that enables practicing artists to speak with teachers? Administrators to speak with artists? Supervisors, community representatives, parents, immigrants and other newcomers, men and women of different social classes?

In her poem "Transcendental Etude," Adrienne Rich writes, in part:

> *But there come times—perhaps this is one of them—*
> *when we have to take ourselves more seriously or die;*
> *when we have to pull back from the incantations,*
> *rhythms we've moved to thoughtlessly,*
> *and disenthrall ourselves, bestow*
> *ourselves to silence, or a severer listening, cleansed*
> *of oratory, formulas, choruses, laments, static*
> *crowding the wires.*
>
> (1978, pp. 74–75)

In writing this, she was (probably without intention) charging people like us to break with pious talk, bureaucratic talk, media talk, with what Dewey called the "crust of conventionalized and routine consciousness." He was always critical of the routine, the thoughtless, the mechanical, and what he called the "anaesthetic"—the opposite of aesthetic, meaning the banal, the repetitive, the solidified. I do not like to admit it, but I have heard a lot of such language in my years in teacher education. Much of it was linked to the preoccupation with measurement, of course, with quantitative research, the counting or the category-making syndrome. Much of it, I suspect, was a function of bureaucracy. We have all had experiences with the difficulty of talking as *who* we are, in our own voices, to those who view themselves as our superior officers, or in a context of "rule by nobody."

Dewey, in *The Public and Its Problems,* described the superficial plane where so many people formed their opinions and made their judgments. But, he went on to say, our lives reach a deeper level that only art can touch. It is, after all, one of the functions of art to break through the crusts and routine, to awaken us and enhance our being in the world. "Common things," wrote Dewey, "a flower, a gleam of moonlight, the song of a bird, not things rare and remote, are means with which the deeper levels of life are touched so that they spring up as desire and thought. This process is art. Poetry, the drama, the novel, are proofs that the problem of presentation is not insoluble" (1988, pp. 183–184). He meant, of course, the problem of articulating or expressing what may seem incommunicable in ordinary, matter-of-fact prose. "Artists," he went on, "have always been the real purveyors of news, for it is not the outward happening in itself which is new, but the kindling by it of emotion, perception and appreciation" (1988, p. 184). Some of us have discovered, and some of us will discover, that aware encounters with art forms (from either the creative or the appreciative point of view) are what make all sorts of awakenings possible. It is after such moments of awakening, moments of "unconcealment," that we find ourselves noticing flowers, moonlight, bird songs, those common things that touch the deeper levels of life. And, indeed, that is one of our hopes, our ends-in-view here at the Institute. Attending to Limón's *The Winged,* in its particularity, helped to notice what is there to be noticed, we will not only unconceal aspects of the body making shapes in space and time, but the fluid soaring and descending of birds, a magic of movement never suspected before. And perhaps we might hear or imagine the song of a bird resonating on the deeper levels of life.

I have said often that the ability to release imagination makes such occasions more likely and more frequent. Imagination is the ability to look at things as if they could be otherwise—to conjure up the as-if world of the tango, of the interplanetary space of *A Wrinkle in Time,* to realize (through such encounters) that there is more in experience than can be predicted.

"It is through imagination," writes one philosopher, "the realm of pure possibility that we freely make ourselves to be who or what we are, that we creatively and imaginatively become who we are, while in the process preserving the freedom and possibility to be yet otherwise than what we have become and merely are" (Madison, 1988, p. 191). Think what that means for teaching and learning, the suggestion that imagination follows us to reach beyond, to reach—not toward the predictable, but toward the possible. It is as important for those of us who teach as it can be for those we hope will become different by learning to learn.

The idea that the arts silently call out to us that (as Rilke wrote in one of his great poems) we can change our lives, that children's lives may be transformed through engagement with art forms that are accessible to them at different stages, poses a great challenge to the teacher. It is not the incorporation of aesthetic education into the school's curricula that makes the significant difference. It is the teachers who make the difference: their own cherishing of experiences with the arts, their own reflections on the way particular encounters have opened vistas, revealed alternative ways of living and being, exposed some of the ultimate mysteries. (The concluding moments of Ionesco's *The Chairs* come back to me. They come after that hectic assembling of chairs on the stage, chairs which turn out to be empty. Suddenly a bright light comes on at the back of the stage, so bright that members of the audience cover their eyes and rear back in their seats. Something has been disclosed, something the audience is not sure it wants to know. And yet, at the end, we are moved to say to ourselves: "I see.")

It is because of the need for a teacher's active engagement, because of the willingness to take risks, to pose the questions, to love the questions, to realize (as James Baldwin said) that the questions are too often covered up by the answers, that I believe partnership must entail face-to-face relationships and the kind of dialogue such relationships make possible. Again I turn to poetry to suggest what this implies—this time Muriel Rukeyser's "Effort at Speech Between Two People." Each verse begins with a variation on "Speak to me. Take my hand. What are you now?" Here is the last verse:

> *What are you now? If we could touch one another,*
> *if these our separate entities could come to grips,*
> *clenched like a Chinese puzzle . . . yesterday*
> *I stood in a crowded street that was live with people,*
> *and no one spoke a word, and the morning shone.*
> *Everyone silent, moving. . . . Take my hand. Speak to me.*
> (1982, p. 10)

Promising as the emergent relations between arts organizations and schools are, coming together in the hope for school renewal and reform, there is always the danger of estrangement, like the feeling of standing in a crowded street with no one to speak to, no one who knows our name.

There has to be talk about the throbbing difficult questions—talk about the meanings of art, the impact of popular culture, the distances that seem to yawn between a theater most of us esteem and the films and concerts young people choose to attend, the videos they buy, the CDs they relish (oftentimes ones of which we have never heard). Remember the youngsters who went to see *Titanic* six, sometimes thirteen times. Recall some of the rap music discs white adolescents buy all over the country. How do we honor what they esteem and at once offer possibilities of what we are convinced may be a heightened, more many-faceted life? How do we open our own imaginations to work we do not care for on first viewing, on first hearing? How important is it for us to "like" what may be an aesthetic experience for others—or described as one? How necessary is it for our students to "like" what we offer? Most important, I believe, is a widening of our grasp, a more intense opening to the world and its multiple offerings, and, at once, a greater ardor with regard to what *we* treasure, what we hope to share.

But what of those teachers who still dread the free fall, the chances they may take as they ponder experiences they have never taken into account before? What of those who still teach to the tests in order to insure predictability, the ones who need to measure in order to justify what they do? What of those who conceive standards as predefined, to be imposed authoritatively from above? What of those immersed in what we call instrumental rationality, seeing themselves as molding the young, treating them as resources for the state, for the business community, for the new technologies, not as existing persons in quest of some significant life—wanting to go beyond having, perhaps, wanting to be?

When we link aesthetic education to conceptions of a different sort of teaching, to what we call school renewal or school reform, I think we have to remember that there are at least three approaches to reform these days, perhaps more. There is the one connected to "Goals 2000: The Educate America Act," centered on increasing general literacy for the sake of readying the new generation for a millennium governed by the new technologies, linked by more and more complicated internets, responding to free market ideologies. There is the one connected to the Christian Right, ostensibly preoccupied with virtue and character education, abstinence, chastity, prayer in schools, school choice, with protection of the young against abortion and homosexuality, the theory of evolution (oftentimes), suspicions of pornography. Then there is the reform that continues the experiential tradition, stemming from Rousseau, Pestalozzi, Emerson, Froebel, moving on to Dewey, Bruner, Gardner, Duckworth, and others familiar to those of you who have kept in touch with that stream in American history running in the direction of personal liberation, awareness, and (in time) a humane, face-to-face community.

I say all this because I believe it so important for us to be informed enough to choose—to recognize what stands in the way of the experience we have had and will have with *The Winged* or Corelli or the ballet, to be clear and articulate about why we feel these moments are valuable. We cannot take for granted a widespread agreement in the educational community on the need for what I call the centrality of imagination. We cannot simply assume that all our colleagues appreciate the wonder of an aesthetic encounter, a bringing a work of art to life, in our experience. I hear too many arguing that the value of such experience is to be found in the contribution it makes to raising standards or improving achievement in mathematics or social studies or even the sciences.

This may be. All of us know how the presence of art activity can alter the atmosphere in a classroom, even in a school. Curiosity and attentiveness are intensified in those involved. We know, too, how significant the sense of oughtness is for an authentic artist—a responsiveness to standards, if you will, to the sense of what might be, what always eludes, what impassions and inspires. We know the sensitivity to manner, to style, to the necessity for rigor that makes possible the wonders created, say, by the Limón dancers. But there remains for me the power of certain works to change our lives, to enable us to feel more, see more, hear more, to make meanings never thought about before. It is not, however, the function of the arts to provide testable knowledge nor to offer answers. It is not the function of the teacher to come into the classroom with reassuring answers or guarantees of any kind. More often than not, novels and great plays confront me with ambiguities, with mysteries, with roads moving off into the darkness, even as they make me feel a consciousness of widened possibility. I think of Toni Morrison's *Jazz* and *Paradise*, of the recent book called *Cold Mountain*, of *As I Lay Dying*, which I am reading again. Great plays come back to me: that wonderful *A Doll's House* production of two years or so ago, *The Beauty Queen of Leenane* (and what does beauty queen mean in that context of an Irish kitchen?), *A View from the Bridge, How I Learned to Drive*, and I remember how deeply each one reached, how they touched upon my consciousness of the human condition—of what I will never fully comprehend. And paintings: Rembrandt's self-portraits, Goya's *Disasters of War*, Picasso's *Guernica*, Monet's Rouen Cathedral changing with each shift of light, meaning differently with every change. And there are Mahler and Bartók, yes, and Phillip Glass, now learning the African *kora*, and Wynton Marsalis, and the recollections of John Cage. Of course more than my cognitive self is involved; they open question after question to my whole being, make me love them as they make me strain in so many directions, make me feel painfully and impatiently alive.

As you learn more and more about noticing what is there to be noticed in the works you encounter and study this summer, as you discover more of what it means to live within the arts for a time, I hope you will feel the responsibility of finding out what it all means for you, how it touches the deeper levels of your own life. So much is up to you, even in this moment of seeming triumph for the arts in education. For some reason I think of Monet again, this time of those lanes bordered with poplar trees, also viewed many times and through many perspectives, opening spaces, new ones for us who have learned to perceive, found out what it means to see. It is a metaphor for today, a kind of metaphor. And that brings me, finally, to Seamus Heaney and a poem called "The Poplar":

> *Wind shakes the big poplar, quicksilvering*
> *The whole tree in a single sweep.*
> *What bright scale fell and left this needle quivering?*
> *What loaded balances have come to grief?*
> (1996, p. 61)

A scale, a needle quivering, refusing balance, refusing stasis. Questions, questions, freedom, and unease. There is much, much for you to do.

Reform, Renewal and the Arts

(Superintendents Day Lecture, 1999)

In this day of what some call educational reform and others educational renewal, attention focuses increasingly on what the public schools can and should be doing. As more and more people enter the conversation, women and men like yourselves—whose professional and personal lives are so focused on teaching and learning—cannot but feel more and more responsibility for choosing yourselves and perhaps redefining yourselves by means of the projects that mark your lives. I am here to talk about the arts and aesthetic education in relation to those projects. I want also to talk about vision, possibility, and membership in an expanding community that is changing day by day. Here at Lincoln Center Institute, there are many of us who—involved as we are in dance, music, literature, theatre, or the visual arts—share what Adrienne Rich called "The Dream of a Common Language." I do not mean only a common language to be used in speaking to one another in the domain of the arts. I mean a way of speaking that enables those of us in partnerships like this to understand and to honor one another, diverse though our backgrounds and perspectives and, yes, obligations appear to be.

Surely we know what she meant. She was calling on all of us to break with esoteric talk or bureaucratic talk, pious talk, media talk, with what John Dewey called "the crust of conventionalized and routine consciousness" (1988, p. 183), no matter what our discipline or specialty.

Dewey was, as many of you know, always critical of the static, the fixed, the banal, the repetitive, and what he sometimes called the anaesthetic—meaning the opposite of aesthetic. In his book on the public, Dewey pointed to the superficial plane in which so many people formed their judgments and went on to say that our lives reach a deeper level that only the arts can touch. For him, it was one of the functions of the arts to break through that "crust of conventionalized and routine consciousness," to awaken us and enhance our sense of being in the world. Common things, he said, "a flower, a gleam of moonlight, the song of a bird, not things rare and remote"—and then he added poetry, drama, the novel, and other works of art—"are means with which the deeper levels of life are touched so that they spring up as desire and thought" (1988, pp. 183–184). Thoughtfulness and desire, I keep saying to myself, remembering all the writers who warn against thoughtlessness and carelessness. And desire—signifying yearning, longing, reaching beyond, striving to be what one is not yet. How, when you think about it, can the questioning that generates learning take place without the desire to become different, to move toward what is not yet?

It is of interest to me that the term "eros" is being used in much of educational writing today, "eros" signifying desire, straining to be, to become. It is interesting also to find so many instances of renewed engagement with Dewey's work: the stress on active learning, collaboration, community, transaction, imagination—the capacity to look at things as if they could be otherwise. Dewey was a visionary, one writer says, a visionary about the here and now, "about the potentiality of the modern world, modern society," yes, and the school. We are eager, here at the Institute, to recapture a consciousness of such potentiality, of the possible as well as the predictable. I often return to Emily Dickinson, writing that "The Possible's slow fuse is lit / By the Imagination" (1960, p. 689). And the imagination, as you surely know, is not only essential to self-expression by means of one or another language of art; it can be released as well through reflective participation in what are thought to be works of art.

Dewey's work has been very influential in our developing an approach to aesthetic education. His *Art as Experience* begins with a chapter called "The Live Creature," and the reader cannot but associate what he said with our notions of the active learner, the making of meaning, the construction of worlds. "The actual work of art," he pointed out, is what the product (painting, sonata, scene from a play, dance performance) "does with and in experience." A wall should not be built around the arts, therefore; they should not be remitted to "a separate realm." He wanted to restore continuity between the intensified experience made possible by engagement with the arts and "everyday events, doings, and sufferings that are . . . recognized to constitute experience" (1980, p. 3).

We had a number of instances of recognized continuity here in the Institute in responses (for all its familiarity) to the rendering of *Romeo and Juliet*, and to the play written for young people called *The Beloved Dearly*. Death in the midst of life, coffins, the sound of weeping, the love of young people for each other, the fragility of the civil order: things become visible that were never visible before; connections appear unexpectedly, the connections, the

patterns that lead to the making of meanings. In our workshops, participants improvise, try out gestures, sketch their own scenes, experiment with
swordplay, summon up memories of crying spells in childhood, move in
unfamiliar ways, seek out modes of rendering darkness and light. There is
no exhausting the poetry, the imagery, the gestural designs in the works at
hand, at least not for those willing to make them objects of their own experience, willing to attend, to grasp them by their own acts of perceiving and
feeling and understanding. Of course there are no neat solutions to the
questions that throb below the surface of *Romeo and Juliet,* for instance:
the questions having to do with adolescent love, with adult hostilities and
interferences, with the role of fatality and the role of chance. They are
questions that keep sounding and resounding; unanswered, perhaps unanswerable, they feed into the ceaseless quest for meaning. They give rise to
wonder, as what is viewed and listened to upon the stage radiates through
experience, as people begin to notice more and more what is there to be
noticed, as they lend what they see and feel before them their own energies, their own lived lives.

I have been describing some of what is involved in what we call aesthetic
education, here offered as a dimension of teacher education or, perhaps,
professional development. It is our belief that experiences like those suggested
may well have a transformative consequence for classroom teaching when
the teachers at the Institute return to their schools before and (we hope) after
visiting artists and performances or exhibitions arrive. Aesthetic education,
as we view it, is a process of empowering diverse persons to engage reflectively and with a degree of passion with particular works of art. It is also,
as I view it, a process of enabling people to release their imaginations, to
ponder alternative ways of being alive and in a world with others, to attend
differently to what surrounds. If we succeed at all in what we try to do here,
the teachers involved and, in time, their students will not only become more
awake to their surroundings. The questions I have been speaking of multiply as the crust of conventionality is broken, and the taken-for-granted
begins to appear differently. We begin noticing the trees in their sudden fullness, the abstract designs the sunlight creates as it glances off the windows
of high-rise buildings, a child abruptly taking center stage in his little canvas carriage, the multiplicity and diversity in the subway car (think of hair
styles, skin colors, baseball caps, T-shirt emblems), the crowds in the street,
the displays of fruit and flowers and pretzels on the sidewalk. Looking at
some of the city paintings or photographs in the present "American Century" exhibit at the Whitney Museum or the photographs, discovering some
of them, uncovering, "unconcealing," as the philosopher says, I see more on

the streets of the city. I go back to Walt Whitman writing about the people coming from around the world to New York in this excerpt from "A Broadway Pageant."

> *For not the envoys nor the tann'd Japanese from his island only,*
> *Lithe and silent the Hindoo appears, the Asiatic continent itself*
> *   appears, the past, the dead,*
> *The murky night-morning of wonder and fable inscrutable,*
> *The envelop'd mysteries, the old and unknown hive-bees,*
> *The north, the sweltering south, eastern Assyria, the Hebrews,*
> *   the ancient of ancients,*
> *Vast desolated cities, the gliding present, all of these and more*
> *   are in the pageant-procession.*
>
> (1982, p. 385)

Here at the Institute, or in one of the programs we try to initiate, we would hope for a professional poet, a city poet, to work with teachers to move them to find words for expressing and communicating what they find in the city crowds, in the subway. Having tried, seeking the right words to communicate—hopefully in metaphor—the complexity of what they feel and see, the learner (a teacher, and later a young student) cannot but read the poem with the eyes of a fellow seeker, someone beginning to treat language as medium, working to find the secret of Whitman's capacity to open new spaces of presentness, new spaces for seeing, new perspectives in which his readers can choose themselves.

Somehow that reminds me of another poet, Philip Levine, starting out in Detroit where he became "hooked" on John Keats, he said once, and going on to New York. In Levine's poem "Salt and Oil," he wrote:

> *[This] . . . is a moment*
> *in the daily life of the world,*
> *a moment that will pass into*
> *the unwritten biography*
> *of your city or my city*
> *unless it is frozen into the fine print*
> *of our eyes.*
>
> (1999, p. 21)

We might recollect the eyes of different young people in and out of schools, sometimes empty eyes, empty of interest or of hope, and we might think what it would signify if they were enabled to make legible the fine print of their eyes, or, to change the image, to make imprints on the world. Levine summons up for me the words of Thoreau saying he never met anyone who was fully awake, of Virginia Woolf talking about a sense of being and of breaking free from the cotton wool of daily life, of Walker Percy saying that, if we are not in search of something, we are likely to be in despair.

I am trying to say that engaged encounters with the several arts, once we are helped to be familiar with the medium involved (paint, sound, the body in motion, language, clay) can set our imagination free, move us into thinking about what might be, what ought to be, what is not yet—move us into transformations and repair. When Dewey spoke about the deeper levels of life and the power of imagination, he spoke also about mastery of technique and the machine, making them serve our human purposes. Of course he knew nothing of cyberspace nor the Internet nor the computer itself, but he knew a great deal about human presentness and connection, even as he knew how important it was that identity is a function of membership, of belonging. Recognizing the testing of imagination that occurs in the computer-dominated realities in which so many of us (including our children) are making our way, I hope we can find connections between participation in the arts and the openings made possible by the arts—and the proliferation of information and images and what are called simulacra. We have all had a remarkable and solemn experience this last weekend with the tragic loss of three young people. Old pictures, films, photographs of all kinds brought back to those of us who can remember what some have called an American family story, a community in part created by television. For those too young to remember, there has been the presentation of a story, a half-familiar myth, perhaps experienced as another television fiction, a created tragedy like that of the "people's princess," some kind of lesson about the glory and the danger of "pushing the envelope," of over-reaching. And I want to find ways of transcending what is now a kind of information by confronting the young with, say, Greek tragedies, if I can, *Moby-Dick,* "The Grand Inquisitor," a series of films, a play like *Death of a Salesman* or *The Iceman Cometh* or Ibsen's *The Master Builder* or *The Wild Duck* and paintings like those of Rembrandt and Vermeer and those heart-shaking Van Goghs at the Metropolitan Museum of Art. I want one world, one community to open into the other; I hope, with the help of people like you, to understand and resist those the critic Denis Donoghue calls the "zealots of explanation" and the "cherishing bureaucracy." He seems to have in mind those who speak possessively in esoteric language about the several arts, who are unsympathetic about the very idea of multiple interpretations and multiple realities. I am well aware, as you must be, that—although most art forms can be opened to people over time—there are differences when it comes to cultural membership, social class, gender, and so on. We cannot expect certain works that may be vitally important to us (Robert Wilson's one-act, one-man rendering of *Hamlet,* say, the opera *Wozzeck,* some of the extreme cases of atonal music, certain novels, even certain of the late plays of Shakespeare) to be vital to everyone. What is important is the making accessible and the effort to engage diverse persons in exploration of different media and, in time, to reflected-on instances of art forms created from that media, representing diverse cultures, symbol systems once given no regard by upholders of the western tradition, of what we have come to call the canon.

What is important is the attention paid to standards. I think, on the one hand, of the disagreements about what the standards ought to be, now that various states are defining their own standards across the board. And I think of the harm that can be done if we focus primarily on uniform standards for all experiences with the arts. For me, the standards that are most meaningful are those we become conscious of when we work with the teaching artists here, faithful to their various art forms, each one presenting himself or herself as (to use Hannah Arendt's term) the best he or she can possibly be. Arendt spoke much of excellence; she holds that we discover excellence when people—in the presence of others—strive for the best way of performing or writing or speaking or painting, with a consciousness of those others, choosing themselves as the best they can conceivably be. I not only think of the example of teaching artists in the workshops here. I think of Wynton Marsalis and that wonderful actress who brings the play *Wit* to life and of Zoe Caldwell rendering the play about Maria Callas (*Master Class*) into something tremulous, impassioned, deeply troubling—and into something that might well change one's life. In my view, standards become meaningful when human beings choose voluntarily to live up to a norm, if you like, if they are freed to engage in dialogue about what they signify. I want to link the idea of standards to the sense of obligatoriness, responding (as Martin Buber would say) to the summons of a norm. And that should draw our attention back to the possibility of a community-in-the-making, perhaps in many ways a moral as well as an interpretive, an aesthetic community.

That takes me to my last point, which I can only touch upon briefly: your participation in the cultural and artistic and critical community, wherever you are. The *New York Times* and a number of the journals many of us read (*The New Yorker, The Atlantic Monthly, Newsweek*) have presented us with a variety of controversies regarding certain works of art—primarily,

I suppose, in theater and film (although there were public arguments about Jackson Pollock's work and Anselm Kiefer's painting, even Picasso's). There is a play called *Art*, in fact, that suggests some of the endless questions about the meaning of art, the high cost of some exemplars, the meaning great paintings and musical pieces have or ought to have in our lives. Some of you recall the disagreements about *Life Is Beautiful*. Some of you have taken note of the controversy greeting Spike Lee's *Summer of Sam*, and you have probably read some of the differences of opinion on Stanley Kubrick's *Eyes Wide Shut*. I am sure you have other memories about Robert Mapplethorpe, Karen Finley, and others who lost the support of the National Endowment for the Arts because their works were called pornographic, more likely because they offended what was then called the moral majority.

I believe that many of you ought to take responsibility as members of an expanding community—surely not to censor, not to bring into being a new kind of witch burning, but to take positions when witches are being burned, to ponder the relationships between illusion and reality (issues raised in the responses to Spike Lee) or the issues raised by recent explorations of sexuality and what it implies for us as educators. We all need to participate in this aspect of the cultural conversation, and to understand the distinction between this and what educators mean when they refer to eros.

PART IV

CULTURAL DIVERSITY
AND COMMUNITY

A esthetic encounters with works of art are situated encounters. That means that the perceivers of a given work of art apprehend that work in the light of their backgrounds, biographies, and experiences. We have to presume a multiplicity of perspectives, a plurality of interpretations. Clearly, this opens aesthetic educators to the likelihood of more than one interpretation of a poem, a dance, a play, a musical piece. At once, the growing diversity in the New York, and other public, schools continues to remind us that we cannot, in the works of art we explore, confine ourselves to what is called the western "canon." In consequence, we have tried to vary our offerings to include works from a range of other cultures (African, Indian, Japanese, Caribbean). Including once unfamiliar musical works and dance performances, for example, we have opened new worlds, new perspectives to ourselves, as well as to the teachers who attend our institutes. At the same time, we have tried to keep alive our commitments to what we have loved within our own traditions. Doing so, the community we keep forming by means of our Institute has opened richer and richer dialogues, and our increasingly diverse numbers have found as many notes of connections as they have new possibilities. "Multiculturalism," therefore, has become more and more multifaceted, more and more open to new interpretations, new ways of viewing works of art, new ways of being in the world.

The Artistic-Aesthetic Curriculum: Leaving Imprints on the Changing Face of the World

(1993)

You have undoubtedly heard me, over the years, exploring some of the meaning of "art," of "aesthetic education," and you are as aware as I that the search can never be complete. There are at hand copies of the two lectures I gave this summer to both new and returning participants; you will find there a continuing effort to communicate a sense of what informed encounters with the several arts can make possible for people young and old, whoever they are. You will notice that I started with an account of the photography exhibition at the Metropolitan Museum of Art, "The Waking Dream." Part of what I said was, as always, an account of my personal response to what I saw on the several occasions I visited the exhibition. Part of it was an attempt to use the show and the experiences it provoked as a kind of metaphor for the awakenings, the unexpected disclosures, the new vistas made possible by what happens and what can happen during the days spent at Lincoln Center Institute. And, yes, I used it all as a lead-in to a discussion of imagination (which I should like to pursue a little further today), the cognitive capacity which has been so overlooked or ignored or denied by both the political leaders and the educational leaders working to define "Goals 2000" and the various "outcomes" considered necessary for this country's economic and technological growth.

Precisely what is that capacity? Why do so-called "postmodern" thinkers give the imagination a centrality when they talk about the ways in which we become involved with our worlds? Why is it overlooked, either deliberately or unthinkingly, by those expressing interest in the "active learner," in enhanced literacy on every level? Is there not some sense in which the inventiveness, the innovativeness presumably sought in a technological society are related to imagination? Why is the activation of imagination (*your* imagination, your colleagues', your students') so crucial in the realization of works of art? If it is indeed the case that an aesthetic experience requires aware participation on the part of the perceiver, the listener, the reader, how can there be such participation without the ability to bring an "as-if" into being, to look through the windows of the actual to what might be and what ought to be?

Always obsessive to some degree about the importance of both imagination and perception, I have perhaps relied too much upon the poets and writers I have loved particularly in the course of my life: Stevens writing about the "blue guitar" and about those rationalists donning sombreros, once they took the risk of looking at "the ellipse of the half-moon"; Bishop writing about inventing the new day, the new year; Woolf yearning for shocks of awareness, for the "moments of being" that depended on disentangling herself from the life of habit, "the cotton wool of daily life"; Walker Percy's "moviegoer" talking about freeing himself from immersion in everydayness and embarking on a "search," a search for new possibilities—about being "on to something," saying that not to be on to something meant being in despair. Always, there is the linking of imagination to the opening of possibility. I have quoted Emily Dickinson: "The Possible's slow fuse is lit / By the Imagination" (1960, p. 689). Can there be any teacher, especially in these days, who can read that without summoning up the faces of apathetic young people, hopeless young people, boys and girls afflicted with a feeling of futility that may well be the worst enemy of education today?

To speak of imagination in relation to encounters with the arts is not to talk of fantasy or castles in the air or false hopes. As I view it (and I know you may not see it in the same way), imagination is what enables us to enter into the created world of, yes, *Charlotte's Web* and *Winnie the Pooh* and *Don Juan*, and Toni Morrison's *The Bluest Eye*, and Shakespeare's *Much Ado About Nothing*, and George Eliot's *Middlemarch*, and Marquez's *Love in the Time of Cholera*, and Puig's *Kiss of the Spider Woman* as novel, film, or musical play. Doing so, we find ourselves creating new patterns, finding new connections in our experience. I quoted Dewey a few days ago on the ways in which art clarifies and concentrates the meanings of things ordinarily dumb and inchoate, and the ways in which works of art can keep alive "the power to experience the common world in its fullness." This would not happen, I am sure, if it were not for the ability to pull aside the curtains of habit, automatism, banality, so that alternative possibilities can be perceived. And it is imagination that makes this kind of experience attainable for people—this break with literalism, this summoning up of the "as-if," the "not yet," the "might be." I think back in my own history and try to recapture what all this has meant and still means for me: the problem of alienation and emancipation in some manner enhanced by my lending Hawthorne's Hester Prynne my life; the matter of the "soul's slavery" generating all sorts of questions after reading *The Awakening;* the new experiences created by those scenes in the Hebrides in *To the Lighthouse;* the startling and renewed vision of Stravinsky's *The Firebird* in the Harlem Dance Theater's production of the ballet; the peculiar realization made palpable by Pecola's wanting to look like Shirley Temple in *The Bluest Eye* and the remembered girl-child wanting the same thing in Tillie Olsen's "I Stand Here Ironing"; the ideas of invisibility and nobodiness etched in my consciousness by James Baldwin and Ralph Ellison; the alternatives to my standard views of time and history discovered in *A Hundred Years of Solitude.* I could go on and on trying to recapture the ways in which encounters with art forms opened windows in experience for a little girl from Brooklyn, and then for a bigger girl continually (although indirectly) taught to accept things as they were and make the best of them. Indeed, I am not sure even now that thinking of that sort may partially explain why the arts are treated as frivolities and thrust, as they so frequently are these days, quite aside in our schools.

In any case, I want to urge you to go back in your own life narratives and try to recover those moments when imagination, released through certain encounters with the arts, opened worlds for you, disclosed new vistas (not always pleasant ones, I grant), helped you look at things as if they could be otherwise. And, yes, helped you play somehow with language, with the thought of carnival, with having (as James Joyce once said) "two thinks at a time." Then, I believe, you might ask yourself how you actually understand what "art" is and what "aesthetic" means. There is no final, authoritative definition of either, I would remind you; but it remains important, if you are to make your own enthusiasm and your own understanding contagious, for you to be as self-reflective here as you are asked to be with regard to other disciplines. Again, do you cherish the arts because they seem to you to bring you in touch with something transcendent, even some universal value, something that moves you to aspire, to strain upwards, beyond yourself? (When I say that, I think of *King Lear,* of Beethoven's Ninth Symphony, of Verdi's *Requiem,* of Martha Graham's *Night Journey,* of the Sistine Chapel, of certain spirituals.) Is this what you hope for for your students— why you wish to initiate them into something grand and lustrous, beyond the everyday? Or do you value art forms because they express (or embody) the feelings and perceptions of certain peculiarly sensitive and observant women and men—Wordsworth, say, Mary Cassatt, Toni Morrison, Nikki Giovanni, Emily Dickinson, Tennessee Williams, Vincent Van Gogh—who saw and heard more, felt more acutely, were more in touch than ordinary folks like thee and me? Or is it the marvelous perfection of certain magically wrought forms—a Mozart symphony, a Yeats poem, a Joyce novel, Flaubert's *Madame Bovary,* T. S. Eliot's *Four Quartets,* Mark Rothko's mysterious washes opening to unimaginable depths?

Or do you value the art experiences you have had here and in other places because of what they have signified for your own sense of the world around, your own pursuits of meaning? Do you take what we think of as a "participatory" approach to the arts, one based on the belief that the active participation of the perceiver or reader or listener is required for the completion of the artistic process, and that this completion is essential for the aesthetic effect? When you, for example, encounter a work as presumably remote in space and time as Molière's *Don Juan,* according to this view, you will not be likely to have a full experience with it if you take a disinterested, distanced view. Here, too, connections have to be found, can be found, to your own lived experience and your own choices and your own activities. This view (sometimes called "pragmatic") is closely related to what is called the "reader response" theory in the study of literature. The emphasis here is on the qualities of the play and on the lived experience of those who attend to it and work to make it, in its enactment, an object of their experience—something to be grasped in its detail and its fullness. And grasped by the total person, not by a particular subjective cast of mind. As you have seen or will soon see, it is difficult to watch Don Juan in what would seem a total amorality without being moved to ponder your own moral choices and the standards governing them, especially at a time when there appear to be no objective standards recognized and acknowledged by all. Our feelings about class and power cannot but be affected, as must our feelings about fidelity and purity and "the war between men and women." In my own case (and I am sure in some of yours), I cannot quite set aside the Mozart opera, nor the Shaw play about Don Juan, the same Don Juan, "in hell." Nor can I set aside the philosopher Kierkegaard writing about the first stage of development being best represented by Don Juan, with his constant flitting, his constant sampling, his refusal to commit himself. He never reaches the "ethical stage," said Kierkegaard, because he cannot gain the "courage to be" (1940). I know this is the Molière version and not Mozart or da Ponte or Shaw or any of the many who rendered noncommittal, irresponsible behavior; but all the other things I have read and heard and seen play into the lived experience I have with this Don Juan, as I work to make it—physically, dialogically, imaginatively, conceptually—an event in the life I live with others. The meaning of the play is not hidden somewhere in the work; it is not predetermined. According to this view, it emerges more and more clearly in the audience involvement or by means of that involvement, and diverse persons achieve what they look upon as meaningful through their particular attentiveness, their willingness to look through the various perspectives the play presents, and against their own lived worlds.

Now there is no requirement for you to take this view of how to render a work of art open to yourself and, in time, to others. You may well think an appreciation has no "right" to appropriate a work in this fashion. You may think that to focus on experience this way is to lose sight of the work of art, glowing there in its own peculiar space, free of the mundane world. You may think that, for all the talk of context, this approach sacrifices the wonder, the glory, even the "sacred" character of the arts. Or that too little is done to bring the appreciator in touch with the creative impulse that burns like a candle in the artist, a candle that may help those coming close to light their own. In the last analysis, it is a choice you have to make as individual and as teacher, struggling to be true to what you know and have encountered in your life, trying at once to communicate to others in a manner that allows them to reach out freely and make Molière's work and Mozart's and Morrison's and, yes, Madonna's authentically and reflectively and critically their own.

One of the reasons for trying to make this clear in your own terms and in accord with your philosophy is that only then will you be able to communicate to colleagues or administrators or school boards the relevance of what we call aesthetic education or its significance for school restructuring and school reform. And, indeed, this may be one of our central responsibilities: to clarify for ourselves and others how what we do here does relate and might relate to what is commonly described as "active learning" and to the emergence of communities in school. Last time, I quoted Dewey on the ways in which works of art that are widely enjoyed in a community are, he said, "marvelous aids in the creation of such a life" (1980). Naturally, we hope (as you yourselves do) that—in your own encounters with others in your schools—you can enable people to recognize that.

All you need to do is picture your life in workshops in previous years and how, through your mutual participation in learning the languages of the various arts and bringing particular works alive, you did indeed bring a community into being. Not only was it one that brought you together with other people, very often very different people, in shared learning and shared creating; it may well have been a community that enabled you to recover a lost spontaneity in yourself—to feel yourself in process of shaping a more distinctive identity for yourself because of your being among and in the presence of others. I have seen this over and over, as participant teachers here have sung in ensembles they created, orchestrated their diverse verses in spirituals or other forms, brought a dramatic scene into existence out of what seemed a discordant variety of voices and improvised gestures, discovered not only how dance movement carves out different designs in space, but how a plurality of movements can be ordered into new patterns—sometimes symmetrical, sometimes not—new relations in space and time.

How, on the various levels at which you teach, can you create the kinds of situations where involvement with the arts not only enables you and your students to combat boredom and banality, but develops among all of you the sense of agency that is most apparent (or so it seems to me) in encounters with the arts? This takes me back, of course, to the participatory approach or to the "reader response" approach. I have in mind the notion that works of art can never be realized by a merely passive attention. There has to be an active, energetic reaching out—so that the noticing we have so often described will take place, so that diverse perspectives can be looked through when it comes to a poem or painting or play, and diverse frequencies can be attended to when it comes to a musical piece. It is with this in mind, of course, that we attach so much importance to the work done with teaching artists—to the moving, and sounding, and rendering that engage you with the actual languages of the arts, with the perceptual landscapes out of which they grow, and with the meanings that can be sedimented upon those perceptual landscapes, the landscapes of pattern and shape and color and sound where our lives began. How can we think of this in connection with the teaching of history, of social studies, or of the interdisciplinary humanities courses we begin to see in the so-called "coalition" schools? How can we show the connection between our attentiveness to the concrete particularities of things in the domains of the arts and the posing of investigative, curious, sometimes impassioned questions that lead to the general descriptions, the overarching explanations of the sciences? How can the problem-solving of the choreographer, of the painter, of any of those who deal with relation, with design, with the shifting shapes of organization, be at once appreciated, participated in, and connect with what it is to "do" math? How can involvement with Hudson River landscapes, and Tuscan landscapes, and British Midlands landscapes, and French impressionist landscapes release visual imagination—and at once provoke questions that lead to doing geography? How can we in public schools play our part in the "blurring of the disciplines," so that aesthetic education becomes resource and provocation, so that the arts become centrally significant even as they open spaces on the "margin" where moments of freedom and presence occur? Here is where your inventiveness—along with that of your teaching artists—comes in. We all have a world to make, in a larger world that does not always understand.

Last time I spoke, I tried to argue for the connection between what we do here and what might happen as we deal with multiculturalism and its multiple demands. I will not repeat again the powerful arguments for paying heed to works thrust consciously or thoughtlessly outside the range of our attention over the years—some of them now regarded as some of the finest human creations in history. I always think of South American literatures, about which I knew so little for so long, about Mexican art over the centuries, about Cambodian dance in its enormous intricacy and symbolic power, about the sculptures of Benin. I could go on; so could any one of you. It seems to me that, if we are to do justice to the works now being brought to our attention, we ought not simply add them to curricula in a kind of categorical way, or with a kind of affirmative action attitude. There is no question that the enrichment and enlargement of the works at hand are necessary and important: children, in so many ways feeling themselves to be strangers, clearly benefit if they find books and plays and other works of art that have to do with people who look like them and act as their families do. But there is more: there is, again, the importance of doing justice to the works from other cultures, of enlarging the experiences of people within our own culture, of making it possible for them to participate well enough in a variety of art forms so as to lend them (as they do more familiar works) their lives. How do we choose? How do we avoid the presumption that all the different art forms of another culture are equally valuable—and, in doing so, imposing another kind of stereotype? The philosopher Charles Taylor addresses "the politics of recognition" in the following passage.

> Indeed, for a culture sufficiently different from our own, we may have only the foggiest idea . . . of in what its valuable contribution might consist. Because, for a sufficiently different culture, the very understanding of what it is to be of worth will be strange and unfamiliar to us. To approach, say, a raga with the presumptions of value implicit in the well-tempered clavier would be forever to miss the point. What has to happen is . . . a "fusion of horizons." We learn to move in a broader horizon, within which what we have formerly taken for granted as the background to valuation can be situated as one

possibility alongside the different background of the formerly unfamiliar culture. The "fusion of horizons" operates through our developing new vocabularies of comparison. (1992, p. 67)

Taylor concludes by saying that we do indeed owe all cultures the presumption that each has something important to say; but, at once we have to try to understand how other cultures make their judgments of worth.

We have to attend to the members of other cultures—to see how they read the materials of their own cultures, and how they interpret the materials of ours. I find myself extraordinarily taken by the African novelist Achebe's reading of Joseph Conrad's *Heart Of Darkness,* because he sees things I never saw. Similarly, Edward Said's reading of Albert Camus' *The Plague* emphasizes the fact that the Arabs who died of plague are, compared with the Europeans in the book, all nameless and faceless. Achebe does not say, however, that we ought not to read Conrad. His reading, like Said's reading of Camus, extends the range of imaginative possibility beyond what we were capable of seeing for ourselves. I admire enormously—and gain inordinately from— Toni Morrison's reading of *Moby-Dick* and of Willa Cather's *Sapphira and the Slave Girl* and of certain Hemingway short stories. Such readings remind us that our canon, our standards, take up a relatively small place in the world; such readings offer us expansion as well as inclusion.

I am reminded of this expansiveness on occasions when a rich dialogue takes place in my classroom after people have read a novel from a participatory or "reader response" point of view, when they have—against the background of their own lived lives—looked through the diverse perspectives the book provides and achieved it as meaningful for themselves. Speaking with their own voices, perceiving from their own locations, they are very likely to articulate a range of meanings. When it is over, the work in question (*The Great Gatsby, Invisible Man, The Bluest Eye,* "Bartleby the Scrivener") is richer, more suggestive, full of more possibilities than it was in my own reading, despite the number of critics I called upon to help me. If we can teach people to notice what is there to be noticed, if we can enable them to reflect upon the medium in use (the language, the paint and canvas, the clay), if we can move them to release their imaginations and break with literal expectations, we are more likely to do justice to a range of works of art, even if we can make no final judgments about their quality.

With what we have said here about expansion and new perspectives and experiential possibilities, we can only welcome the challenges of multiculturalism. Multiplicity means a new opening, after all, in an often monological world. And we are learning that we cannot cover everything that comes to our attention: we can only make them exist as possibility for our students. If our students are attentive, if they are authentic, if they are aware of the fact that all the works they encounter belong to diverse contexts that on some level must be understood, our teaching can be the kind of teaching that moves all kinds of persons to take their own initiatives as they learn how to learn. Perhaps, as they move toward the "fusion of horizons," they can make their own judgments in collaboration with others. They can, at once, attend to the judgments made by members of other cultures—not only of what is valuable in their worlds but of what demands confrontation in our own. Yes, we want our students, in the expanding communities in which they will live their lives, to attend to particulars, to engage, to move in the spaces opened by works of art, each of which (we may discover) makes its own distinctive demands. We need to hold in mind somehow that many works of art (wherever they come from) address themselves to human freedom— meaning the capacity to choose and (we would hope) the power to act in a changing world. We want our students to choose themselves and to be strengthened in their choosing by art experiences that open doors, that allow them to realize how wide and various and enticing the contemporary world can be. I have been trying to say throughout that we are all in process, we who are teachers along with those we teach. And in a pluralist world, with newcomers appearing every day, we somehow have to realize that no one of them is fixed forever, identified forever by a culture, a religion, a class, an ethnic identity. Like ourselves, they may be aware of their roots, of their beginnings, but like ourselves, they need to use their imaginations "to light the slow fuse of possibility." Feeling our own new beginnings, we have been learning here—as the seasons give way to new seasons, as things change and change again—what it means to break with anchorage, what it means to move with others, to care for others, to reach beyond where we are.

... We Have Found the Wonders of Difference ...
(1994)

$\mathbf{M}$y themes have to do with opening new pathways in lived experience, breaking with the taken-for-granted, setting aside the crusts of mere conformity. It takes work, as we know, as so many have reminded us, work to be done on the part of those of us who are perceivers lending some of our lives to the works before us as we attend to and gather together the particulars, the details that are there for us. "The one who is too lazy, idle, or indurated in convention," wrote John Dewey, "will not see or hear" (1980, p. 54). Jean-Paul Sartre, describing the mutual interdependence of artist and perceiver, talked about how we have to create what the artist discloses to us, to work along with the artist in bringing into being the universe of *Hamlet*, let us say, or Doctorow's *The Waterworks,* or "The Wind as a Knife." If, Sartre said, we are "inattentive, tired, stupid, or thoughtless," most of the relations will escape us; we will never manage to "catch on" to what is before us (in the text, on the stage, on the wall) in the sense that fire catches or does not catch (1949, p. 43). Both Dewey and Sartre were paying tribute to the potential of those who come, through their own free choosing, to make certain works objects of their experience—to attend to them with the particular kind of effort that allows them to become works of art. It is, as you already recognize, the concern of the aesthetic educator to enable persons to exert that effort in whatever way they can, to break with the automatic or with purely conventional norms, to awaken themselves from passivity so they do not simply wait to absorb.

We have shared a number of experiences that make some of this particularly clear. Friday afternoon, as those who were here recall, we saw the sky darken outside the windows, the clouds gather, and a storm begin. Watching the light change, the rain pour down for a few minutes, remembering what I said the other day about having aesthetic experiences with nature, I asked myself about the difference between what I was seeing outside the window and what, say, the painter Turner made me see when it came to storms, steam, mist—or a Hudson River painter rendering clouds gathering over the Catskills. And I thought about the haze in the hours before the rain here in the city and about Monet's painting of mist—in that work called "Impression: Mist." If Monet or Turner had been here on Friday and had been moved to make the look of the city the subject of a painting, we might have waited for a rendering of the storm as Turner or Monet saw it, but neither one would have captured it at the moment, as we do when we take a snapshot; he would have kept looking, trying to see it in terms of oil paint, pondering later what he had seen, finding new possibilities of color, of vaguely emergent form, transfiguring the storm we saw on 65th Street into a concretion, something called formed content, something—at last—that never existed in the world before. And if we reached out to understand, to engage with its shapes and colors and relationships, we would discover a wholly new storm-on-65th Street, something we could not conceivably have anticipated, and perhaps something new about storminess and the meaning of sudden darkening, curtaining, storming in our experience—which might have changed that experience in some fashion even as it altered our perceiving of city storms in time to come and offered us different perceptions of the city itself, perceptions that might play against one another—as they do when we read novels about the city (Toni Morrison's *Jazz*, Doctorow's work) making us ask ourselves what do we (here in the first person) really see.

I hope you think about the wonder of multiple perspectives in your own experience. I hope you think about what happens to you—and, we would all hope, to our students—when it becomes possible to abandon one-dimensional viewing, to look from many vantage points and, in doing so, construct meanings scarcely suspected before. That makes me think of another experience many of us shared: David Gonzalez telling the story of Orpheus and Eurydice—because he tapped so many styles of sound and movement, moving us to actualize one of the most familiar tales there are in multiple and unfamiliar ways. Again, we had to *be* there with him, let our imaginations work so that, in collaboration with him, we could make visible and palpable the musician Orpheus and the lost wife he goes in search of to the underground. We had to be personally participant, imaginatively participant when he tried not to look back until he and Eurydice were back on earth; we had ourselves to be drawn to look back, to assure ourselves that the "as-if" Eurydice was really there—even though we knew. What we shared was an enactment of art-making—someone raising up a world before our eyes through movement and the sound of his voice and the expressions of his face. It reminded me of a Rilke poem called "Initiation" that begins with going out into the evening and lifting one's eyes from the worn-out door-stone—and then:

> *slowly you raise a shadowy black tree*
> *and fix it on the sky: slender, alone.*
> *And you have made the world (and it shall grow*
> *and ripen as a word, unspoken, still).*
> *When you have grasped its meaning with your will,*
> *then tenderly your eyes will let it go.*
>
> (1940/1974, p. 21)

It reminded me of it because it seemed to ask of me the same effort—to raise something against the sky by means of my imagination—and then choosing it in some way meaningful, making it my own.

None of this signifies that you are required to like these works or that you are bound to discover openings within them. I am pointing to, suggesting to you the possibilities opened by imagination—possibilities that something may happen in your experience, that something may open to a new way of seeing or feeling or coping with the world. I want—to extend the point I am trying to make about perceiving and imagining and opening—to refer to another experience some shared, the listening to the Mendelssohn octet, which I well realize sounds differently to each of us, which may well be heard differently—phase by phase, phrase by phrase. I could not but recall an essay that has always meant a good deal to me. It is called "Making Music Together" and was written by a philosopher named Alfred Schutz. He looked at a performance like the one we heard as a particular kind of "web of social relationships," a mutual "tuning-in relationship" by which, he wrote, the " 'I' and the 'Thou' are experienced by the participants as a 'We' in vivid presence." He spoke of listeners coming into communication with a composer through the mediation of the performers, and he also spoke of the relation among the performers and "the flux of tones unrolling in inner time and an arrangement meaningful" to composer and listener and performers "because and in so far as it evokes in the stream of consciousness participating in it an interplay of recollections, retentions, protensions and anticipations which interrelate the successive elements" (1964, p. 173). He saw this as one of the best examples of persons communicating, becoming mutually concerned with one another, creating a relationship founded upon a common experience of living simultaneously in both inner and outer time. There are other ways of explaining the musical experience, but this is one that, at least for me, relates it to the other participatory experience we are having here and, at once, suggests what can happen in situations here and in our classrooms when, by means of a performance, an enactment, a reading, or an exhibition, a "We" can emerge in vivid presence—something crucial to our lives.

Now I know, as all of us now concerned about cultural diversity know, that there are other kinds of music than the Mendelssohn, other kinds of arrangement in inner time than the one Schutz had in mind. I know, for example, that the experience of listening to Indian music is different from the experience of listening to Mendelssohn; I know that the Indian aesthetic is different from ours—with its emphasis upon an intuitive grasp of what is happening in an art form and a move outward from that art form to a transcendence of the sensory world and an escape to a state of superior pleasure, practical betterment, and spiritual bliss. We will be in some way participant in Indian dance this week and the sounds that accompany it, and I would like to believe that, for all the difference in aesthetic theory, we can somehow experience the "I-Thou" moment Schutz described when listening to Indian music. It is interesting to read that dance and music are thought to outrank sculpture and painting in Indian culture because of the Indian belief that art should have a dimension of time. While paintings, for instance, freeze the action of the subject in a single instant, music and dance unfold in time. Without sharing the religious resonances, I think many of us have experienced the moments of "vivid presence" in, say, the music of Ravi Shankar.

Our object, where public school children and young people are concerned, is to provide increasing numbers of opportunities for tapping into long unheard frequencies, for opening new perspectives on a world increasingly shared. It seems to me that we can only do so with regard for the situated lives of diverse children and respect for the differences in their experience. But this need not mean shutting the doors to the possibility of making music together, not always the same music, not music governed by the same norms. The point seems to me to be experiential, not theoretical. My own experience opened when I first heard Ravi Shankar (who helped me, as time went on, listen to Philip Glass, to attend to the *Mahabharata,* to push back my horizons, to realize there were multiple musics and multiple ways of making music together—but that I was entitled to listen to the musics of other cultures against my own lived situation, on my own ground. It may be that some day we will find our studies revealing what some scholars call a "single Calliope"—Calliope, the daughter of the goddess of memory and of

Zeus, Calliope who gave us the gift of art. It may be that some day we will find a common unity shared by art around the world as more disparate artists work to imbue sensuous media with potential meanings. We have not yet found it, but we have found the wonders of difference, the wonders of diversity, and the possibility of experiencing the "I" and "Thou" in particular cases and with regard to specific art works as an emergent "We."

I believe that this is more likely to happen if the participatory engagements we are involved with here become more likely in the schools around the country. Working together to discover Indian dance movements, learning something about the importance of styles, young people will open themselves to the language of Indian dance—on the basis of who *they* are and what they are willing to explore. Some of us have had this experience with African dance, some with Mayan symbols and images in literature as well as visual art. We have not become African or adopted Mayan creeds, but some of us, along with the young strangers in our classrooms, have reached out as reflective knowers in a world changing daily in the light of views from what used to be the margins, in the light of new eyes looking, new voices speaking. We all have to look out as persons somehow in pursuit, somehow leaning toward a future of possibility. Empathy is required, the kind of empathy that imagination, of all human capacities, makes possible. An imaginative reaching out and toward is needed, as we learn—all of us, old and young—to look through more and more perspectives at what we hold in common—and as, using our imagination, we become able to imagine what Cynthia Ozick describes as "the familiar heart of the stranger" (1989).

Opening ourselves, putting one-dimensionality aside and shallow conventions, we can nurture a desire or *communitas* by means of art experiences while preserving differences. We need to affirm ourselves and touch our own horizons as we work to fuse with others, as we offer more and more pathways out of the fixed and the ordinary, pathways toward what might be. I like what Sartre wrote about pathways, after writing that we all perceive things against the background of our world.

> If the painter presents us with a field or a vase of flowers, his paintings are windows which are open on the whole world. We follow the red path which is buried among the wheat much farther than van Gogh painted it, among other wheat fields, under other clouds, to the river which empties into the sea, and we extend to infinity, to the other end of the world, the deep finality which supports the existence of the field and the earth. So that, through the various objects which it produces ... the creative act aims at a total renewal of the world. (1949, p. 57)

And, now forgive me. I need to end with a woman's words, words written by a woman poet, Muriel Rukeyser, writing (yes) about Orpheus in her "The Poem as Mask," in which things come together with "their own music." First, she tells of writing about dancing wild women, singing, and she says it was a mask when she wrote of Orpheus, exiled; it was really herself, "unable to speak, in exile from myself."

And, wonderfully:

> *There is no mountain, there is no god, there is memory*
> *of my torn life, myself split open in sleep, the rescued child*
> *beside me among the doctors, and a word*
> *of rescue from the great eyes.*
>
> *No more masks! No more mythologies!*
>
> *Now, for the first time, the god lifts his hand,*
> *the fragments join in me with their own music.*
>   (1982, p. 435)

It is not only renewal. It is a wholeness for each of us, for ourselves.

I Still Wonder at How Unaware I Was of So Many Frequencies . . .

(2000)

Windows have been opening for many of us. There have been sounds we never heard, images we never saw. There has been a program of contemporary music played by an amazing pianist, Nurit Tilles. She played a sonata by Samuel Barber and part of one by Charles Ives. Both were American, both became known to the public (to some degree) at mid-century. Both experimented with dissonance, with the rhythms of jazz, with tonalities still unfamiliar to many of us. Barber enclosed the extremely modern in a classical frame; Ives made folk songs, hymns, and marching tunes part of his startling harmonizations. To attend to their music even today is to find ourselves pushing back the boundaries of what we have thought of as beautiful music. I still wonder at how unaware I was of so many frequencies; and I wonder how many remain unheard. Encouraged, challenged by our teaching artists, asked to explore for ourselves the modalities of sound, many of us have found entries into this "new" music. We have had what we now think of as aesthetic experiences we might never have had without the kind of listening made possible by our teaching artists, without the exercises we accomplished together, without the unfamiliar perceptions of structure and form. Not only did our musical experience expand and deepen; the sounding world around mysteriously changed.

We were fortunate enough, as a growing community, to be present at a workshop performance of a brief version of Mozart's *Così fan tutte*, called in its adaptation *Così Cosa*. The wonder of it came in part from the way, from the first moments, it tapped our imagination and drew us into an "as-if" world brought into existence on the bare floor of a studio room. Made conscious of the performance as one still in the making, we became vicariously participant as members of a small audience, each with memories of Mozart and, perhaps, that great comic opera. Some of us felt the relation between *our* Mozart and modern composers like Barber and Ives, all three perceived anew. And there were the feelings aroused by the singers, the actors: their young voices, their gestures, their facial expressions. And there was the tantalizing thought of its becoming, of what the scenes that followed would be like, what was still to come and was not quite yet devised. Openings again, a sense of the unpredictable, of the incomplete—and of our own agency in helping to bring the work of art alive.

As you can guess, I am trying to convey what we mean when we speak of aesthetic education and when we say, as John Dewey did, that the opposite of aesthetic is anaesthetic. The simplest explanation is that it is a mode of nurturing an increasingly informed attentiveness to a diversity of art forms. We often make the point that the more we know, the more we see and hear. And we realize that our seeing and hearing are often enhanced by whatever explorations we have done in the media of the different arts—how we have sought our own symbols, our own images, even our own melodies; how we have tried to make imprints upon the world.

You are familiar with the importance of encouraging encounters with subject matter (including the arts) that involve a sense of agency, of achieving dimensions of that subject matter as meaningful, not uncovering some hidden meaning others have predefined. We know as well the range of understandings that are necessary in the ongoing effort to *create* meanings, efforts going beyond the cognitive, to include intuition, imagination, feeling, perception—all the acts of consciousness, perhaps especially where the arts are concerned. This becomes particularly clear when we become engaged with works of literature, considered as an art form. Some of us, reading *The Bluest Eye* by Toni Morrison this summer, made conscious efforts to find out what it signified, to approach it in the light of gender, color, class, the intersections in which we were located in the world. Each of us made the text an object of our experience, grasping the language, the figures of speech, the images in such a way that new perspectives kept opening on the events and characters being revealed. As in the case of other works of art, the text (like a dance performance, or a play) exists at what is called the "artistic" pole. Created by an artist, we can assume, it presents itself to be felt, interpreted, resonated to, on a number of levels understood. The perceiver or the listener exists at what is called the "aesthetic" pole, at which a consciousness reaches out to grasp the work, to lend it (if you will) the perceiver's or the listener's or the reader's life. In the space that opens between the two poles, Pecola (let us say) is brought to life, certainly from the narrator's perspective, but a perspective affected by the reader's lived life, memories, injuries, moments of pleasure—or desire, or delight. What happens in that space is always distinctive, an event like and unlike the event of others' reading.

Aesthetic education focuses on that space and what may happen there as a work of art is realized or fulfilled by a human being, present as *"who, not what"* he or she is, to quote Hannah Arendt (1958, p. 182). And the questions must multiply and not be covered over by the answers. A reader who has at any time sought to construct a narrative or write a poem is more likely to attend to the work of literary art with a different quality of interest, even of empathy. Like the experiences in our workshops here of shaping kinetic patterns in space and time with our own bodies, or trying to render in water color our perception of sky outside or a neighbor's profile, we may relate our sense of what it is to shape or construct or to give form to raw material to our experience with dance performances or paintings— or whatever is encountered as a work of art. If we do so, the mystery may deepen, but we may come closer to what we think of as an aesthetic moment.

We are forever hoping that the feelings, indeed the passions so often palpable here can be kept alive as the reflective and (I trust) ardent teacher works to involve her own students (with due allowance for age, level of development, life experience) with works of art. Her capacity to do so, I am convinced, depends in large measure on her capacity to keep her wonder and sense of mystery alive and the questions open. It is in connection with this that I think of a poem by Mary Oliver my poet-friend Madeleine Holzer shared with me. It is called "The Swan." The poet writes first about the delicate white swan floating near, turning its dark eyes and trailing its webbed foot, rearranging "the cloud of its wings." Then the questions, perhaps the necessary questions arise:

> *Oh, what shall I do*
> *   when that poppy-colored beak*
> *   rests in my hand?*
> *   Said Mrs. Blake of the poet:*

> *I miss my husband's company—*
> *   he is so often*
> *   in paradise.*
> *   Of course! the path to heaven*

doesn't lie down in flat miles.
It's in the imagination
with which you perceive
this world,

and the gestures
with which you honor it.
Oh, what will I do, what will I say, when those white wings
touch the shore?

(1999, pp. 27–28)

Read it as you will, as you choose. You cannot (I cannot) subdue the questions that touch upon the aesthetic experience and the risks it makes us run.

That makes me think of the energizing character of dance, even in the face of emotional risk, often the risk of experiencing something new, for which we do not feel prepared. Some of us know the bond that can develop between perceiver and audience, the muscular sympathy and emotional empathy, the ways in which visual and imaginative activity combines with bodily perception to provide a kind of unity of being. A signal experience that marked the summer for some of us was the experience we had with a dancer who transmuted poetry into movement, most movingly Elizabeth Bishop's poem, "One Art." She spoke it aloud as she danced; and it is difficult to communicate the effect it had on those who were participants and spectators at once, feeling the universe expand, feeling the symbol become fused with the world. I will read it because it is brief and somehow necessary to read, and it is up to you to imagine, if you can, the movement, the shimmering moments. And (yes, again) the mystery.

The art of losing isn't hard to master;
so many things seem filled with the intent
to be lost that their loss is no disaster.

Lose something every day. Accept the fluster
of lost door keys, the hour badly spent.
The art of losing isn't hard to master.

Then practice losing farther, losing faster:
places and names, and where it was you meant
to travel. None of these will bring disaster.

I lost my mother's watch. And look! my last, or
next-to-last, of three loved houses went.
The art of losing isn't hard to master.

I lost two cities, lovely ones. And, vaster,
some realms I owned, two rivers, a continent.
I miss them, but it wasn't a disaster.

—Even losing you (the joking voice, a gesture
I love) I shan't have lied. It's evident
the art of losing's not too hard to master
*though it may look like (*Write *it!) a disaster.*
                                              (1997, p. 178)

For most of those present, I believe, the dancer (Susan Thomasson) made possible a complex and memorable emotional experience, one that highlights for me important aspects of the aesthetic experience. There is the origin in the concrete and the ordinary (keys, wasted time), the transition to abstract places, lost opportunities—none of it truly painful. The odd calm in losing a mother's watch and then the houses, an expansion now to a continent, perhaps to the cosmos itself. But what is beyond disaster is the loss of the particular person, the desperately induplicable. Perhaps the only way of mastering the loss is to write about it—a poem, conceivably, a savage scrawl. Who can know? Who can guess? What part can be played by the arts?

What can be pointed out is the number of modalities that come into play when engaging actively and authentically with a work of art—be it a Vermeer painting, a Bach cantata, a Shakespeare (or a David Mamet) play, a Twyla Tharp dance. Imagination, cognition, intuition, emotion: all interweave, highlighting one another. Maurice Merleau-Ponty (1962/1967), speaks of a "network of relationships" (p. xx), says in fact, "We *are* network of relationships." And, in another place, he says we are "condemned to meaning" (p. xix). It seems to me that encounters with the arts, because of the interrelating of capacities, the play of human powers, lead to the kinds of insight and awareness unlikely in other contacts with the objects and living beings in the world. When we connect such insights with the kinds of communities that form when people come together with their unanswered questions and their sense of mystery, the diversity of perspectives about what is shared makes possible a unique dialogue.

In a chapter called "The Search for the Great Community" in *The Public and Its Problems*, John Dewey had much to say about the potency of the arts. He spoke about people's conscious life of opinion and judgment often proceeding on a superficial and trivial plane.

> But their lives reach a deeper level. The function of art has always been to break through the crust of conventionalized and routine consciousness. Common things, a flower, a gleam of moonlight, the song of a bird, not things rare and remote, are means with which the deeper levels of life are touched so that they spring up as desire and thought. This process is art. Poetry, the drama, the novel, are proofs that the problem of presentation is not insoluble. Artists have always been the real purveyors of news, for it is not the outward happening in itself which is new, but the kindling by it of emotion, perception, and appreciation. (1988, pp. 183–184)

When we ponder our experiences here as audiences and as participants in workshops, we cannot but recognize what Dewey meant by saying that our lives "reach a deeper level" when touched by the arts. And we would add, especially when we know enough to be reflective in our engagement with them, critically conscious of what is happening in our encounters, eager to break through that crust Dewey described.

The so-called partnerships may lay a groundwork for a community attentive to the deeper level, so long as they are conceived in interpersonal and not simply inter-institutional terms. Much remains to be done if we are indeed to find a language of community, perhaps a common language stemming from dialogues that had their origin in spaces some of us have opened and may continue to open in the corridors and studios and even the classrooms of our schools. In her poem, "Transcendental Etude," Adrienne Rich writes, in part:

> *But there come times—perhaps this is one of them—*
> *when we have to take ourselves more seriously or die;*
> *when we have to pull back from the incantations,*
> *rhythms we've moved to thoughtlessly,*
> *and disenthrall ourselves, bestow*
> *ourselves to silence, or a severer listening, cleansed*
> *of oratory, formulas, choruses, laments, static*
> *crowding the wires.*
>   (1978, pp. 74–75)

She appears to be charging people like us, as Dewey did in his way, to break with pious talk, bureaucratic talk, media talk, technicist talk and with, again, "the crust of conventionalized and routine consciousness" (1988, p. 183).

I find myself reaching back once more to Elizabeth Bishop's words; and then I recall the virtuosity of the storyteller and the part he plays in breaking through that crust—if only by giving up the linearity of a single voice, a single direction in a children's story. And there was Ronald K. Brown's "March," his duet enabling us to hear the words of Martin Luther King afresh through their being put into motion by dancers. Not all touch the "deeper levels" in the same fashion, but because they break with the customary and the overly familiar, they move us to reflect upon the way we apprehend them. They may move us to trace the networks in our experience, the web of relationships that free us to construct new meanings, to shape new visions of what is and what might be.

We are teachers after all; and many of us are eager to communicate some of the passion we feel about openings, about possibilities. We want our desires to be contagious, like our excitement about the several arts. We want to celebrate the sense of agency, every young person's right to go in search of her/his own voice, and own vision, even while recognizing the connection between freedom and discipline that makes the arts what they are. And if indeed the arts are the "chief purveyors of the news," I hope that what they purvey gives rise to a dialogue that has to do with decency, compassion, and concern. I quoted Sartre a while ago writing that "at the heart of the aesthetic imperative we discern the moral imperative" because "the work of art, from whichever side you approach it" (1949, pp. 62–63) is an act of confidence in the freedom of human beings. We feel that freedom here—to interpret, to reflect, and (now and then) change our lives.

I trust as well that such freedom can become an act of confidence in human connection. "Only connect," it resounds. And then there is Edward Said writing about traditions and continuities and telling us that "survival is about the connection between things; in Eliot's phrase, reality cannot be deprived of the 'other echoes [that] inhabit the garden' " (1993, p. 336). For Said, and I think many of us, it is more rewarding to think concretely and sympathetically about others than only about "us." But this also means not trying to rule others, not trying to classify them or put them in hierarchies or to silence them. And—I want to add—to prevent them from coming in touch with that deeper level so many of us have touched through our encounters with the arts. There is so much to do, so much to imagine, so much that is not yet. Remember that Emily Dickinson quote once more: "The Possible's slow fuse is lit / By the Imagination." A slow fuse, indeed. The questions remain open. The work remains incomplete. But what work it can be!

PART V

SPREADING
THE WORD

The opportunity to speak at an occasion sponsored by the New York State Board of Regents was particularly significant, not only for me, but for the Institute. We are, and have been, eager to see ourselves as full members of the educational community, as well as the arts community. It was especially meaningful because the Regents were giving awards that evening in dance, literature, music, and drama—with an emphasis on "the creative spirit."

No matter what the year, a connection with the Regents, so distinctively representative of those concerned with teaching and learning, would be memorable. To find ourselves playing a part in the celebration of the best, most humane, most imaginative of human capacities in this context could not but give us hope for the young people of New York and for art in their lives.

The Creative Spirit:
Keys, Doors and Possibilities

(Address to the New York State
Board of Regents, 1984)

"The Kingdom of Numbers is all boundaries / Which may be beautiful
and must be true," wrote W. H. Auden in his poem "Numbers and
Faces" (1976, p. 473), and he knew, as we do, that—as significant as numbers are, and boundaries, and necessary truths—there are times when we
must move beyond. To think of the creative spirit is to think of moving
beyond into spaces where we can live now and then in total freedom. It is
imagination that releases us, that discloses alternative possibilities—imagination that is the "health," as Emerson put it, of every human being. It was
surely imagination that revealed the shape of the Brooklyn Bridge before it
was built, the "swift, unfractioned idiom" (to use Hart Crane's words) of
that bridge. It was imagination that opened the likelihood of the Erie Canal,
of the railroads, of the highways, of the malls. And, yes, it was imagination
that enabled Anne Sexton to picture riding an elevator into the sky, to a floor
where there was "a very large key, / that opens something— / some useful
door— / somewhere— / up there" (1981, p. 427).

Those images—the sky, the key, the door, the opening, and that "somewhere" with its overtones of the unpredictable—summon up (how can they
not?) the arts and the part the arts might play, ought to play in the lives of
New Yorkers, young and old. Granted, the arts can be called marginal when
we ponder the serious problems confronting our state and its schools. The
critic Denis Donoghue has written: "I want to say that the margin is the place
for those feelings and intuitions which daily life doesn't have a place for, and
mostly seems to suppress. . . . It's enough that the arts have a special care
for those feelings and intuitions which otherwise are crowded out in our
works and our days. With the arts, people can make a space for themselves,

and fill it with intimations of freedom and presence" (1983, p. 129). Marginal, yes, but not trivial. Beyond the everyday and the actual, yes, but not mere frills and frivolities. I would want to add that engagements with the arts, informed and aware engagements, provide the key to the door of the imaginative life. And that means a key to untapped possibility, to a sense of what is not yet.

First, I would affirm the value of making, shaping, expressing—of releasing as many persons as we can into the adventure and discipline of working with the materials of paint, sound, language, body movement, clay, voice, film. There is no human being, no matter what age, who cannot be energized and enlarged when provided opportunities to sing, to say, to inscribe, to render, to show—to bring, through his or her devising, something new into the world. But there is more. It is largely through some immediate involvement with "making" (or, if you like, creating) that individuals who are not themselves artists can begin to get a sense of what is demanded by what might be called artistry. To understand on any level what excellence implies in this domain is to be acquainted with more than visible or audible products and achievements. It is to know something of the process, the craft. It is to become in some way acquainted with the long trying, the self-reflecting, the rehearsing, the remaking, even the doubting. Excellence, after all, refers to a quality of being, to the ways in which people go about their lives, attend to their work; it is not simply a mark for a final product. To communicate some of this to the young may well be to help them see what standards mean, what doing things with style can mean. If we can provide occasions for more and more to incarnate this somehow, make it integral to what they do day by day, then we will be able to tell ourselves that we are authentically in search of excellence—excellence as a way of conducting one's life, one's very being in the world.

But there is more. I want to argue for the kind of education that allows for an increasingly informed awareness of the events, performances, and created things we categorize as the arts. We have all seen the accounts of the numbers of people now attending museum exhibitions and dance performances. We know, perhaps particularly in New York, how vast the audiences (actual and potential) are for the arts in all their manifestations. There are many reasons for this, but I choose to believe that at the core (most often unarticulated) is a desire for those spaces filled with "intimations of freedom and presence." It is not enough, however, to experience the desire; nor is it enough to have tickets in hand for the Van Gogh in Arles exhibition, or for the Motherwell show, or for a Balanchine series at the New York State Theater. People must be empowered to notice what is there to be noticed.

They must know what it is to move within paintings and among the masses of sculptures, to live in music, to attend to bodies in motion on a stage—not solely with eyes and mind, but with nerves and muscles and pulsing blood. What I have in mind is not art appreciation in any of its customary senses: appreciation imposed on passive people sitting still to be improved. Nor am I talking about anything that can be easily subsumed under art history or the humanities. Affective education does not describe it; nor is it to be understood as a predominantly intellectualized engagement—musicological, literary critical, philosophical aesthetical—with selected works in the artistic domains.

It can be called aesthetic education; it can be called education in being present, personally present as imagining, feeling, perceiving, thinking beings to works of art. And, because of that achieved presentness, this can also mean an enhanced capacity to come in touch with the appearances of things, the sound and smell and touch of things in the sensible and opened world. (I so much want my students, for instance, to be able to perceive such phenomena as the calligraphy of the black tree branches against the winter sky; to pay heed to the glint of apples or the sheen of grapes on fruit stands, to the pink and brown faces of hooded children playing in strained sunlight. And, yes, I want them to attend as well to the shattered places—the burnt-out building shells, the bodies on the benches, the hushed lines of applicants—where there are gaps that need closing, breaks that need to be repaired.) I believe that attentiveness of this sort, openness, wide-awakeness may arise out of involvements with the arts, with making *and* attending, if those involvements are reflective, educated, authentic, and informed.

For me, teaching is not mainly a matter of informing people or enabling them to know *that* such and such is the case in one or another dimension of their lives. It is not of overriding significance for students to know that Aaron Copland grew up in Brooklyn, went to Paris, and wrote *Appalachian Spring;* or that the peculiar emptiness of Edward Hopper's painted city streets is due to a distinctive handling of light and form; or that the central symbol in *The Great Gatsby* is that billboard over the valley of ashes; or that Balanchine's abstract ballets depend crucially on mirroring and symmetries. Of course these pieces of information are meaningful, but teaching, for me, is fundamentally a matter of discovering what I can do to empower people to move into such imaginary worlds and to *achieve* them variously as meaningful, to realize them—in their own experience—as aesthetic objects, works of art. I mean enabling them to attend, to notice what is there to be noticed, to let their energies go out to the musical piece, the painting of the city, the novel, the dance performance in such a fashion that each can emerge in the consciousness of the one attending with increasing clarity and intensity. If that occurs, it is highly likely that dimensions of experience will be illuminated that may not have been noticeable before.

It is altogether evident to me that Aaron Copland—like Chopin, Berlioz, and Charles Ives—makes me hear sounds, tempi, tones I never suspected were audible. It is as if each one pushes back the horizons of silence and opens up new frequencies to which I can attend. Hopper's New York paintings, and Jasper Johns's, and Larry Rivers's disclose concealed shapes and surfaces and shadings that add entirely new dimensions to urban, and indeed to modern, existence. I might say something similar about Elizabeth Bishop's "Letter to N.Y.," with those surprising images startling the reader into seeing: "and coming out of the brownstone house / to the gray sidewalk, the watered street, / one side of the buildings rises with the sun / like a glistening field of wheat" (1997, p. 80). And surprises, you will admit, like the unpredictable, are an aspect of that space where we find ourselves (if we are aware and lucky) to be free.

Saying that, I think of June Jordan's "Toward a City That Sings," which begins with a plane landing into the topaz of Manhattan and goes on: "I will never tell you the meaning of this poem: / Just say. 'She wrote it, and I recognize / the reference.'"—and ends with a comment that the speaker wants to clean up everything in sight "for your possible / discovery" (1980, p. 48). ("Possible discovery": how wonderful when one is trying to speak about the arts. They offer possible discoveries and discoveries of the possible, after all.) I think of Herman Melville and of Fitzgerald again, of the beginning of *Moby-Dick* with its rendering of the inlanders who come to the water side from the lanes and alleys where "of week days" they have been "pent up in lath and plaster—tied to counters, nailed to benches, clinched to desks" (1979, p. 3). Melville presents them heading for the ocean on Sunday afternoons, looking outwards, fixed in reveries. He involves his readers with those inlanders' searches for something beyond the margins, beyond the constraints of the ordinary. And oftentimes (because Melville was an artist) those readers (we ourselves) begin yearning outwards in quest of their own spaces of freedom, their presence to themselves. And there is *The Great Gatsby* still making me confront—and question and wonder at—the radiance and the meretriciousness and the persistence of the American enchantment, the American Dream. You remember the green light at the end of the dock, and you may remember those last words, "tomorrow we will run faster, stretch out our arms farther. . . . And one fine morning—" (1995, p. 228). I think I am still and shall be forever trying to realize that book, deal with the questions it raises for me, discover the new patterns and jagged places and holes and shimmers of light it introduces into my experience.

I can say similar things about Dustin Hoffman in *Death of a Salesman,* transforming himself into a nerve-wracked, lurching Willy Loman trying to remain hearty, to remain alive. I can say them about the sound of the horn in August Wilson's *Ma Rainey's Black Bottom* and about the movements in Alvin Ailey's *Revelations* and about Anna Sokolow's rendering of Solzhenitsyn's *The First Circle* through dance, and about the Haydn Trio I heard the Chamber Music Society of Lincoln Center perform. Each one, in its own fashion, opened doors for me, made me see and hear and feel what I had never seen or heard or felt in quite the same way. Each one released me— marvelously, mysteriously—to look at things as if they were or could be otherwise. That means, as you surely know, to break with petrifactions and fixities, to perceive alternative realities, to begin breaking free.

Now I want to suggest that the ability to break with the conventional and the taken-for-granted—the capacity to pay heed to metaphors, gestures, tonalities—does not come naturally. I think that people have to be enabled to crack the codes, to enter in, to take the risks, to uncouple—if only for a while—from ordinary, commonsensible reality. And I think everyone *can* be enabled to enter in—to break through the screens of preciousness, profundity, postmodernism, and the ever-present "hype." I am convinced that efforts to free persons in this way, to help them break with passivity or automatism or fear or somnolence ought to be central in education wherever education occurs. I feel particularly strongly about it in places where the vocational or the technical or the "skills" emphasis is uppermost. Our system in this country has been so practical, so moralistic, so utilitarian that the way of experiencing I have been trying to describe has been reserved for the relatively privileged. For those not so privileged, art has meant Halloween pumpkins and Valentine cards and playing in the band and now and again (seldom these days) participating in a busy, "popular" play. Few of these undertakings have fed into experiences with actual works of art.

You may be thinking that I am speaking out of an elite orientation, the orientation of someone lucky enough to go to Lincoln Center, to have been introduced to museums early in life, to have had books available through the years. You may be thinking that the tradition in which I seem to be enmeshed is the upper middle-class tradition, and that I have no right to assume it can or should offer the same riches to everyone. What is wrong, some of you may murmur, with popular culture or with ethnic art, folk stories, folk dances? Nothing, I would of course respond. I would agree that the creative spirit speaks through these forms as well. You may be thinking that people can very well enjoy Alvin Ailey and Arthur Miller if they can simply respond to the drama and the power of the surfaces, the whirling shapes on the stage, the sound of that remarkable phrase, "attention must be paid." Is it absolutely necessary, you might ask, for someone to look at an Edward Hopper scene and do more than remark that the luncheonette must actually have looked like that? What is wrong, you may ask, with plain showing, plain looking, finding whatever one wants to find?

I simply want to communicate the idea that there is always more to be found, horizons to be breached, limits to be broken through, always untapped possibility. Indeed, in a world so focused on objectives and results, efficiency, effectiveness, and the rest, I would lay particular stress on what lies beyond the moment's grasp, on the uses of defamiliarizing the overly familiar (and thus invisible, inaudible) world. Indeed, that is my major response to the questions some people raise. I am not disturbed by the reminder that most Americans can live perfectly decent and even enjoyable lives without hearing Haydn or seeing an Arthur Miller or a Sam Shepard play or watching the Ailey dancers or the New York City Ballet perform magic in virtual space and time. Nor do I have a required list of works that must be comprehended and enjoyed by anyone I would call a good citizen or be willing to treat as my friend. I like Ray Charles, and I admire Michael Jackson, and I think Linda Rondstadt and Meryl Streep are remarkable. I have watched break-dancing on New York street corners for a half-hour at a stretch (although I do not enjoy it as much as watching Jacques D'Amboise's many children dance). I know little about soap operas; I happen not to like *Dallas* or even *Falcon Crest;* but I do sometimes get pleasure from *St. Elsewhere* and *Hill Street Blues*. It is only that I do not think we offer the young enough live options, options they feel good enough to seize. I do not think we take the arts seriously enough as worlds that can be opened to all sorts of individuals if only they are provided opportunities to move, media to work with, keys for the doors, if they are enabled to crack the codes. Most significantly, I think we too often forget that the primary purpose of education is to free persons to make sense of their actual lived situations— not only cognitively, but perceptually, imaginatively, affectively—to attend mindfully to their own lives, to take their own initiatives in interpreting them and finding out where the deficiencies are and trying to transform them. And discovering somehow that there is no end to it, that there is always more to see, to learn, to feel.

We need to hold in mind the fact that the arts are almost always inexhaustible. There is no using up of a painting or a concerto or a poem. If they have any richness, any density at all, they are inexhaustible; there is always more. I have seen the Van Gogh show twice, and each time, for all the sur-face familiarity of some of the paintings, my experience has often been star-tling, indeed shattering. It has been an experience of discovery of new pat-terns in the landscapes, whorls, curves, twisting forms—dark blue, dark green moods, of chilling cold even in the yellow glare of the sun; and, if I were to go back tomorrow, I would see even more. The same would be true in encounters with Balanchine's *Apollo,* with *Carmen,* with *The Color Pur-ple,* with William Kennedy's wonderful *Ironweed.* It may be because I would be different each time, or because I might have fondled and tried to shape more words, more sounds—or because I might have read a particular poem, observed a bird's wing, felt someone's hand in mine. And, even as these works were to open up to me, I would find myself able to make finer dis-tinctions in my lived world, to see more, hear more, feel more, to be wide-awake as I could never be without the arts—and more alive.

And that is what the arts and encounters with the arts can do in many—perhaps most—human lives. That is what the blue guitar can do. You may remember Wallace Stevens's metaphor for imagination and the image of the man with the blue guitar who will not play things as they are. "Things as they are," he says, "Are changed upon the blue guitar" (1982, p. 165). And, at the end: "You as you are? You are yourself. / The blue guitar surprises you" (p. 183). It surprises, yes, as it opens doors. And it enhances the sense of personal agency, since, clearly, each of us has to be there in person and fully present if dance is to come alive, if the landscape is to fulfill itself, if the sonata is to run its course, if the poem is to be achieved. We cannot send representatives to see *The Magic Flute* for us or a Motherwell drawing or *The Prodigal Son,* or any of the works I have named. It can only be we our-selves, among other selves, and this is true of the young among us as well—who may be opened to the surprise of self-discovery in this fashion, as they are to the sense of craft, of discipline, of taste, of standard, as they become aware of what excellence can mean. That, for me, is what the creative spirit signifies, and it is our obligation to devise occasions for its flowering, more and more occasions for all the children and for presumably grown-up New Yorkers who can themselves be provoked to come awake and find new visions, new ways of living in the fragile human world.

Appendix

The lectures compiled in this book include many references to works of art in the Institute's repertory at the time each speech was given. A selected listing of the Institute's repertory referred to in each part for the pertinent years is provided below for the reader's reference. An asterisk (*) is used to indicate works which were produced by Lincoln Center Institute. When groups of works are listed for a single performer, information specific to individual works within the group is indented below the name of the work and information that pertains to all works in the group is not indented. The Visual Arts and Architecture components appear at the end as separate categories.

PART I

Selected Lincoln Center Institute Repertory

1980

Dance

Haiku
The Garden of Villandry
choreographed by Martha Clarke, Robby Barnett, Felix Blaska
performed by Martha Clarke, Robby Barnett, Wesley Fata

Brandenburg Fourth*
choreographed by Jean-Pierre Bonnefous
music by Johann Sebastian Bach
performed by senior students from the School of American Ballet

Games
choreographed by Donald McKayle
directed by Mary Barnett
performed by members of the Juilliard Dance Ensemble

Contrasts in Ballet
two excerpts from works choreographed by George Balanchine
performed by Harriet Clark and Afshen Mofid of the School of
    American Ballet

*Four**
choreographed by Kenneth Rinker
music by Sergio Cervetti
performed by Beth Davis, Laura Delano, Nancy Nasworthy, and
    Marcia Trees

Music

Quartet No. 2
composed by Béla Bartók
performed by the Emerson String Quartet

String Quartet
composed by Maurice Ravel
performed by the Emerson String Quartet

Ancient Voices of Children
composed by George Crumb
conducted by Arthur Weisberg
performed by the Contemporary Chamber Ensemble

Clarinet Quintet in A-Major, K. 581
composed by Wolfgang Amadeus Mozart
performed by the Emerson String Quartet and Loren Kitt, clarinet

French Suite No. 5 in G
composed by Johann Sebastian Bach
performed by Joyce Lindorff, harpsichord

Twelve Poems of Emily Dickinson (Excerpts)
composed by Aaron Copland
performed by Linda Wall, soprano, and Myron McPherson, piano

Theater

A Midsummer Night's Dream (Excerpts)
written by William Shakespeare
directed by Jack O'Brien
performed by members of the Acting Company

Citizen Kane (film)
directed by Orson Welles

Home
written by Samm-Art Williams
performed in a Broadway production

Children of a Lesser God
written by Mark Medoff
performed in a Broadway production

1981
Dance

Aureole
   music by George Frideric Handel
3 Epitaphs
American Folk Music
choreographed by Paul Taylor
performed by members of the Juilliard Dance Ensemble

Four
choreographed by Kenneth Rinker
music by Sergio Cervetti
performed by the Juilliard Dance Ensemble

Music

Sonata in A-flat, Op. 110
   composed by Ludwig van Beethoven
Poissons d'or
L'Ile joyeuse
Soirée dans Grenade
   composed by Claude Debussy
performed by Richard Goode, pianist

Verklärte Nacht
composed by Arnold Schoenberg
performed by Joyce Hammann, Jennifer Cowles, Miriam Hartman,
   Mary Rowell, Bonnie Thron, and Julian Rodescu

Theater

Miss Julie
written by August Strindberg
directed by Thomas Allen Bullard
performed by Kate McGregor Stewart, William Russ, and Diane Venora

The Duck Variations
written by David Mamet
directed by Helen Burns and Michael Langham
performed by Richard Ooms and Dennis Bacigalupi

1982

Dance

Unsung
choreographed by José Limón
performed by the José Limón Dance Company

Ballade
    music by Alexander Scriabin
A Short History and Lecture Demonstration on the Evolution of Ragtime
    music by Jelly Roll Morton
choreographed by Anna Sokolow
performed by Anna Sokolow's Players' Project

The Steadfast Tin Soldier
choreographed by George Balanchine
music by Georges Bizet
performed by dancers from the School of American Ballet

Eight Easy Pieces
choreographed by Peter Martins
music by Igor Stravinsky
performed by dancers from the School of American Ballet

Music

Harpsichord Concerto
composed by Manuel de Falla
performed by Joyce Lindorff, harpsichord

Divertimento in E-flat Major, K. 563
composed by Wolfgang Amadeus Mozart
performed by members of the Primavera Quartet

Theater

Schubert's Last Serenade
written by Julie Bovasso
directed by Kenneth Grantham

Aria da Capo
written by Edna St. Vincent Millay
directed by Mark Harrison

Scooter Thomas Makes It to the Top of the World
written by Peter Parnell
directed by Paul Lazarus
performed by Bill Macy and Peter Frechette

PART II

Selected Lincoln Center Institute Repertory

1987

Dance

Bonsai
choreographed by Moses Pendleton with the assistance of Daniel Ezralow,
    Katherine Komatsu, Carol Parker, and Christopher Stahl
staged by Moses Pendleton and Cynthia Quinn
music by Hisao Tanabe and Osamu Kitajima
performed by Lauren McDonough, Rebecca Stenn, George Callahan,
    and Duane Cyrus

*Monday Morning**
choreographed by David Parsons
music by John Adams
performed by the Juilliard Dance Ensemble

Little Improvisations
choreographed by Antony Tudor
performed by Louisa Santarelli, Scott Sharff, and Carla D'Ottavio

Lovers Duet from *Magritte, Magritte*
choreographed by Anna Sokolow
music by Alexander Scriabin
performed by Pamela Zaley, Owen Taylor, Lisa Baldyga, and Paul Dennis

Rhythmetron (Excerpts)
   choreographed by Arthur Mitchell
   music by Marlos Nobre
Don Quixote (Pas de Deux and Coda)
   choreographed by Marius Petipa
   music by Leon Minkus
Preludes
   choreographed by Hector Tello
   music by Claude Debussy and George Gershwin
Rags 'n' Things
   choreographed by Mark Schneider
performed by the Dance Theatre of Harlem Workshop Ensemble

Music

Entr'acte
   composed by Jacques Ibert
Madrigals, Book III (Lorca)
   composed by George Crumb
Lute Songs
   composed by John Dowland
Duettino Concertante
   composed by Ingolf Dahl
Four Songs
   composed by Igor Stravinsky
performed by the Vocal Chamber Ensemble

Brandenburg Concerto No. 2
   composed by Johann Sebastian Bach
Ocho por Radio
   composed by Silvestre Revueltas
Capricorn Concerto
   composed by Samuel Barber
conducted by Don Jennings
performed by the Juilliard Chamber Orchestra

Clapping Music
    composed by Steve Reich
Percussion Music in 3 Movements
    composed by Gerald Strang
Snow in Kalamazoo
    composed by Koos Terpstra
Jalterang
    composed by Alex Lubet
Variations on an Indian Tala
    composed by David Schrader
performed by the Maelstrom Percussion Ensemble

Theater

Antigone
written by Jean Anouilh
directed by Paul Lazarus

1990

Dance

Day on Earth
    choreographed by Doris Humphrey
    directed by Muriel Topaz
    music by Aaron Copland
Improvisation
    directed by Rebecca Stenn
performed by the Juilliard Dance Ensemble

Natural Selection
    choreographed by Victoria Marks
    music by Douglas Wieselman
A Last Place
    choreographed by Victoria Marks
    music by the Bulgarian State Radio and Television Female Vocal Choir
performed by the Victoria Marks Performance Company

Swan Lake
  choreographed by George Balanchine
  music by Peter Ilyich Tchaikovsky
A Midsummer Night's Dream (Titania and Bottom Pas de Deux)
  choreographed by George Balanchine
  music by Felix Mendelssohn
Agon
  choreographed by George Balanchine
  music by Igor Stravinsky
Stars and Stripes
  choreographed by George Balanchine
  music by John Philip Sousa, arr. Hershy Kay
performed by dancers from the School of American Ballet

Music

*East of the Sun and West of the Moon**
composed by Robert Dennis
written by Stephen P. Policoff
directed by Joshua Major
produced and performed by the New York City Opera

Theater

*Alice in Wonderland**
written by Lewis Carroll
adapted and directed by Christopher Markle
performed by the DearKnows Theater Company

*Krapp's Last Tape**
written by Samuel Beckett
directed by Thomas Allen Bullard
performed by W. Alan Nebelthau

Romeo and Juliet
written by William Shakespeare
directed by Leon Rubin
produced and performed by the Acting Company

1995
Dance

The Particle Zoo
  choreographed by Robby Barnett, Michael Tracy, and Jonathan
    Wolken
  music by Abercrombie, Darling/Rypdal, Eno, Garbarek/Shanker,
    Hyde, Ponty, Rypdal
Day Two (Excerpts)
  choreographed by Daniel Ezralow, Robert Faust, Jamey Hampton,
    Carol Parker, Moses Pendleton, Peter Pucci, Cynthia Quinn, and
    Michael Tracy
  directed by Moses Pendleton
  music by Brian Eno, David Byrne, and the Talking Heads
performed by the Pilobolus Dance Theatre

*Peach Flower Landscape**
choreographed by Nai-Ni Chen
music by Qizhang Pu
performed by Nai-Ni Chen Dance Company

Three Dances with Army Blankets
  choreographed by Shapiro and Smith
  music by Toby Twining
Escapades
  choreographed by Alvin Ailey
  music by Max Roach
performed by the Alvin Ailey Repertory Ensemble

Music

Quintets for Winds
produced and performed by the Juilliard School

Theater

True West
written by Sam Shepard
directed by Joe White

1996

Dance

Lamentation
    music by Zoltán Kodály
Errand into the Maze
    music by Gian Carlo Menotti
choreographed by Martha Graham
performed by the Martha Graham Dance Company

The Stomp Dance
Girlfriends
I Don't Know, but I Been Told ...
choreographed by Jawole Willa Jo Zollar
performed by the Urban Bush Women

Music

Music of Monk
composed by Thelonious Monk
performed by the Eric Reed Trio

John Somebody
composed by Scott Johnson
performed by Jon Herrington, guitar

The Trout Quintet
composed by Franz Schubert
performed by the Phantasy Chamber Players

Theater

*The Broken Jug**
written by Heinrich von Kleist
translated by Jon Swan
directed by Liviu Ciulei

*Ali Baba and the Forty Thieves**
taken from the Arabian Nights
directed by Donald Brenner
performed by Celeste Varricchio

*The Well Done Chef**
created and performed by Bob Berky

1997

Dance

Facing North
created by Meredith Monk in collaboration with Robert Een
performed by Dina Emerson and Theo Bleckmann

Septet
    choreographed by Merce Cunningham
    directed by Robert Swinston
    music by Eric Satie
Signals
    choreographed by Merce Cunningham
    directed by Robert Swinston
    music by John Cage, Tkehisa Kosugi, David Tudor
performed by the Cunningham Repertory Group

The Stomp Dance
Girlfriends
I Don't Know, but I Been Told . . .
choreographed by Jawole Willa Jo Zollar
performed by the Urban Bush Women

Music

Music of Monk
composed by Thelonious Monk
performed by the Eric Reed Trio

Theater

*Krapp's Last Tape**
written by Samuel Beckett
directed by Thomas Allen Bullard
performed by W. Alan Nebelthau

2000

Theater

Julius Caesar
written by William Shakespeare
directed by Robert Richmond
performed by the Aquila Theatre for Young Audiences

PART III

Selected Lincoln Center Institute Repertory

1985

Dance

Aureole
  music by George Frideric Handel
3 Epitaphs
American Folk Music
choreographed by Paul Taylor
performed by the Juilliard Dance Ensemble

The Moor's Pavane: Variations on the Theme of Othello
choreographed by José Limón
music by Henry Purcell, arr. by Simon Sadoff
performed by the José Limón Dance Company

Music

Permutation Seven*
  composed and conducted by Tania León
Sonata for Two Pianos and Percussion
  composed by Béla Bartók
performed by Christina Kiss and Paul Shaw, pianists; John Leister
  and Randy Max, percussionists

Theater

A Family Tale*
written by le Clanché du Rand
directed by Eric Booth

The Winter's Tale*
written by William Shakespeare
directed by Andy Wolk

1994

Dance

Baroque Journey
conceived and written by Catherine Turocy and Paul Shipper
performed by the New York Baroque Dance Company

Bharata Natyam
classical dance and traditional drum of Southern India
performed by Swati Bhise and Arundhati Chattopadhyaya

Three Dances with Army Blankets
    choreographed by Shapiro and Smith
    music by Toby Twining
Escapades
    choreographed by Alvin Ailey
    music by Max Roach
performed by the Alvin Ailey Repertory Ensemble

Music

Jazz Masters
performed by the Roy Hargrove Quintet

Theater

A Popol Vuh Story
written by Cherrie Moraga
conceived and directed by Ralph Lee
produced and performed by INTAR, Hispanic American Arts Center

Hamlet
written by William Shakespeare
directed by Kevin G. Coleman
produced and performed by Shakespeare & Company

Orpheus & Delgadina
as told by David Gonzalez

1995

Dance

*Peach Flower Landscape**
choreographed by Nai-Ni Chen
music by Qizhang Pu
performed by Nai-Ni Chen Dance Company

Music

Songs of Kings and Warriors
performed by Papa Susso, Salieu Susso, Basirou Jobarteh, and
    Nakoyo Susso

Quintets for Winds
produced and performed by the Juilliard School

Jazz Masters
performed by the Roy Hargrove Quintet

Theater

True West
written by Sam Shepard
directed by Joe White

1997

Theater

Krapp's Last Tape*
written by Samuel Beckett
directed by Thomas Allen Bullard
performed by W. Alan Nebelthau

1998

Dance

Limón Dance Company
Heartbeats (Excerpt)
    choreographed by Donald McKayle
"Suite" from *The Winged*
    choreographed by José Limón
directed by Carla Maxwell
performed by the Limón Dance Company

Music

Four Nations Ensemble
composed by Arcangelo Corelli, François Couperin, and Antonio Vivaldi
directed by Andrew Appel
performed by Ryan Brown, Loretta O'Sullivan, Claire Jolivet, Olav Chris
  Henriksen

Theater

A Wrinkle in Time
written by Madeleine L'Engle
adapted by James Sie
directed by Meryl Friedman

1999

Theater

*The Beloved Dearly**
written by Doug Cooney
music by and directed by Elizabeth Swados

Romeo and Juliet
written by William Shakespeare
adapted and directed by Kevin Moriarty
performed by the Hangar Theatre

PART IV

Selected Lincoln Center Institute Repertory

1993

Music

*Symphony No. 40 in G-Minor**
composed by Wolfgang Amadeus Mozart
conducted by Gerard Schwarz
performed by the Mostly Mozart Orchestra

Theater

Charlotte's Web*
written by E. B. White
adapted by Joseph Robinette
directed by Joe White

Don Juan*
written by Jean-Baptiste Molière
adapted by Joseph Chaikin and Bill Coco
directed by Joseph Chaikin
performed by the Juilliard Drama Division

1994

Dance

Bharata Natyam
classical dance and traditional drum of Southern India
performed by Swati Bhise and Arundhati Chattopadhyaya

Theater

A Popol Vuh Story
written by Cherrie Moraga
conceived and directed by Ralph Lee
produced and performed by INTAR, Hispanic American Arts Center

Hamlet
written by William Shakespeare
directed by Kevin G. Coleman
produced and performed by Shakespeare & Company

Orpheus & Delgadina
as told by David Gonzalez

2000

Dance

Ronald K. Brown/EVIDENCE
choreographed by Ronald K. Brown
performed by members of EVIDENCE: a Dance Company

Music

Così Cosa*
based on Così fan tutte by Wolfgang Amadeus Mozart
conceived by Orchestra of St. Luke's and Lincoln Center Institute for
    the Arts in Education in collaboration with David Briskin and
    Joshua Major
music direction by David Briskin
stage direction by Joshua Major

Twentieth Century Solo Piano
Piano Sonata, Op. 26
    composed by Samuel Barber
Piano Sonata No. 1
    composed by Charles Ives
performed by Nurit Tilles

Theater

Julius Caesar
written by William Shakespeare
directed by Robert Richmond
performed by the Aquila Theatre for Young Audiences

VISUAL ARTS AND ARCHITECTURE

Visual Arts

1980–1983

In 1980 Lincoln Center Institute in association with the Metropolitan
Museum of Art presented its initial offering in the visual arts. The visual arts
component was led by Randolph Williams, painter and museum education
staff member. The visual arts Summer Session met each morning in galleries
and studios at the Metropolitan and moved to the Juilliard Theater for afternoon general sessions. In 1982, visual arts seminars also met at John Jay College. In 1983, visits to the Whitney Museum of American Art were added
to the program.

1984–1986

After three years of initial forays into the world of the visual arts, the Institute joined forces in 1984 with the Cooper Union, and that school assumed prime responsibility for those components of the Institute program dealing with painting, sculpture, architecture, and other visual and graphic arts. Beginning with the 1984 Summer Session, teachers had the option of working in the visual arts in Cooper Union's building on Astor Place, and teachers continued this work in their schools in the fall with Cooper Union's roster of teaching artists. The collaboration between Lincoln Center Institute and the Cooper Union continued through 1986.

1987–present

In 1987, The Museum of Modern Art began to conduct visual arts units for Lincoln Center Institute, offering schools a wide choice of museum visits and portfolios of original artworks for in-school study. Participation by visual artists and visits to The Museum of Modern Art became a part of every Summer Session workshop for entering teachers. Schools in the Institute program selected in-school units of study based on original works of art lent by the museum or half-day visits led by teaching artists to museums of choice.

Beginning in 1994 the Brooklyn Museum of Art joined the Museum of Modern Art in conducting the visual arts component for the Institute. Today, the outstanding collections of The Museum of Modern Art, the Brooklyn Museum of Art, the Whitney Museum of American Art, and the Metropolitan Museum of Art serve as repertory for the visual arts.

Architecture

In 1997 the study of architecture was added, conducted in partnership with the New York Foundation for Architecture, working with Learning By Design:NY, which uses buildings in New York City and local school neighborhoods as the focus of its work.

References

Aldrich, V. (1963). *Philosophy of art*. Englewood Cliffs, NJ: Prentice-Hall.

Anouilh, J. (1973). *Antigone* (adapted by L. Galantiere). New York: Samuel French.

Arendt, H. (1958). *The human condition*. Chicago: University of Chicago Press.

Arendt, H. (1968). *Between past and future*. New York: Viking Press.

Auden, W. H. (1976). *W. H. Auden: Collected poems* (E. Mendelson, Ed.). New York: Random House.

Berger, J. (1977). *Ways of seeing*. New York: Penguin Books.

Bishop, E. (1997). *The complete poems, 1927–1979*. New York: Noonday Press; Farrar, Straus and Giroux.

Brenson, M. (1990, July 22). Is 'quality' an idea whose time has gone? *New York Times* [Late Edition], sec. 2, p. 27.

Brooke, R. (1977). *The complete poems*. New York: AMS Press.

Broudy, H. (1972). *Enlightened cherishing: An essay on aesthetic education*. Chicago: University of Illinois Press.

Buber, M. (1978). *Between man and man*. New York: Macmillan.

Burke, K. (1953). *Counter-statement*. Los Altos, CA: Hermes Publications.

Camus, A. (1971). *The plague* (S. Gilbert, Trans.). New York: Knopf.

Conrad, J. (1967). Preface to The nigger of the *Narcissus*. In *Great short works of Joseph Conrad* (pp. 56–57). New York: Harper and Row.

Conrad, J. (1999). *Heart of darkness*. New York: Modern Library.

Crane, H. (1926, October). A discussion with Hart Crane. *Poetry Magazine, 37*.

Crane, H. (1933). *The collected poems of Hart Crane*. New York: Liveright.

Cunningham, M. (1985). *The dancer and the dance: Merce Cunningham in conversation with Jaqueline Lesschaeve*. New York: Marion Boyers.

Cunningham, M. (1997). The impermanent art. In D. Vaughan (Ed.), *Merce Cunningham: Fifty years*. New York: Aperture. (Original work published in 1955)

Dewey, J. (1931). *Philosophy and civilization*. New York: Minton, Balch.

Dewey, J. (1966). *Democracy and education*. New York: Free Press.

Dewey, J. (1980). *Art as experience*. New York: Perigee Books.

Dewey, J. (1988). *The public and its problems*. Athens, OH: Swallow Press.

Dewey, J. (1994). *Experience and nature*. Chicago: Open Court.

Dickens, C. (1996). *Hard times*. New York: Cambridge University Press.

Dickinson, E. (1960). *The complete poems of Emily Dickinson* (T. H. Johnson, Ed.). Boston: Little, Brown.

Donoghue, D. (1983). *The arts without mystery*. Boston: Little, Brown.

Dostoyevsky, F. (1945). *The brothers Karamazov* (C. Garnett, Trans.). New York: Modern Library. (Original work published 1879–1880)

Duckworth, E. R. (1996). *"The having of wonderful ideas" and other essays on teaching and learning* (2nd ed.). New York: Teachers College Press.

Dufrenne, M. (1973). *The phenomenology of aesthetic experience.* Evanston, IL: Northwestern University Press.

Eliot, T. S. (1952). *The complete poems and plays, 1909–1950.* New York: Harcourt, Brace.

Ellison, R. (1994). *Invisible man.* New York: Quality Paperback Book Club.

Fitzgerald, F. S. (1995). *The great Gatsby.* Thorndike, ME: G. K. Hall.

Freire, P. (1997). *Pedagogy of hope* (R. Barr, Trans.). New York: Continuum. (Original work published 1994)

Frye, N. (1964). *The educated imagination.* Bloomington: Indiana University Press.

Gold, S. (1997, July 13). Maniacal about acting, as well as privacy. *New York Times,* sec. 2, pp. 5, 7.

Gombrich, E. (1965). *Art and illusion.* New York: Pantheon Books.

Goodman, N. (1988). *Languages of art* (2nd ed.). Indianapolis, IN: Hackett.

Gotshalk, D. W. (1962). *Art and the social order* (2nd ed.). New York: Dover.

Grubin, D. (Producer and Director), Haba, J. (Ed.), & Moyers, B. (Author). (1995). *The language of life: A festival of poets* [Film]. Boston: Newbridge Communications.

Heaney, S. (1995). *The redress of poetry.* New York: Farrar, Straus and Giroux.

Heaney, S. (1996). *The spirit level.* New York: Farrar, Straus and Giroux.

Hofstadter, A., & Kuhns, R. (Eds.). (1964). *Philosophies of art and beauty.* New York: Modern Library.

Hughes, L. (1959). *Selected poems of Langston Hughes.* New York: Knopf.

Jordan, J. (1980). *Passion.* Boston: Beacon Press.

Kearney, R. (1988). *The wake of imagination.* London: Hutchinson.

Keats, J. (1975). *The poetical works of Keats.* Boston: Houghton Mifflin.

Kierkegaard, S. (1940). Stages on life's way. In R. Bretall (Ed. and Trans.), *Kierkegaard.* Princeton, NJ: Princeton University Press.

Kinnell, G. (1985). *The past.* Boston: Houghton Mifflin.

Langer, S. (1957). *Problems of art.* New York: Scribner's.

Lasch, C. (1984). *The minimal self.* New York: Norton.

Lee, L.-Y. (1990). *The city in which I love you.* Brockport, NY: BOA Editions.

Levine, P. (1995, October 29). Keats in Detroit. *New York Times,* p. E13.

Levine, P. (1999). *The mercy.* New York: Knopf.

Lévi-Strauss, C. (1969). *The raw and the crooked* (J. & D. Weightman, Trans.). London: Cape. (Original work published 1964)

Lorca, F. G. (1995). The Tamarit divan (C. Brown, Trans.). *Federico García Lorca: Selected verse* (C. Maurer, Ed.). New York: Farrar, Straus and Giroux. (Original work published 1940)

Madison, G. B. (1988). *The hermeneutics of postmodernity.* Indianapolis: University of Indiana Press.

Malitz, N. (1996, July 14). Trying to reinvent summer in the city. *New York Times* [Late Edition], sec. 2, p. 1.

Marcel, G. (1949). *Being and having* (K. Farrer, Trans.). Westminster, UK: Dance Press. (Original work published 1935)

Marcuse, H. (1978). *The aesthetic dimension* (H. Marcuse & E. Sherover, Trans.). Boston: Beacon Press. (Original work published 1977)

McKayle, D. (1969). The act of theatre. In S. J. Cohen (Ed.), *The modern dance: Seven statements of belief* (pp. 53–61). Middletown, CT: Wesleyan University Press.

Meier, D. (1995). *The power of their ideas: Lessons for America from a small school in Harlem.* Boston: Beacon Press.

Melville, H. (1979). *Moby-Dick.* Berkeley: University of California Press.

Merleau-Ponty, M. (1967). *Phenomenology of perception* (C. Smith, Trans.). London: Humanities Press. (Original work published 1962)

Morrison, T. (1974). *Sula.* New York: Knopf.

Morrison, T. (1988). *Beloved.* New York: Plume Fiction.

Morrison, T. (1999). *The bluest eye.* Thorndike, ME: Thorndike Press.

Oliver, M. (1999). *Winter hours.* New York: Houghton Mifflin.

Ondaatje, M. (1997). *The English patient: A novel.* Thorndike, ME: Thorndike Press.

Ozick, C. (1989). *Metaphor and memory.* New York: Knopf.

Paley, V. G. (1995). *Kwanzaa and me.* Cambridge, MA: Harvard University Press.

Percy, W. (1961). *The moviegoer.* New York: Knopf.

Piercy, M. (1989). *Circles on the water.* New York: Knopf.

Polanyi, M. (1967). *The tacit dimension.* Garden City, NY: Anchor Books.

Poulet, G. (1969). Phenomonology of reading. *New Literary History, 1*(1), 53–68.

Rader, M. (1974). The imaginative mode of awareness. *Journal of Aesthetics and Art Criticism, 33*(2), 136.

Reid, L. A. (1958). Beauty and significance. In S. K. Langer (Ed.), *Reflection on art.* Baltimore: Johns Hopkins University Press.

Reid, L. A. (1968). Art, truth and reality. In H. Osborne (Ed.), *Aesthetics in the modern world.* New York: Weybright and Talley.

Reid, L. A. (1969). *Meaning in the arts.* New York: Humanities Press.

Rich, A. (1978). *The dream of a common language.* New York: Norton.

Rich, A. (1989). *Time's power.* New York: Norton.

Rich, A. (1995). *Dark fields of the republic.* New York: Norton.

Rilke, R. M. (1974). *Selected poems* (C. F. MacIntyre, Trans.). Los Angeles: University of California Press. (Original work published 1940)

Rilke, R. M. (1993). *Letters to a young poet* (H. Norton, Trans.) (Rev. ed.). New York: Norton. (Original work published 1934)

Rilke, R. M. (1996). *Uncollected poems: Rainer Maria Rilke* (E. Snow, Ed. and Trans.). New York: North Point Press.

Rose, M. (1995). *Possible lives.* Boston: Houghton Mifflin.

Rukeyser, M. (1982). *The collected poems of Muriel Rukeyser.* New York: McGraw-Hill.

Said, E. (1978). *Beginnings: Intention and method.* Baltimore: Johns Hopkins University Press.

Said, E. (1993). *Culture and imperialism.* New York: Knopf.

Sartre, J.-P. (1949). *Literature and existentialism* (B. Frechtman, Trans.). Secaucus, NJ: Citadel Press.

Schutz, A. (1964). *Collected papers* (Vol. 1). The Hague: Nijhoff.

Schutz, A. (1967). Making music together. In *Collected papers* (Vol. 2). The Hague: Nijhoff.

Sexton, A. (1981). *The complete poems.* Boston: Houghton Mifflin.

Simic, C. (1996). *Walking the black cat.* San Diego: Harcourt Brace.

Smith, A. D. (1993). *Fires in the mirror.* New York: Anchor Books.

Stevens, W. (1951). *The necessary angel.* New York: Vintage Books.

Stevens, W. (1982). *The collected poems of Wallace Stevens.* New York: Knopf.

Strand, M. (1980). *Selected poems.* New York: Atheneum.

Taylor, C. (1992). *Multiculturalism and "the politics of recognition."* Princeton, NJ: Princeton University Press.

Tennyson, A. (1962). Ulysses. In *The Norton anthology of English literature* (pp. 1463–1465). New York: Norton.

Walker, A. (1982). *The color purple.* New York: Washington Square Press.

Walsh, W. (1959). *The use of imagination.* London: Chatto and Windus.

Warnock, M. (1978). *Imagination.* Berkeley: University of California Press.

Whitman, W. (1982). *Poetry and prose.* New York: Viking Press.

Williams, W. C. (1988). *The collected poems of William Carlos Williams: Vol. 2. 1939–1962* (C. MacGowan, Ed.). New York: New Direction Books.

Woolf, V. (1985). *Moments of being* (J. Schulkind, Ed.) (2nd ed.). San Diego: Harcourt Brace.

Woolf, V. (1989). *A room of one's own.* San Diego: Harcourt Brace.

Woolf, V. (1990). *To the lighthouse.* New York: Harcourt Brace.

Wordsworth, W. (1984). *William Wordsworth: Selections* (S. Gill, Ed.). New York: Oxford University Press.

Yeats, W. B. (1997). *The collected poems of W. B. Yeats* (R. J. Finneran, Ed.) (2nd ed.). New York: Simon and Schuster.

Index

About the Authors

MAXINE GREENE is a professor of philosophy and education and the William F. Russell Professor in the Foundations of Education (emerita) at Teachers College, Columbia University, where she continues to teach courses in educational philosophy, social theory, and aesthetics. She earned her B.A. degree (1938) at Barnard College. After a decade of work and child rearing, she took her M.A. degree at New York University. She has honorary degrees in the humanities from Lehigh University, Hofstra University, the University of Colorado at Denver, the University of Indiana, Goddard College, Bank Street College, Nazareth College, McGill University, College Misericordia, and Binghamton University. Teachers College awarded her its medal of honor in 1989. Before joining Teachers College, Greene taught at Brooklyn College, Montclair State University, and New York University. She also taught during the summer at the University of Hawaii, the University of Illinois, and Lehigh University. In 1990, Greene presented some of her work in New Zealand on a three-week Fulbright lecturing fellowship.

Greene's primary concerns today are with the arts, aesthetic education, literature, and social thought. She has written more than one hundred articles in these fields and over forty book chapters for collections and anthologies. The most recent of her six books is *Releasing the Imagination* (1995). Greene is a past president of the Philosophy of Education Society, the American Educational Studies Association, and the American Educational Research Association. She has also served on various state and municipal commissions for curriculum and assessment. Greene is presently nurturing the development of a Center for the Arts, Social Imagination, and Education. Her work and life are the subject of a new documentary film by Markie Hancock entitled *Exclusions & Awakenings: The Life of Maxine Greene*. Greene's dedication to aesthetic education stems in large measure from her continuing twenty-five-year association with Lincoln Center Institute for the Arts in Education as its Philosopher-in-Residence.

MADELEINE FUCHS HOLZER is Program Development Director at Lincoln Center Institute for the Arts in Education. Previously Director of Arts in Education at the New York State Council on the Arts, she holds both a doctorate in education from Teachers College, Columbia University, and a masters degree in creative writing from New York University. A poet and educator, her essays and poetry have appeared in *New York Newsday, Education Week, Black Fly Review,* and *Footwork: Paterson Literary Review,* among others. She has taught at Cornell and New York Universities and at Fox Lane High School in Bedford, New York. She has also been a poet-in-residence at the East Side Community High School in New York City, and was Senior Editor for English/Language Arts at Sunburst Communications, where she developed educational multi-media CD-ROMs on *Romeo and Juliet* and on multicultural American poetry.

SCOTT NOPPE-BRANDON is Executive Director of Lincoln Center Institute. He serves on the steering committee of the Arts Education Partnership and its research and higher education task forces. Mr. Noppe-Brandon joined Lincoln Center Institute in 1987 as associate director and took over management of the Institute in 1995. He is also President of the Association of Institutes for Aesthetic Education, an organization of twenty institutes based on the Lincoln Center model. A former dancer and teaching artist, he previously served as consultant to state agencies including the Ohio Arts Council, where he developed arts-in-education programs with special emphasis in program philosophy and structure, curriculum development, and criticism. He is certified to teach K–12 arts education and has been part of planning teams that designed eleven schools nationwide. In Ohio, he led a successful statewide effort to certify dance and theater as subject areas within the schools.